AF360122

Advance Praise for *Unshackling the Elephant*

'Finally, here are sound, sensible answers to deliver quick and fair justice to every Indian citizen!'

Gurcharan Das
Author, *The Difficulty of Being Good*

'A passionate plea for legal reform, *Unshackling the Elephant* stands out for clarity of thought, felicity of expression and scholarship that traverses the country's historic, legal and political landscape. It is an invaluable addition to the literature on legal reform with concrete suggestions for action by policymakers.

The book is a must-read for all those interested in reinforcing the role of law as an instrument of justice amid declining standards of political and social morality.'

Ashwani Kumar
Former Union Minister for Law and Justice,
Senior Advocate, Supreme Court of India

'India's legal system is now the single biggest hurdle to its rise as a global economic power. There is no doubt that it needs urgent surgery and radical ideas. In this very readable book, Anand Prasad provides many views that break with convention. Agree or disagree, India needs to engage with such new thinking.'

Sanjeev Sanyal
Economist and author

'A nation's economic vitality and the strength of its democracy rest on the relationship between the citizen, the market and the state. This book offers a provocative and brilliant reimagining of that relationship for a 21st-century India. It courageously confronts the legacy of an "imperial" legal mindset and proposes reforms that are fundamental to a modern liberal market economy: making the state liable for its actions by reconsidering sovereign immunity, enhancing whistle-blower protections to deter corporate fraud and even empowering citizens to defend themselves when the state fails. This is the intellectual ammunition needed to dismantle the old structures and build a legal system that fosters both prosperity and freedom.'

Ajay Shah

Professor, National Institute of Public Finance and Policy, New Delhi

'A powerful and timely contribution to the national discourse on legal reform. With the clarity of a seasoned practitioner and the vision of a public-spirited reformer, Anand Prasad navigates the complex intersection of law, policy and governance. As India's startup ecosystem grows, a modern and responsive legal framework becomes even more critical. This book is a must-read for policymakers, lawyers and entrepreneurs alike. It diagnoses deep-rooted structural issues and proposes bold, thoughtful ideas that challenge many of our common assumptions.

From rethinking contract law to discourage non-compliance, using technology to accelerate dispute resolution, proposing a robust whistle-blower framework for better corporate governance, and ensuring true agency for women within legal and institutional frameworks, Anand invites us to imagine a legal system that is more efficient, just and inclusive.

Its nuanced and fresh perspective on widely discussed themes makes this book particularly compelling. Even readers who may not agree with every recommendation will find the ideas provocative and intellectually rigorous.'

Shweta Rajpal Kohli

President and CEO, Startup Policy Forum

'Anand has a bunch of radical and thought-provoking suggestions. Debating these and legislating the ones that draw a wider consensus will hopefully make us a fairer nation, one with greater ease of doing business and living, a better nation.'

Lalit Bhasin

President, Society of Indian Law Firms

'In the worlds of economic or social development, reforms related to India's judicial system rarely find their rightful space – largely because they seem complex and foreign. This book is an excellent attempt at making the judicial world more approachable to a development sector professional. It spans a range of ideas – from accelerated and transparent justice to unshackled economic growth to gender inclusion. Eye-opening for any development professional ... gave me a peek into the world I knew existed but had not dared to experience. The book felt like my first deep-sea dive.'

Seema Bansal

Vice-chairperson, Punjab Development Commission

'This well-researched book presents a distinct perspective on India's legal system. Steering away from being a dry legal commentary, it deals with hard and complex legal concepts economically and justifies the necessity of improvement.

The book dissects why most traditional legal ideas, though impeccable on paper, fail in India's complex sociopolitical reality. Some of these concepts may be radical, but they're grounded in rationale and conviction about what 21st-century justice ought to be.

It is a book that looks into the future and imagines how we as a people could move from the inevitability of a dysfunctional legal system to one that delivers quickly – a new experience with the law, easy to trust and rely on, one that could quickly bring about a new age of ease of doing business and ease of living.'

S. Niranjan Reddy

Member of Parliament, Rajya Sabha, and Senior Advocate, Supreme Court of India

'When following the law becomes a handicap and breaking it a badge of honour, what hope remains for a nation?

In this call to action, Anand Prasad, a founder of one of India's top law firms, lays bare the slow and dangerous corrosion of the rule of law in India – a corrosion so normalised that most citizens have ceased to notice it. He argues that India today resembles the proverbial frog in boiling water – incrementally adjusting to the rising heat of legal decay until it's too late to escape.

Drawing from decades of legal experience, Prasad dissects the moral and institutional failures that have allowed corruption, injustice and impunity to become systemic. He explores how legal inefficiencies stifle entrepreneurship, enable crime and hollow out public trust, while also exposing the colonial hangovers and elite biases embedded in India's judicial apparatus.

But this is not a book of despair. It is a blueprint for hope. With a bold agenda – ranging from lifetime judicial appointments and contingency fees for lawyers to AI-driven justice delivery and decolonisation of courtroom culture – Prasad reimagines a legal system that could once again command public confidence and constitutional integrity.

This book invites readers to reclaim the Indian dream of Ram Rajya – not as mythology, but as a society anchored in justice, equality and the rule of law.'

Sanjay Hegde
Senior Advocate, Supreme Court of India

'Anand's iconoclastic book on legal reform does not pull its punches on what ails India's legal system. I see the book as encapsulating a core principle – that human beings surrender aspects of their inherent freedom to the state on the basis of a moral and legal contract with that state. And the state is failing to deliver on its side of this contract, one of the most important features of which is to ensure the rule of law for its people.

With characteristic boldness, Prasad argues for greater accountability for the two arms of government not subject to oversight by the public through the ballot box – the bureaucracy and the judiciary. His suggestions on AI-assisted courts, reforming the judiciary through lifetime appointments on the one hand and performance review on the other, and creating better incentives for the various actors in the drama of the legal system are both radical and achievable. I welcome his focus on better implementation of existing laws in the short term while working towards deeper reform, which includes aligning Indian law with Indian values rather than colonial legacies.

The book is a welcome contribution to the thinking on legal and economic reform in India.'

Akshay Jaitley
Co-founder, Trilegal, and founder, Trustbridge

'India's courts were built for a different century – yet every day, millions stake their futures on a system groaning under the weight of delay, opacity and soaring costs. This book describes a step-by-step overhaul of the Indian judicial system to make it ready for the future. From livestreamed hearings to AI-assisted benches; from whistle-blower bounties to a Supreme Court split in two, Anand Prasad presents a clear and ambitious roadmap that draws on a lifetime's worth of experience as a commercial lawyer. You may differ with him on the pace or extent of some of his proposals, but there can be no question that the problems he seeks to fix deserve serious and urgent attention.'

Rahul Matthan
Co-founder, Trilegal

'India has a legal system, but it does not provide justice. Anand's book focuses on this most important of India's handicaps and suggests wide-ranging and innovative changes – from process improvements to deep structural reform to seemingly trivial but deeply significant cultural norms. You may not agree with all of them, but they will all provide food for thought in an area that we must fix for Indians to lead better lives.'

Rahul Ahluwalia
Founding director, Foundation for Economic Development

'The book rejects blind imports from Western social science, such as the US-based Critical Race Theory's oppressed–oppressor framework, which simply doesn't apply to India's distinct context. We've adopted these ideas without scrutiny, and Prasad rightly calls for reforms grounded in our own truths. What truly captivates me is his unflinching commitment to genuine equality, especially in reimagining women's rights: treating women as autonomous adults with full agency rather than as fragile beings requiring government-mandated shields. This rejection of patronising "protection" aligns perfectly with my disdain for self-righteous moral posturing by authorities, emphasising empowerment through dignity, independence and choice. A must-read for anyone tired of colonial-era hangovers and ready for a legal system that serves the people, not the elite.'

Rahul Dewan

Tech entrepreneur, angel investor, and founder, Srijan Technologies, Hindu Network Foundation and Sangam Talks

Unshackling the Elephant

Unshackling the Elephant

Transforming Indian Law, Culture and Economy

Anand Prasad

BLOOMSBURY
NEW DELHI • LONDON • OXFORD • NEW YORK • SYDNEY

BLOOMSBURY INDIA
Bloomsbury Publishing India Pvt. Ltd
Second Floor, LSC Building No. 4, DDA Complex, Pocket C – 6 & 7,
Vasant Kunj, New Delhi, 110070

BLOOMSBURY, BLOOMSBURY INDIA and the Diana logo are trademarks of Bloomsbury Publishing Plc

First published in India 2025

Illustrations by Capt. Sanjay Gehlot

ISBN: HB: 978-93-56402-27-0; eBook: 978-93-56402-20-1
2 4 6 8 10 9 7 5 3 1

Typeset in Minion by Manipal Technologies Limited
Printed and bound in India by Thomson Press India Ltd

Contents

1

The Frog on a Slow Boil: A Quest for True Freedom

Where the law is subject to some other authority and has none of its own, the collapse of the state, in my view, is not far off.

Plato (350 BC)

YOU MAY HAVE HEARD the fable of the frog placed in a vat of water being slowly brought to a boil. If it had been thrown into water that was already very hot, it would jump out instantly. However, because of the slow increase in temperature, the frog keeps adjusting to the increasing discomfort until it is killed when the water begins to boil.

This frog is like the average Indian citizen, who keeps adjusting to the slow increase in temperature, that is, the gradual diminishing rule of law in our country. We have become so used to accepting the increasing injustices in the country that we will not notice when we come to live in a jungle raj, where dishonesty and might are right, and the idea of a just and fair State remains confined to the textbooks. We will be unprepared when, ultimately, there is a total breakdown of the law and our nation-state descends into anarchy.

So, how do we get our vat of water off the fire to stop the boil? That is what this book explores in an endeavour to identify a few significant reforms in the legal space that could save our nation from what looks to be an inevitable descent into mayhem.

Why this book

In today's India, compliance with the law or a contract has become an option, with non-compliance becoming a real and inexpensive choice. Many Indians are beginning to nurture the perception that law-abiding citizens are fools who lack the courage and talent for 'innovation' to find their way around legal restrictions. The 'smart' Indian finds solutions, legal or otherwise; he or she cheats, bribes and escapes the law without any guilt and succeeds in life. Many even boast about the original ways through which they have avoided paying a tax, wriggled out of a fine, cheated in an exam, conned someone or even lied before a court of law. All of this is perfectly acceptable – even admirable – in many quarters, particularly in urban India, where such behaviour has become the norm. This means that India is facing a problem in which its people not only openly and proudly break the law but also benefit from this behaviour.

Consequently, a process of slow decay in governance and the rule of law has set in, leading to a steep deterioration in public morality. This could eventually create a lawless and hollow system where rules mean nothing. Because the section of the population that is lying in every domain of life is increasingly successful, and with such sections becoming role models, confidence in the legal system dips, leading to a weakening of integrity levels in Indian society.

Am I saying that we Indians are a rotten lot? Certainly not. Ask any of our grandparents, and they will tell us how integrity levels were higher at the time of India's independence. Our behaviour is not entirely our fault but is attributable to the failings of the Indian State. When the costs of complying with the laws or contracts are much higher than the combined costs of bribes, penalties, fines, compensation and punishments for evading them – and throwing in the frustrations and humiliations often faced when dealing with the bureaucracy – this kind of behaviour is bound to be the outcome.

Right now, the common citizen remains largely apathetic to the pressing need for legal reforms in the country because they do not know how intertwined it is with their own daily life. They have come to accept the slow decay of the rule of law in India as part of the '*chalta hai*' culture. A survey of over 2,70,000 Indian voters in 2019 revealed that they are mainly concerned with getting their basic needs met. The common Indian citizen wants better jobs, better healthcare, drinking water and roads.[1] Legal reforms do not appear in the top ten issues that bother them. The farthest they will go is to ask for better policing, seeing this as necessary to address crime prevention. It is really unfortunate that the average Indian does not see the connection between the problems in his daily life and the cracks in the Indian legal system.

The low standards of municipal infrastructure, air quality and drinking water, as well as the disappearing green cover, are all a result of poor enforcement of municipal and environmental laws. Similarly, inadequate enforcement of commercial and financial laws allows for dishonest advertising, substandard and overpriced goods and services, and real estate or financial frauds. The legal system also fails us when it comes to fake news and partisan journalism. Because the average Indian cannot see the connections between the legal system and the world around them, it appears frustrating at every turn.

The legal system is fundamental for the establishment of a just, fair and happy society, but unfortunately, cracks in this system are not as obvious as other problems such as potholes, water shortages or electricity outages. Therefore, the need for legal reforms is only felt and discussed among the business, academic and intellectual circles but is not a topic in electoral debates. With no public pressure to address the matter, the political class is happy to ignore it. Legal reforms do not offer the instant voter gratification that can be had from well-made roads, tall buildings, free healthcare and other subsidies. They do not hold the power to win the attention of the common person. The responsibility, therefore, weighs on the political and intellectual elite of the nation to bring legal reforms into focus.

There are already several warning signs. Colonial-era sedition laws – originally intended for the British Raj to suppress India's freedom movement – are often used to quell dissent today. Police departments continue to try to prosecute using criminal offences that have been read down or even prohibited by the Supreme Court, harassing citizens by attempting to penalise them for conduct that has been declared to be lawful.[2] Our jails are filled with more people under trial than with proven criminals.[3]

There are fewer visceral signs too. Our courts continue to be swamped by an astronomical and continually increasing number of pending cases,[4] with one government report noting that 'it would take 324 years just to clear the present backlog at the current rate of disposal'.[5] There is data to further underline this. In 2020, India was ranked 69 out of 128 countries on a global Rule of Law Index (RLI) compiled by the World Justice Project. The index is based on a country's performance on factors such as its government's openness, upholding of fundamental rights, civil and criminal justice systems, and efficacy in containing corruption. Even Belarus – which has been described as Europe's last dictatorship – was ranked one place above India, while Africa's Burkina Faso – which has been rocked by numerous military coups – was ranked one below us.

These statistics make the problem look like a lost cause for our country. But is it so? We need to make legal reforms a more prominent subject in public discourse and make it a matter that at least figures in electoral debates, if not actually being the decisive factor in elections. To do this, we must have champions for legal reforms – political leaders who see the need for them and are willing to take up the challenge of cutting through the red tape and other obstacles imposed by an insensitive, indifferent establishment.

We must strive for a system that is significantly superior to the current one. The solution does not lie in passive resistance towards reforms but in realising their scope and capabilities for India, and in using a feedback-loop system to keep improving them. We cannot kill reforms by focusing on abstract concepts. It is wiser to establish a time limit within which they must be enforced. This will create an urgency for constant feedback, and for the law ministry and other governmental stakeholders to take full responsibility for the enforcement of the reforms.

This is where this book comes in – with two aims. First, to encourage public discourse on legal reforms by making the legal system easy to understand and relatable. Second, to offer a set of legal reforms that can be championed.

In this context, the book takes a look at a few options to find a fix for this mega problem.

Analysing some of the problems

Compliance-cost arbitrage

Nowhere is this tendency to circumvent legal obligations more evident than in entrepreneurship. Explaining this with a few examples: while Indian businesses are bound by regulations for proper garbage disposal, optimum employment conditions, care for the environment and other quality controls, they find it terribly expensive to fulfil all these obligations. Those ticking all the boxes soon find that they have been undercut by their 'smart' peers who have circumvented all these 'inconveniences'.

Entrepreneurs in India increasingly find that it is necessary to cut corners if they want to provide a competitive and cost-optimal product. In fact, as a result of the massive failure of our legal system, the entire process of economic growth in our country involves such practices, that is, becoming inexpensive by not complying. It's more expensive to follow the law than to break it. This has resulted in the glorification of practices such as flagrant non-compliance, bribery, incomplete filing of paperwork, exploitation of the workforce, delaying or not paying vendors, and so on.

So, there is a compliance–cost arbitrage that keeps us Indians from sticking to the straight and narrow. Many of us personally know people who refuse to comply with the law. For example, some may not install an environmental-protection system at a factory because it would be less expensive for them to deal with the consequences later than to spend on compliance. Others may delay paying their electricity bills, their vendors and even their employees. This kind of behaviour is seen as the 'smart way' rather than wrongdoing. It also helps build cheaper products, making 'cheap is best' a terrible idea.

No sanctity of law or contract

India's glory of becoming the fifth-largest economy in the world is sullied by the fact that there is no sanctity of contract and generally poor regard for the law in the country. It is sad that even China might be an example for India to emulate in many matters. China has used AI to deal with simple legal matters such as disputes about the sale of goods, intellectual property rights, e-commerce and product liability, resulting in cases being resolved in less than forty days. In our country, however, should you be cheated in business or as a customer, your case will easily take three or four years to be heard at a trial court, not to mention the appeals that could follow!

In the context of criminal law, the conviction rates in India also indicate why it is better to cut corners than follow the law.

For major crimes in India, the conviction rates are less than 10 per cent, whereas in first-world countries such as Japan, the US and the UK, they are close to 90 per cent. It is absolutely shocking that the conviction rate for crimes against women in India is around 15 per cent, dropping to a negligible 3.01 per cent in rape cases. So essentially, rapists have a free run in our society. The more depressing aspect of these conviction rates is that most of the convicted criminals are those who cannot afford a proper defence, while conviction rates among the wealthy are significantly lower. Of course, the low conviction rates are also a reflection of poor investigative work by the police, but that is a separate issue in itself. Hence, the upside of committing a crime is much higher than the downside.

Trial is the punishment

Bail is the rule while jail is the exception. This is an old and established legal norm in criminal law. However, this norm has come under pressure in today's India. Over the last several years, our courts have been reluctant to give bail even to people who are entitled to it, keeping them imprisoned for the course of the trial. This seems to be because there appears to be an increasing acceptance that a criminal or, say, the accused, would eventually be acquitted even if guilty and would suffer no penalty. Hence, it would appear that the judicial establishment has come to an unstated view that the trial itself has to serve as the punishment. This is the working of a crude and immature criminal justice system, which has no place in a country that aspires to become an advanced economy in today's world.

If the people lose trust in the justice system, governance will become very difficult because people will eventually lose confidence in democracy and in the nation-state itself. It is already impossible to function without *saam, daam, dand, bhed*[6] in the political system. This principle will find its way into our daily lives as a result of the loss of confidence in the rule of law, and then the concept of a happy society will get lost too. Why should this be so? Is this the atmosphere that our nation-state must create for its people, that is, an Asuric Rajya, or should it aspire for a form of Ram Rajya[7], that is, a society where the rule of law is upheld?

The elusive Ram Rajya

After the Constitution was drafted, the artist Nandalal Bose and his students created illustrations for handwritten prints of the document with images from both Indian history and mythology. Among them are representations of Nalanda University and Akbar's court, Arjuna and Krishna from the Mahabharata and the deities Shiva and the Buddha. These illustrations frame the first page of each part of the Constitution of India.[8] The first page of Part III of the Constitution – which covers the fundamental rights of citizens – is framed by an illustration from the Ramayana, depicting Ram, Sita and Lakshman returning victorious from the battle with Ravan.

This painting has been subject to various interpretations. The framers of our Constitution evidently considered Ram to be a great national figure, and the events of his life were accepted by the Constituent Assembly as 'realities having taken place to establish rule of law and discipline'.[9] Courts have relied on it to accept claims that Ram was not merely a mythical figure, while political commentators have cited it as proof that the Constitution of India was written with the principles of Ram Rajya in mind. In Mahatma Gandhi's opinion, the illustration intended to depict India as a true democracy that guaranteed equal rights for all, where 'the meanest citizen could be sure of swift justice without an elaborate and costly procedure'.[10]

When we consider the idea of Ram Rajya from the common Indian citizen's perspective, it becomes easier to see why this idea has mass appeal and explains the efforts to include it in our Constitution. Today, an average citizen of our country can only dream of a system of governance that meets the requirements set out by Gandhi. They are far more likely to be found praying for divine intervention before trying to navigate red tape, such as filing a court case or making a complaint to the police. This situation has arisen because of our failure to deliver the rule of law.

Rule of law

In simple terms, the rule of law is a concept in which the law applies equally to all in a democratic State – including those in power. Every citizen – whether they are an elected leader, a member of the business elite or part of the bureaucracy – should act according to the law. Every person shall also receive equal treatment and protection before the law. Extending this further, government authorities must not act arbitrarily, nor abuse or exceed their powers.

This principle may not be mentioned in our Constitution, but it is considered to be an integral part of it and of our legal system – noted on several occasions by the Supreme Court.[11] While long-standing philosophical debates on its interpretation may continue, the purpose and value of having this principle and what it demands are at least in theory unquestioned by all.[12] But for the vast majority, the rule of law is missing where it is needed the most.

As alluded to earlier, before Independence, one's word held great importance in society, and the system ran on the basis of verbal promises. It was considered true dharma to keep one's word. Both a king and a common man would be bound by their word for this system to flourish.[13] This rule of dharma is considered to have been significantly distorted by invasions from foreign lands that resulted in the imposition of Turko-Mongol and European ideas, philosophies and law on the Indian population. However, is this idea true? Is it truly foreign rule that has brought us to the present state of legal system distress? Remember, at the time of Independence, the ideals of nobility, integrity and honesty were valued very highly, at least higher than they are today. Hence, it's probably a diminishment in the rule of law in post-Independence India that is the true villain.

In the past, rules and social principles that evolved out of religion helped establish the law, justice and fair play in the State – I am ignoring the religious norms unacceptable in a modern world for the moment and speaking only of the norms that would be relevant today. The religiously minded Indian people were compliant with these rules. Therefore, there is a strong case to suggest that it is the subsequent de-legitimisation of religion by the independent Indian State which pushed our society away from religion and threw the good in religion along with the bad. As a consequence, we have descended into an atheistic world of cold logic and rank materialism, and the socio-economic philosophy of 'greed is good' has become the guiding principle of modern Indian society. It is considered more important to accumulate material wealth and gain social acceptance than to stay true to rules of honesty and fair play embedded in religion. The lack of adherence to the traditional value system has made even scarcer the ideals of nobility, integrity, decency, kindness and empathy, which have now been replaced by greed and dishonesty.

Ram Rajya is not just a Hindu concept: the Bible too states that true religion consists of honouring promises made to another,[14] and the Quran declares that keeping one's word is one of the foundational values of Islam. It is considered one of the biggest sins to break a promise.[15] But even though the concept held immense value historically, the British era and post-colonial India diminished the sanctity of the verbal promise by laying greater emphasis on the written contract. The unintended consequence has been that people began to make frivolous promises with no intention of fulfilling them, in the belief that commitment only applies when written down. With that, we have lost one of the oldest and most treasured Indian values. Therefore, legal reforms will play a pivotal role in improving public morality and in reviving the importance and legitimacy of verbal commitments and promises.

The lack of confidence in the word of an individual tends to make our existence a little more complex in society and will also affect the country's business environment adversely. All business and corporate entities now expect paperwork to be exhaustive to minimise loopholes. Elaborate paperwork takes up both time and money, slowing down simple corporate procedures and ultimately the economy as a whole. Reforms can revive the value of verbal commitments and increase confidence in them. Lightly drafted written documents would reduce long negotiations on contracts and deals, speed up the economy and induce greater confidence in the system.

Let's discuss solutions

A practical approach to legal reforms

Typically, the method adopted to fix our slow and ineffective legal system has been to change the substantive law in the hope that big-ticket changes will fix everything. An example of this is the focus on increasing the punishment for rape instead of focusing on delivering speed and certainty of conviction and punishment. There is no need for new laws when our problem has been the implementation of existing laws. The same holds true in the space of civil and commercial laws as well. If we can implement them well, we will not need to introduce special legislation. Yet, the reaction to any failure is to bring in a new set of laws, which either subvert established principles of democratic law, as in the case of the bail provisions in the PMLA,[16] or are likely to be equally ineffective because the real problem of implementation would not be addressed, as in the case of an increase in punishment for rape.

Although some of the problems with our legal systems are a legacy of the British Raj, veteran lawyers and judges will tell you that the laws were much better implemented in the past. In my view, only a few changes are required to bring about a large impact. My first suggestion for change is to move away from thinking in terms of new laws and to think more in terms of speedy implementation of existing laws. It would be more practical to focus on enhancing the level of justice rather than postponing all reforms until we have the perfect solution. For enhancement of the speed with which cases are handled, we would need to use a combination of technology measures, some processes and fewer structural changes. Technological innovations will be a great enabler for this.

The other important requirement would be to create an environment where the balance lies in favour of compliance rather than transgressions, and where the common man is in natural alignment with the laws of the land. When the Indian mindset is in sync with the law, compliance comes naturally to the citizens. In addition, the imperial legal principle of ignorance of the law being unacceptable as an excuse ought to be done away with, and instead the government should be tasked with educating all citizens about their legal obligations.

Finally, there are a few general changes that will have to be made to reinforce the independence of the justice system. Greater professionalism would bring about a service-provider orientation in the judiciary and bring back a common-sense approach to law and its enforcement.

Liberating the higher judiciary

Many of our judges work under the principle that the State can do no wrong unless proven otherwise. In some instances, they may even have their post-retirement opportunities in mind. In many countries, judges are appointed for life, at least in the higher judiciary, instead of having a fixed retirement age. In our country too, judges must be allowed to go on working for as long as they are able to do their job. This will free them from having to kowtow to the powers that be. Even if a judge is appointed by an autocratic prime minister, he can still function with independence. Of course, if judges are going to have lifetime tenures, then there must be provisions for their easier impeachment too.

While the executive is not sufficiently reviewed in India, judges are not subject to review at all, except in lower courts in cases of appeals. This is because of the belief that we must have an independent judiciary that exercises sovereign authority and whose decisions cannot be subject to review. But I think that this is an imperial idea – a European idea, not Indian. There must be a mechanism to review the actions of judges, and there is also a need to have judges do more judicial reviews of legislation and administrative decisions instead of taking the lead in administrative issues.

When the government takes decisions, it has better means of gathering information than judges do. But when a court takes such decisions, they will be based only on the information gathered from the people appearing before it, which results in suboptimal outcomes. However, they cannot be subject to judicial review as the judiciary is on a higher plane when it comes to administrative and statutory action. It points to one of the country's biggest concerns – that governance is not working.

The citizenry cannot rely on the executive for reasonable administrative decisions, so the courts are stepping in – but with imperfect solutions. To not clutter up the courts as a consequence, we must create special quasi-judicial tribunals for public interest litigation (PIL), whose decisions will always be subject to judicial review. When you have an unresponsive executive, you do need recourse to some authority – but it does not have to be a judicial authority, because once judicial courts take suboptimal decisions, there is nobody to review those decisions.

Judges' performance must also be subject to review. Rather than viewing themselves as custodians of sovereignty, judges should see themselves as service providers – and as specialists, not generalists. The era of the all-purpose judge is largely over, with few exceptions. Specialisation is essential: a judge who has handled landlord–tenant disputes for years cannot seamlessly shift to company law, nor can a long-time criminal judge be expected to adjudicate tax matters mid-career. Yet our high courts and the Supreme Court continue to operate this way, resulting in judges ill-equipped to handle complex, specialised cases.

To allow the Supreme Court to focus on its core responsibilities, the number of appeals should be restricted: one appeal from lower courts to the high courts, and from there only to division or higher benches within the high courts. This would free the Supreme Court to function primarily as a court of constitutional and statutory interpretation, focusing on questions of law rather than routine appeals.

Stamping out the myriad arbitrages

For a litigant, going to court can be very expensive and hiring a lawyer even more so. This economic inequality would create arbitrage. The idea of mobile courts has been under discussion for some years now, at least for some kinds of cases in which the court can go to the litigants rather than the other way round. Our community of lawyers is already adjusting to virtual courts, and this began even before the COVID-19 pandemic. In a virtual court, the case does not have to be heard by a particular judge, and cases can be heard from a different city if necessary. This makes it very efficient.

Technology can also be employed to flatten 'knowledge' arbitrage. As a lawyer, you quickly realise that not all judges operate at the same level. Their grasp of the law, engagement with legal literature, understanding of precedent and judicial temperament can vary widely. In today's world, justice should not depend on the individual capabilities of a judge or lawyer. To address this, we could develop a centralised knowledge grid to support judges by keeping them updated on relevant case law. Rather than relying solely on memory or personal research, a judge could access the latest legal developments through a simple phone call or email, leading to more consistent and informed decisions.

I was also struck by the idea of templated pleadings, which I encountered while working at a major law firm and observing international practices. For example, in the US they have institutionalised legal capability to such an extent that even average lawyers produce high-quality work. There's no reason we can't do the same in India. For instance, in landlord–tenant disputes, most possible scenarios have already occurred after decades of such cases. A template-based system could guide litigants through a drop-down interface – no need to draft in English – allowing AI to generate pleadings. Where a case involves unique facts, users could manually enter those details. Many global law firms already rely on such templated systems. Entire practice areas such as insolvency and bankruptcy are increasingly driven by technology and AI. There's no reason

India's courts shouldn't adopt and scale these innovations as well.

Templatised pleadings not only save time but also reduce the arbitrage some lawyers gain from superior language skills – especially in English. Justice must be equal for all, not dependent on how eloquent or articulate one's lawyer is. It should not be the case that hiring Lawyer X gets you justice but hiring Lawyer Y does not. We no longer need to accept that inequity. We can use Big Data to segregate, club and dispose of similar cases, and have special courts at all levels for grouped cases to rake out the backlog we face today.

Templated systems also enable computers to analyse cases, not just ensuring the outcome would not depend on a judge's legal ability but also removing more subjective factors like the temperament or integrity of judges. Any lawyer will tell you that a judge's mood can alter the outcome. We have long operated under the burden of unpredictable courtroom dynamics and had no option but to function with the handicap of a judge in a foul mood sitting in the high chair. But if we now have an option to take away this handicap, we must.

Recording and broadcasting proceedings can also enhance transparency and accountability. Public scrutiny would curb many forms of misconduct and intimidation seen in courtrooms today. When proceedings are recorded and archived, lawyers and judges alike will be far less likely to engage in inappropriate behaviour. Once the proceedings are known to be in the public space and can be recorded for eternity, lawyers will be less inclined to act in the unsavoury or intimidating manner they sometimes do.

Taming the lawyer

The other point that needs to be dealt with is the handling of perjury, or lying in a court of law. Anybody with knowledge of Indian courts will admit that there is always somebody or other lying in court. We do have perjury laws, but they are never used. Reflecting the citizenry's macho attitude towards breaking the law, Indian lawyers boast about how they get away with bluffing in court. We should not allow such attitudes to exist in a system that is trying to deliver justice and fairness. We must take greater action against perjury.

Lawyers must be incentivised to finish their cases quickly, and one way of doing so would be through allowing them to charge contingency fees. You often hear litigants say that their lawyers appear not to be interested in their case and that there are many delays and adjournments. The reasons may be many, but clients suspect that their lawyer may be trying to extract higher fees from them. The system of contingency fees for lawyers exists in various parts of the developed world. In it, the lawyer gets a basic fee, which becomes larger if he wins the case. Essentially, the fee is based on the outcome. This gives the lawyer an incentive to bring the case to a conclusion as quickly as possible and also ensures that their focus is on success and speedy justice.

A famous example of lawyers working for a contingency fee was the Erin Brockovich[17] case, which raised the issue of water contamination causing terminal illness in an American town. This case brought attention to the dangers of environmental pollution and corporate negligence and was one of the largest environmental lawsuits in the US, with a settlement amount of $333 million. The lawyers representing the case received a contingency fee, working in a high-risk, high-reward situation that incentivised them to focus on success.

It has been seen that lawyers function in a more efficient manner when working under a contingency fee system. The fee will also reduce the upfront burden on clients. Any compensation awarded to the client would help to cover the legal fees in cases where the client cannot afford them at first. This ensures that the high cost of legal representation does not hinder a client's ability to seek justice. Therefore, the contingency fee also takes care of the affordability arbitrage.

Trapping the wrongdoer

On the business front, the compliance arbitrage available from breach of contract must be wiped out. I believe that we must follow the American system, where damages are consequential and penal, and costs are awarded on actuals. In India, the losing party has to pay fixed costs, but the lawyer's fees will actually be much higher for the winning party. Costs must be rewarded on the basis of actual losses or damages incurred, because it is natural justice that the victim must be restored to a position identical to where they were before the breach occurred.

It is my strong opinion that perpetrators of corporate and financial fraud must be rendered impoverished. It is shocking that in India corporate fraudsters are happy to go and sit in jail. They know that they can finance a not-very-uncomfortable life for themselves in jail for the period of five years or so that they are punished for, and then emerge from behind bars to continue enjoying their vast wealth gained through illegal means. This means that jail time is hardly a disincentive for such crimes. We need to gravitate towards high financial penalties rather than imprisonment for corporate offenders – people like Vijay Mallya or Nirav Modi should end up poor. That would be the strongest disincentive for anyone following in their footsteps.

We also need effective whistle-blower legislation – laws that go beyond merely protecting the whistle-blower. In the US, individuals who expose corporate wrongdoing are rewarded with 25 to 30 per cent of the penalties recovered from the offending company. In India, employees may often find themselves under pressure to act unethically. But if offered a similar monetary incentive, those with a sense of integrity and courage may be more inclined to come forward. As a result, corporate fraud would likely decline, since management could no longer assume that employees will always comply with dishonest practices. Such legislation must be accompanied by a robust witness protection system, including the ability to give whistle-blowers new identities if necessary to ensure their safety.

Decolonising Indian law

Some of my ideas may not be immediately accepted because we have all been brainwashed for over a century about the manner of implementation of the law. But we need to make the law more acceptable and in alignment with the culture and instinctive sense of justice cherished by a majority of the population. My first suggestion is to move our courts towards being more inquisitorial, instead of being adversarial as they are now. This would make it closer to the European systems instead of the US and English systems.

In the latter system, the entire burden of proving the case is on the plaintiff in a civil case, or on the prosecution in a criminal case. The defendant is not obliged to reveal the entire case from their point of view. This imbalance is more pronounced when it comes to criminal cases. The judges in the adversarial system are slow at determining the facts for themselves instead of just looking at what is presented before them. But in the European system, the judges are more focused on delivering justice. That divides the burden of proof more equally between the two litigating parties.

I believe that the Indian mindset is more aligned with the European one. An Indian with no formal knowledge of the law is likely to agree that justice must be delivered instead of being 'won' with a better argument. This leads us to the other imperial idea of presuming that citizens have knowledge of the law. Under this idea, ignorance of the law is no defence. I believe that India must make efforts to allow ignorance, if proved, as a defence.

Sovereign immunity

Sovereign immunity is not an Indian idea. We have many examples in our mythology, history, folklore and literature of rulers acting in good faith but paying for it if their actions turn out to be a mistake. Therefore, even if you are a sovereign – and even if you did not intend to cause harm – you must bear the consequences of your actions. There is a provision for mitigation of consequences in our tradition, but there is no concept of full sovereign immunity. Even the rishis, devatas or kings of olden times never enjoyed full sovereign immunity in India.

Europe, however, has always had the concept of the king being the representative of the divine and thereby having sovereign immunity. It is an Anglo-Saxon idea that the State must not punish even a single innocent person, even if it means that many guilty also go free. But I believe that a bureaucrat or court must not be entitled to get away with a mistake just because they acted in good faith or on behalf of the sovereign. In the US, one can sue a state authority for wrongful prosecution. Such action is generally accepted and acted upon. With this principle, nobody is afforded unfettered immunity in the country, and liability can be imposed for mala fide acts.

Other countries – such as the UK, Germany, Canada, Australia, Sweden, Italy and South Africa – also allow individuals to sue the authorities for wrongful prosecution or miscarriage of justice. We in India too must discard the principle of sovereign immunity and bring in the practice of class-action suits for wrongful prosecution. This will not only enhance the justice mechanism but also improve the quality of justice served.

Approach to punishment

In India, punishment is concurrent instead of cumulative. If someone in our country is found guilty of robbery as well as murder and trespass in the course of it, the sentences for these offences are served concurrently. However, in countries like the US, they run in a cumulative fashion, which means that the offender has to finish one sentence before the next one starts. That is a great deterrence, because one could be in prison for decades for multiple crimes committed at once.

Even the police should be prosecuted if they are found to have used illegal force in the course of an investigation or arrest. But there is not much public support for such a view. Perhaps one should allow our police to use force but also place on them the burden of proving that they used an appropriate level of violence. For example, there is widespread public support for the Uttar Pradesh police and their method of law enforcement, in which they behave as both judge and executioner.

Reforms in the legal profession

In a democracy, should the laws only reflect what the elite believe, or ought the sentiment of the masses be recognised to bring about greater compliance? We need to strike a balance. The legal profession itself must be freed from unnecessary regulations. For example, lawyers in India face many restrictions on the kind of websites they can have, but from my experience, in other countries, lawyers without a decent website are considered unreliable. Indian law firms are also prohibited from entering into partnerships with non-lawyers, but the rest of the world is moving towards multidisciplinary partnerships in which lawyers, company secretaries and chartered accountants offer integrated services.

However, while freedom is essential, so are accountability and performance review.

This book explores many other ideas as well, and some of the above ideas in greater detail. Read on, democratise the idea of the law and its workings, and let the law truly be a function of a realisation, a decision by an informed majority.

2

Digitising Justice: Advancing Courtroom Technology

TECHNOLOGY HAS INCREASINGLY BECOME an all-pervasive aspect of our lives, as can be seen in our use of the internet, communication systems or e-governance platforms. There is no doubting the ease that technology has brought to our lives. The question is no longer one of 'whether' but of 'how' technology can be leveraged to improve the speed, quality and cost of justice delivery.

It's not as if Indian courts have not tried technological solutions in the past. However, these attempts have been ad hoc, consisting of electronic filing of documents, posting of court lists and orders online, use of legal research tools and, more recently, online hearing of cases. While these measures have certainly helped, we are nowhere close to transforming the justice system. Such a transformation calls for a detailed strategy, the key aspects of which are discussed in this chapter.

But what does 'transformation' mean in the context of Indian courts? The transformation I envisage for our judicial system would consist of the following:

i. Speedy disposal of cases: Private disputes of a civil or contractual nature should be concluded within 12 weeks, and prosecutions for minor and petty offences within 12 months. Complex civil and criminal litigations should take no longer than 2 years, and appeals from all cases – including final decisions at the high courts and the Supreme Court – should be completed within 18 months.

ii. Transparency: The litigants must get a clear view of how their cases are handled and decided in the courts. They should be able to know the exact reasons that lead to the court decisions affecting them.
iii. Consistency in decisions: Full awareness of the relevant laws, prior judicial decisions, and applicable customs and practices in the transformed judicial system will help courts across the country arrive at similar decisions in similar cases. This will strengthen a legal adviser's ability to predict the outcomes of disputes and provide better advice to prospective litigants.
iv. Cost reduction for litigants: The high cost of employing lawyers in India is due to the scarcity of legal talent in our country. There are a few high-quality lawyers practising law in any court here. Because of the limitations of physical courts, it is difficult or nearly impossible for any lawyer to appear in more than one court. As a consequence, a talented lawyer who appears in one court is generally limited to that court. Online courts would resolve this issue and lead to increased competition among lawyers, who would no longer be restricted by physical location. This would result in lower fees.

Does all this sound unrealistic? In my view, it is perfectly possible to achieve all these goals. The technological advances over the last decade and a half in every field of human activity have been so astonishing that there are now myriad ways to do so. From an implementation standpoint, the biggest challenge to ushering in a technological revolution in the Indian courts is the lack of vision, imagination and courage on the part of the state machinery.

Of the various categories of legal reforms mentioned in this book, technology reforms ought to be the least controversial as technology is politically agnostic. Such reforms would not require stepping on any political or bureaucratic toes and would provide the most cost-effective impact as they can be scaled up quickly and widely implemented. Any opposition to technological reforms could come from the players entrenched in the present system and lording over it – the lawyers, judges and court administrators. These individuals have become used to a certain style of practising law and administering justice, and any radical change would require much relearning on their part. Therefore, they are the ones who would tend to resist change.

While thinking of tech solutions, it is relevant to remember that we have an open court system in India – which means courtrooms are open not just for the litigants but also for the public to sit in and watch the proceedings. However, like elsewhere in the world, the open court system in India too has physical constraints and cannot accommodate more people than the room's physical capacity. Therefore, in my view, the prospect of a technological solution that removes the constraints of the physical courtroom should be welcomed. The system needs to adjust its old ways to fit the new world of technology.

Any suggested reform would have its critics, but India needs to move forward with essential changes. The reforms that would receive less political and social criticism should be implemented first, before moving on to the more challenging ones. With that approach, technological reforms for our judicial system would be the easiest to start with. The aim of this chapter is to describe the kind of solutions technology can offer to overcome some of the current problems troubling our legal system and to touch on the benefits these solutions can create for all the stakeholders in the system, principally the citizenry.

I advocate for wider and more urgent adoption of technology-driven courtrooms and suggest four sets of reform measures to achieve this. They are ordered by ease of implementation, starting with the least difficult.

i. Live-streaming of court proceedings across all levels of courts

Live-streaming of court hearings is already done for certain key cases argued in the Supreme Court. While the quality of the streams could be better, they make courtrooms transparent like never before. If the live-streaming feature is extended to all courts and tribunals across the country, it will lead to a better understanding among citizens about how cases are argued, what arguments find greater favour with the courts, how the country's laws work and operate, and how they are applied. This knowledge will, one hopes, trigger a greater understanding of and respect for the law, compelling people to comply with it.

Litigants will also see their lawyers in action, and this will pressure the lawyers into dropping several of their disagreeable practices in court – in particular, the unnecessary adjournment of court hearings, which they manipulate to their benefit. It is a big malaise that afflicts Indian courts. The professional negligence on the lawyers' part, often witnessed in the physical courts, will also be visible to a wider public. Therefore, it is certain that live-streaming of hearings would improve the quality of advocacy in our courts and expedite decision-making.

In addition, after witnessing the performance of various lawyers in court, prospective litigants can use their own judgment to choose who represents them rather than rely only on references as they currently do. The visibility of a particular lawyer's performance will give the client more information about the lawyer's knowledge, skills and capabilities. Live-streaming can also be expected to pressure lawyers and judges into behaving better in the courtroom.

ii. Creation of a knowledge grid

A common complaint about today's courts is the lack of consistency in decision-making by judges. This can be seen not just across courts but even within a court, where two judges in adjacent rooms can deliver very different judgments in similar cases. Their differing ideological inclinations can be one significant reason for this, but another is the variance in their levels of knowledge. This problem is further compounded by the differences in the capabilities of the lawyers arguing the cases.

Most lawyers and judges do not have encyclopaedic knowledge. That is why easy access to legal know-how is key to the high-quality administration of justice. Traditionally, this was achieved by building robust libraries, particularly in courts. One problem with this is the physical limitations of the court in buying and storing books. While the Supreme Court and high courts in India have very good libraries, the same cannot be said of the lower courts. Another problem is accessing updated books with the latest legal amendments. Also, having only one or a limited number of copies of a particular publication often leads to books being unavailable for long periods.

These limitations often lead judges to make decisions *per incuriam* (that is, without knowledge of law or precedent), causing the inconsistencies we see in rulings across our courts. Why should today's court system be held hostage to 18th-century systems of physical libraries, given the technological advances of today? In contrast, modern-day commercial law firms commonly use legal databases or knowledge management systems containing the latest judgments, legal opinions and partner advice. This system enables lawyers to take note of the positions taken by different lawyers across the firm on a particular subject or situation and ensures that the firm offers consistent advice to its clients regardless of the lawyer providing the advice. If the same facilities were made available to judges and lawyers across the country, they too would be better informed, and judicial decisions in the country would witness greater consistency.

The fix I suggest is the creation of a database of judgments, statutes, the latest changes in the law, and the latest social and commercial trends. This database must be updated continually, and all judges across the country must have access to it. This will help iron out the variance in knowledge levels in courts across India, and therefore the variance in the judgments passed by them. In addition, the benefits from such a database could multiply manifold if trained research teams were able to use it to support judicial officers in their decision-making.

This would radically transform the inconsistency in justice delivery across the country, as well as elevate the quality of the justice delivered.

Access to this knowledge grid must be enabled by highly advanced research tools, more sophisticated than those offered by the existing online legal libraries. It should be as easy to use as an online search engine.

iii. Virtual or online courts

India lacks the resources to significantly expand its physical courtrooms – either in size or number – to tackle the current backlog of cases or the volume of future disputes. There are practical limits to how many people a courtroom can hold. Moreover, reaching courts, especially in crowded Indian cities, is often burdensome due to traffic congestion, public transport inefficiencies and commuting costs. Building new courts also demands substantial budget allocations from an already resource-constrained state. Virtual or online courts offer a compelling solution to these challenges.

Unlike physical courtrooms, online courts can accommodate far more participants and observers. They eliminate travel time for litigants, lawyers and judges, and reduce costs significantly. Funds that would have gone into constructing new buildings could instead be directed towards developing digital infrastructure and expanding the judiciary's capacity through technology. Compared to the time and expense required to build physical courts, setting up virtual ones is quicker, cheaper and more scalable. In short, one solution addresses multiple problems at a fraction of the cost and time.

India has already experimented with virtual courts, especially during the COVID-19 pandemic. As physical gatherings became unsafe, the crisis forced the Supreme Court and other judicial bodies to adopt video hearings. These online sessions helped move cases forward. However, the experience was far from seamless. Many participants struggled with poor internet connectivity and inadequate technology, highlighting the need for better digital infrastructure. Lawyers and litigants frequently experienced dropped connections, and the platform also struggled to accommodate the high number of participants.

Another major limitation was the use of smartphones and laptops. Their small screens significantly diminished the courtroom experience for everyone involved. Yet, these problems are not insurmountable. With thoughtful planning and relatively modest investment – far less than what would be required to expand physical court infrastructure – simple technological upgrades can dramatically improve the online court experience.

Shifting from physical to virtual courts has the potential to transform the delivery of justice and reinvigorate the rule of law. Every stage of the process – listing, arguments and decision-making – stands to become far more streamlined and efficient than it is today.

iv. Use of AI and holographic technology

The use of AI represents the next stage in the evolution of judicial technology. Initially, AI could assist judges in decision-making, particularly in straightforward cases, and may eventually evolve to replace human judges in certain contexts. In the early stages, AI could be deployed to evaluate pleadings in simple disputes – such as sale-of-goods cases or other matters that do not require witness testimony and can be decided purely on documentary evidence. As familiarity with technology grows and AI systems mature, they could be applied to increasingly complex cases, starting with those where the legal process remains relatively straightforward.

Indian law, including the Code of Civil Procedure, 1908 (CPC) and various special statutes, already allows for the summary disposal of such cases. However, lawyers often exploit legal loopholes to delay proceedings even in these straightforward matters in an effort to serve their clients' interests.

This misuse of procedural law is especially common in cases involving bounced cheques, bank loan defaults and enforcement of guarantees. Accused parties in such matters frequently try to avoid summary trials, aiming to prolong proceedings indefinitely and frustrate the process. Even when all evidence is present – for instance, in criminal cases where a charge sheet has been filed – prosecutors may still oppose summary trials, instead insisting on full-length hearings. This undermines the purpose of summary procedures, which are designed to deliver swift justice.

It would be a while before AI could assist in cases involving intricate facts, such as murder trials and other serious offences. But it could already serve as a digital judicial assistant – similar to a law clerk – providing judges with preliminary drafts of judgments. In the next phase, AI could operate independently, delivering judgments without human intervention by analysing the pleadings and documents submitted. Eventually, it may be capable of handling more complex cases, taking on a greater share of the judicial workload.

The need for translation services will be keenly felt to hear cases in a multilingual nation like India. The Indian government is already working on plans for the creation of online courts with translation services, which could become operational in the not-too-distant future.

Besides AI, another new advancement is 3D or holographic video conferencing. Holographic technology was utilised by Prime Minister Narendra Modi in his election campaigns in 2012 and 2014. He used technology developed by a company called MDH Hologram to design and manage his holographic mass addresses. A lifelike 3D hologram of Modi was projected onto the stage at his party's campaigns. This technology enabled him to extend the reach of his campaign's message and provided him the opportunity to 'appear' before his electorate at approximately 1,500 locations and 'personally' address about 100 million voters without having to be physically present in front of them.

With the ever-emerging advancements in technology and its facilities in every region of the country, holograms and 3D video conferencing could become a cheaper, more effective means of communication. It will not be long before courtrooms adopt advanced 3D technology to create simulations of all the stakeholders – lawyers, litigants, witnesses – at a trial, making court proceedings more accessible from any location.

Live-streaming

The year 2018 was pivotal for the Indian judicial system due to the revolution introduced in the courts by the *Swapnil Tripathi v. Union of India* judgment.[1] This case was filed to bring greater transparency to legal matters of constitutional importance, and the petitioners succeeded in their effort. A law student named Swapnil Tripathi was interning at the Supreme Court in 2017 and struggled to attend hearings as an intern due to the limitation of space in courtrooms. He filed a PIL seeking access to live-streaming of Supreme Court proceedings within its premises so that people could witness the hearings without crowding the courtrooms.

As a consequence of this PIL, in September 2018 Chief Justice Dipak Misra and Justices A.M. Khanwilkar and D.Y. Chandrachud held that cases of constitutional and national importance should be broadcast to the public via live-streaming over the internet. This judgment recognised the need for live-streaming of court proceedings and encouraged it as it would lead to greater transparency and judicial accountability. The three-judge bench in the case referred to practices in countries such as Israel, France, the US, Canada, Singapore and Germany in identifying live-streaming as an essential aspect of judicial dispensation. Their view was that live-streaming of court proceedings would lead to better accessibility to justice for citizens.

The Supreme Court opined that 'publicised justice' is an essential aspect of connecting the entire system to the litigant, or a case to all those who wish to observe it closely.[2] The aim was to foster a system that catered directly to litigants and favoured them without undue bias towards lawyers and judges. Courts need to be made approachable for litigants seeking justice and protection of their rights, and this is possible only when there is transparency in the country's legal system.

It was not until three years later in 2021 that the 'Model Rules for Live-Streaming and Recording of Court Proceedings'[3] were introduced to foster better access to justice for the people. The rules aimed to encourage inclusivity and expedite the creation of the necessary infrastructure for recording and live-streaming of court proceedings. They instruct that hearings not live-streamed must be recorded and provided to the litigant.

The idea underlying the concept of open courts is judicial transparency. In simple terms, this principle instructs that judges must not act discreetly but rather conduct their business publicly. An old English law theory prescribes that 'justice must not just be done but also be seen to be done'.[4] This theory is based on the notion that where there is no publicity, there is no justice.[5]

Traditionally, all courts were open courts, except for some sensitive cases that were concealed from the public eye. In theory, this concept of open courts may work well, but in practice, the physical limitations discussed earlier make it impossible for everyone who wishes to witness the proceedings to fit in a courtroom. With virtual courts, it will be possible for a large number of spectators to view the hearings. As previously mentioned, this will contribute to inculcating a sense of professionalism and transparency among judges and lawyers.

In a country like India, where decision-making does not solely rely on a plain reading of the law, it is important that checks are imposed on judges and lawyers so that the essence of justice is not compromised. Digitisation of the court system and courtrooms might be the most efficient method of achieving this. This idea has been adopted in many jurisdictions which, willingly or unwillingly, inherited English law, such as India.[6]

The open-court principle is not an absolute one. Some exceptions are recognised. For example, judges can ask the public to leave the court to protect the identity of victims in sexual offence cases or of the parties involved in matrimonial disputes. The general idea is that exceptions to open hearings may be made where publicity could compromise justice, sovereign interests or the right to privacy of the litigants. Court proceedings can be recorded on video, which is beneficial to litigants in appeals as they can use the recordings in the appeal process to point out procedural flaws in the trial court. It can also allow judges hearing appeals to monitor the lower judiciary better and to ensure that laws are more systematically applied across the country.

The connection between transparency and the rule of law can be explained with the example of any competitive game or sport. The loser of a contest only accepts the outcome if the game has followed fair procedures, and, more importantly, if the loser can *see* those procedures being applied fairly.[7] Our practical life experiences affirm this and also explain why transparency is so necessary.

If a person is accused of a crime, it is more likely that they will be treated fairly in an open trial than in a closed one because the presence of the general public will pressure prosecutors and judges to be fair and to follow the law to preserve their own credibility. It also affords observers the opportunity to point out flaws in the directions issued by the court and make a fair assessment of its ruling in the case. It offers citizens a role in their judicial system and gives them confidence in the judiciary.

While people's opinions may not change the result of a trial, they have the power to compel judges to make informed decisions that are not influenced by immoral or illegal motives. Transparency is an efficient means to induce judicial integrity. Courts can only win the confidence of the people if they expose themselves to public scrutiny by making their proceedings open and showing a willingness to educate the public. Any right-thinking lawyer will also endorse the open-court principle. Lawyers know clients will not come to them if they cannot see for themselves that the system works fairly and produces fair outcomes – justice must be *seen* to be done.

Without live-streaming, if clients are unable to be physically present in court, their lawyers are their only source of information about what happened at the hearing of their case. There is no other mechanism by which clients can monitor the proceedings, leaving their lawyers completely free to give their own ambiguous version of events. A common example of this is when lawyers agree to non-serious adjournments and insist that the court forced the adjournments on them. This kind of behaviour has contributed significantly to the common person's loss of confidence in the judicial system.

With online courts and live-streaming, clients can directly view for themselves the progress of their case, reducing their reliance on their lawyers.[8] They can understand whether frivolous adjournments were sought and if they are being misled by their lawyers. Even if they don't view the hearings, the fact that they *can* choose to do so is sure to make lawyers more cautious about being dishonest with them. Remote access to courtroom activity ensures that lawyers cannot take undue advantage of their clients' absence from court.

Another aspect that live-streaming and recording of proceedings could resolve is in the matter of appeals. This relates to a peculiarity in the manner in which judgments are delivered. The general rule is that a court has to address all arguments raised in a proceeding, and its judgment must explain why each one has been accepted or rejected. In practice, however, court judgments sometimes overlook a few arguments, often because a judge believes those arguments are irrelevant or minor. The problem for the litigant arises when these arguments are raised in an appeal before an appellate court, which then refuses to deal with them because they were not addressed by the lower court. If the proceedings in the lower court had been recorded, it would be easy to establish whether the arguments had indeed been made earlier or were being raised for the first time in the appeal.

There are some courtroom episodes from India worth recounting to underline the importance of live-streaming and recording of court proceedings. In 2022, a complaint was filed by Justice Sushri Arpita Sahu of the Allahabad High Court, accusing Advocates Ritesh Mishra and Mohan Singh of using offensive language towards her in the courtroom. The court directed the police to review footage from recordings of the court proceedings in question as part of their investigation into the matter.[9] Live-streaming is a necessity in unfortunate situations such as this one.

Misbehaviour in court can also occur on the part of judges, and their conduct is often compromised. With live-streaming or recording, they will now be compelled to maintain courtroom etiquette. If there is some form of surveillance and public monitoring, the likelihood of displays of disrespect in courtrooms will be lower. Transparency is the greatest disinfectant a murky system can have. Live-streaming also allows litigants to better evaluate and choose their lawyers based on the quality of their arguments in earlier cases and their courtroom conduct. They can also review recordings of hearings from courtrooms across the country when deciding on their lawyer, reducing dependency on personal recommendations to find the right one.

As of 2022, the official estimate of pending court cases in India is at an all-time high of 70,000. The Supreme Court places the blame for this seemingly insurmountable backlog on the adjournments sought in almost every matter that comes up for hearing before the courts.[10] Aggrieved and accused parties are often caught in a rut of court visits as their cases make no progress. The absence of key participants at hearings and the repeated adjournments only lead to further agony and delays.[11] Even when court cases are delayed by the inefficiency of the judiciary, the costs of these delays are always borne by the litigants. Court reforms could not only reduce the backlog of cases but also create a system with integrity and accountability. The current lack of public confidence in the system can be erased if justice is made more accessible.

Brazil has allowed live video and audio broadcasting of court proceedings since 2005. The coverage includes the deliberations and voting process undertaken by the judges. The relentless gaze of TV cameras enables transparency in the courts and leads to better professionalism and discipline among both judges and lawyers as they are constantly under public scrutiny. This transparency will ultimately uplift democracy itself.[12] In the US, live audio feeds of all courtroom arguments have been streamed since 1955.[13] The lack of video helps protect the privacy of the parties concerned while still allowing for public scrutiny. People can listen to proceedings across the country's courtrooms through the live audio feeds and thereby hold lawyers and judges accountable.

This degree of public scrutiny will also lead to a reduction in the number of appeals going from the trial courts to the higher courts, with cases being resolved at the lower courts. This will also chip away at the backlog in the higher courts in India. Recordings of proceedings at the trial level can be reproduced in the appellate courts, and by examining these recordings the appellate courts can evaluate the arguments and decisions made earlier. This will lead to speedier justice and appropriate application of the law. Such a system will also restrict lawyers from filing frivolous appeals based on vexatious claims.[14]

Live-streaming comes with some of its own concerns and challenges, of course. Recordings of court hearings might be deliberately misused or misrepresented. Extracts of these recordings could be presented out of context. Lawyers are already complaining about clips from live-streamed proceedings being circulated on social media and being sensationalised or misrepresented.[15] This is a real concern as court proceedings should not be used for media trials or for unfairly criticising the judicial process. However, this concern can be mitigated by putting in place a statutory regime to regulate the use of live-streamed content, with stringent policing and penalties for violations. Software-based restrictions could also be applied to prevent recordings and live-streamed content from being downloaded, edited and circulated on other platforms.

Live-streaming would also compel lawyers to do away with the casual banter of the courtroom. That may take away a small degree of enjoyable casualness that exists in courts today, but the trade-off would be worth it. Perfection is a mirage, so the goal of reforms should be to strive for a system that is more refined. Millions will eventually be able to witness courts in action from the comfort of their homes.[16] Of course, many judges and lawyers will resist this increased transparency because they are comfortable with the way things are. However, given that our court systems are public institutions marked by gross underperformance, the comfort of lawyers and judges should probably not be factored into the decision.

This reform will not only hasten the delivery of justice but also function as a regulatory authority, constantly assessing the judicial system and facilitating continuous growth and legal advancements in doing right 'by' the people, 'for' the people. It will certainly rein in the lawyers and judges who currently play to the gallery. The performance of a court will now be judged in a more direct fashion by the people, and that will make courts more accountable.

Live-streaming of hearings can initially be implemented in the Supreme Court, the high courts and the tribunals, and gradually extended to the lower courts. The law and the rules for this are already in place. Gradually, capacity will have to be built to enable this at scale. It is important, however, that from the outset all types of cases – not just the exciting and controversial ones – are live-streamed. Even the 'boring' cases are important to the litigants and to those studying the court system. There will also be sensitive cases that some will want to prevent from being live-streamed. However, our courts are truly independent, and it is their duty to keep in check any elements trying to spoil the system.

As more and more cases are live-streamed, judges will also have to evolve and nuance their position on when to grant exceptions and restrict public access to recordings or live-streaming to protect the privacy of litigants, given that the Supreme Court has recently affirmed the fundamental right to privacy for all Indians.[17] Practical solutions to address the problems are easy to conceive and implement, even if they do not exist today. However, we cannot cite the present lack of adequate safeguards against possible misuse of live-streaming as a justification for abandoning it altogether. Technology should be leveraged to make all court proceedings available to as many relevant people as possible.

Knowledge grid

Justice is placed before liberty, equality and fraternity in the Preamble of the Constitution of India. Without social, economic and political justice we cannot have the other three concepts present in society, and the people then have to turn to the judiciary for their rights to be enforced.[18]

Judicial decision-making relies heavily on the application of mind and appropriate execution of the law by the judges. It is important to assess the Indian justice delivery system to see if it is ensuring the people their rights as declared in the Constitution.

Quality justice is consistent, standardised and uniformly delivered to all citizens. But if judicial discretion is allowed and each judge interprets and applies the law differently, justice is often compromised. One must keep in mind that present-day decisions will set the precedents for future cases. So, improper application of mind by judges will set the entire Indian judiciary system back for generations. The proposed knowledge grid will serve to avert this kind of situation.

The grid will consist of a robust and comprehensive database of legal information, including judgments, statutes, interpretations and applications of such statutes, subsequent rules and regulations, legal commentaries and expert comments. The grid will templatise and organise this knowledge to ensure that all judges and lawyers have easy access. This should lead to an end of the culture of judicial isolation as judges could be constantly updated on the latest legal developments in the country.

It is very important that the interface of the knowledge grid is efficient and user-friendly so that judges and their assistants can navigate the vast ocean of legal, business and cultural information with ease and efficiency. The search tool should be as easy to use as an online search engine. I believe that India already has the resources to develop such a grid and bind the legal fraternity to one knowledge pool. It would greatly reduce the hours of isolated research that would otherwise be required.

The idea of a justice system outsourcing the gathering of know-how is not unique and has been implemented in other parts of the world to varying degrees.[19] Here are some notable examples of European countries where technology has been effectively deployed to create repositories of judicial knowledge:

i. In the Netherlands, there are legal forums that supply such information, and their work is held in very high regard. They have strong authority, even though their advice is not binding on the judge. The quality of their inputs is sufficient to function as a guideline for the judiciary.
ii. In Spain, the Association of Judges for Democracy provides judges with access to two blogs – one on issues of criminal law and the other on matters of social law. These blogs offer information on case law, documents and legal analysis.[20]
iii. In France, there are several 'discussion lists' and 'blogs', both created and used by judges, each dedicated to a particular legal function or field. Some of them are: Civilnet (for judges performing civil functions); Instru (for investigating judges); Jafnet (for family judges); Justepeine (for judges enforcing sentences); Themis (for administrative judges); and Jprox (for local judges and lay judges). These tools enable judges to exchange information on legislative and jurisprudential developments as well as articles on doctrine and decision-making models.
iv. In Finland, within the jurisdiction of one of the five courts of appeal in the country, the courts have organised working groups composed of judges – and sometimes also external experts such as prosecutors and lawyers – to improve the quality of decisions delivered by those courts and to harmonise practices among them.

A comprehensive knowledge grid that institutionalises expertise and supports judges across the nation and the judicial hierarchy can transform the quality of justice delivered in our courtrooms. This will significantly enhance the performance of judges, reducing the worry for litigants about the quality of judges in the town where their case is being heard.

Experts in the field consider the European e-Justice Portal to be the future of legal practice. It provides information on all kinds of laws, practices and cases. It was created with the aim of improving access to justice for everyone and provides updates on legal news and blogs that are accessible to the portal's subscribers. By standardising availability and access to knowledge for the legal fraternity and binding the European countries to a common platform, the portal has made the delivery of justice more efficient.[21]

Such knowledge systems have existed for a few decades now in private commercial organisations such as the big multinational consulting and accounting firms. Now many international as well as Indian law firms are also adopting similar systems to support their client-facing professionals. This results in clients having a uniform experience when working with any of these firms, regardless of which consultant they are assigned or which part of the world the service is delivered. The hope is that we will have a similar outcome with our justice delivery system once a knowledge grid is created for it.

Certain vital considerations have to be kept in mind when creating a knowledge grid. They include the following:

i. The grid will have to be kept relevant and updated to always function as a cutting-edge tool. Collaborations will have to be forged with reputed legal institutions – such as bar associations and legal research organisations – to gather the latest judgments, legal developments and changes in legislation. The knowledge grid must constantly evolve to keep pace with the ever-changing legal landscape.

ii. The grid must have a powerful search engine capable of presenting the most appropriate material from the database for any search. Judges should be able to seek and obtain immediate responses to their queries, with the search functionality providing tailored results based on specific keywords, case citations or legal topics. Needless to say, advanced filtering and sorting options will have to be provided. They should be able to refine their search results based on jurisdiction, court level, date or legal principles, allowing them to find the most relevant and applicable legal precedents.

iii. Data security and confidentiality are of paramount importance, so stringent measures such as encryption protocols, access controls, regular backups and strict adherence to data protection regulations would need to be in place to protect the integrity of the knowledge grid.

iv. Comprehensive training and support programmes would be required to familiarise judges with the functionalities and features of the grid so that they can use it to its full potential.

v. Judges, senior lawyers and academics must be encouraged to contribute their responses to judgments – their insights could be in the form of annotations and summaries. This would enrich the database by reflecting the collective wisdom of the country's bench and bar.

vi. Campaigns and training sessions to spread awareness among judges, legal professionals and relevant stakeholders would promote adoption of the knowledge grid and should be conducted across the nation.

The knowledge grid can easily be funded by the taxpayer. An alternative would be to finance it as a public–private partnership. But for this to happen, certain services would have to be put behind a paywall. The fee-based system will help sustain the infrastructure. This model can foster a sense of appreciation for the services offered by the knowledge grid among the legal fraternity while also ensuring its long-term sustainability. Ultimately, any cost reduction for lawyers should result in a proportionate cost reduction for clients and litigants.

As the knowledge grid spreads its roots, judges will find that they have a powerful tool at their disposal. Divergent viewpoints will become fewer as the system gets honed. The quality and consistency of judicial decision-making will improve across the country, and justice delivery will be transformed.

Virtual courts

The next step to live-streaming of court proceedings is the establishment of virtual or online courts. This would lead to even more benefits for litigants, lawyers and judges.

One of the positives to have come from the COVID-19 pandemic was that several organisations – whether government or private – have moved from physical offices to online platforms and a work-from-home model for their employees. But only some courts have gone online. The pandemic unintentionally became a catalyst for legal reforms through the use of technology. In a breakthrough decision, the Supreme Court of India mandated the use of video conferencing in judicial proceedings on 6 April 2020. Until then, the use of technology in Indian courts had been very limited.

On 11 September 2020, the Parliamentary Standing Committee on Personnel, Public Grievances, Law and Justice released an interim report on the functioning of virtual courts after the COVID-19 pandemic.[22] The report recognised the importance of introducing virtual hearings and noted that over 1.5 million court hearings had been conducted via video conferencing during the lockdown. The one thing that became apparent through this limited exercise was the advantage of online courts over physical courts.

Some of the key limitations of physical courts are as follows:

i. They are woefully inadequate in number.
ii. Their design is archaic and their physical infrastructure sub-standard.
iii. They are generally inefficient, which impacts the time that will be taken by the courts to dispose of a case.
iv. They are usually very crowded, which makes for a difficult work environment, particularly when it comes to the important task of justice delivery.
v. They are very expensive to build and establish.
vi. Physical courtrooms automatically limit the presence of expertise in the courtroom.
vii. For litigants, the distance they have to travel to get to a court can be a big burden.
viii. Lastly, appearing in court can be an intimidating experience for the litigant.

All these problems can be addressed by moving hearings to virtual courts.

The momentum gained with the initial rollout of online courts in India has meant that the time is ripe for a comprehensive technological overhaul. This revolution does not need changes to substantive laws and can be achieved with some basic amendments to the civil and criminal procedural codes. It will build on the foundations of the past while embracing the possibilities of a technology-led future.

The online court hearings during the pandemic highlighted the advantages of online courts. It became evident that the money that would have been spent on creating physical infrastructure could be redirected towards improving the technological capabilities of courts and even towards enhancing the remuneration of judges. Video conferencing also simplifies the process of obtaining witness testimonies, removing the unnecessary formalities associated with physical courtrooms and allowing for significant improvements in the enforcement of time limits on lawyers' arguments.

The cumbersome task of recording witness statements can be streamlined and could even be pre-recorded to be presented in a virtual court later. No longer will the system be constrained by witnesses who become disinterested on account of delays or by the archaic evidence-taking process, as they can now provide their testimony from any corner of the country. In sensitive matters such as cases of sexual offence, witnesses are often apprehensive about appearing physically in court and attesting to the crime. But an online hearing may make them less inhibited and more likely to divulge details. Also, virtual courts can eliminate the need for the physical presence of defendants in specific courts. Transporting defendants to courtrooms is often a risky exercise that demands elaborate logistics.

The marriage of technology and justice has the potential to reshape the Indian legal system. Physical courtrooms and virtual courts can coexist, each complementing the other in pursuit of a consistent, fair and efficient judicial system.

However, the digital divide is still a matter of concern as a stark gap exists between those who have access to technology and those who do not. It is a divide that needs bridging, for justice should know no boundaries. Efforts will have to be made to bring high-speed internet connectivity and the necessary electronic devices to people living in remote areas and to those with limited financial resources. Digital literacy programmes could empower more individuals with the knowledge and skills required to navigate the system. Also, such a transformation will need significant upgrades to the existing technology infrastructure. Internet bandwidth would have to be increased to ensure seamless live-streams, and more advanced cameras and high-resolution screens would need to be used in courtrooms.

I envisage these technological changes happening in three phases. The first phase would consist of the deployment of technology that streamlines and improves online hearings at the Supreme Court and high courts. Once the technology is perfected at the higher court levels, it can be implemented at the lower courts. The second phase would see the transformation of each court in the country into an online court, while the third phase would have all the online courts interconnected.

This would entail changes to procedural law to allow judges with similar experience and expertise to hear cases dealing with subjects in which they have personal expertise, regardless of their location. Similarly, clients could have lawyers with specific expertise from anywhere in the country represent them, as the lawyers would no longer be bound by their physical location. The best lawyers would be able to handle cases in courts across the country, all from the comfort of their chosen location.

With these changes, lengthy arguments by lawyers that unnecessarily delay trials could become a thing of the past. Judges would have the ability to force lawyers to conclude their arguments in an efficient manner. Lawyers could also be given timeslots and told exactly when their matter would be heard, and for how long. Allotted timeslots would put pressure on lawyers to hone their arguments and present more concise and succinct points. With judges and lawyers sitting in different physical spaces, the merits of the case would begin to count more at hearings than the personality of the lawyers. Time limits for presenting arguments can bring more discipline to hearings by discouraging showmanship and ensuring swifter verdicts. Lawyers and litigants would no longer have to wait hours for their case to be heard.

Another aspect of the courts that technology can change is 'court craft'. This refers to the conduct of lawyers and how they understand and present their cases. More senior lawyers have usually honed their skills in court craft and are better able to get judgments in their favour. The craft involves aspects such as the lawyer's physical appearance, style of speech, camaraderie with the bench, and their ability to dominate the courtroom. It often plays a crucial role in the outcome of a court hearing. But in the case of virtual courts, this aspect of court craft is diminished. Online courts would handicap lawyers who rely more on court craft and familiarity with the judges and have established a certain dominance from practising for years at a particular court. These lawyers would see a visible reduction in their practice as the politics of intimidation would be removed from the courtrooms.

Well-prepared junior lawyers would then have a better chance against more senior lawyers with bigger reputations. This would definitely lead to a greater degree of fairness in judicial decisions as they would be based on the application of law and the facts of the case rather than the personality of the lawyers. One consequence of this would be a reduction in the fees of the better-known lawyers. In India, the fees charged by a lawyer are determined by their seniority. Lower fees would allow litigants to hire lawyers with greater expertise in their area of need.

In online courts, lawyers could supplement their oral pleadings with audiovisual support, enhancing the strength of their arguments. This would mean a dramatic shift in the skills lawyers would need to win cases, and that is something they will need to adjust to and train themselves for. The move from physical to electronic formats for court records would lead to easier operation, lower risk of tampering and faster transmission of documents between institutions. Electronic copies of pleadings and related documents would be quicker to sift through than paper records.

In addition, litigants would benefit from the uniformity and accessibility of e-filing, which has seen limited adoption in India. Electronic filing of documents has been a great success in the US since the protocol was introduced in 2007. India can follow their example to allow case documents such as pleadings, motions and petitions to be filed online with the court. Of course, a transition to virtual courts would require lawyers to overcome any initial scepticism or reservations and familiarise themselves with the latest online technologies. Concerns may be raised about the efficacy of digital proceedings and the limitations of our infrastructure, and the initial costs to lay a sound digital foundation would be significant. The government has to power past the objections of people resistant to these changes.

In the UK, public users of virtual courts are reportedly highly satisfied with the commercial and civil cases being conducted online. However, judges and practitioners of law feel that complex criminal matters are relatively less suited for online hearings because intense back-and-forth arguments can be difficult to conduct online. But there is no doubt that virtual courts have advantages that any legal system can benefit from. When a document or a piece of evidence is referred to during an online hearing, every participant in the case can immediately view it on their screens. Legal teams can access their own private version of the document with the notes and comments they made during the preparatory phase. This effective digital presentation of evidence makes proceedings more efficient, saving significant trial time. It is also useful for litigants, who can view the entire courtroom conveniently on their screens, away from the crowded and intimidating physical environment of a regular court.[23]

Australia considers virtual courts a safer option in cases involving high-profile prisoners as they mitigate the risks tied to their public movement and safety. Children and other vulnerable witnesses also feel a sense of confidence and are more forthcoming in giving their testimonies online. It is also easier to seek the active assistance of interpreters and sign-language experts, as they simply have to join virtually rather than be physically present. However, Australian judges find it more efficient to assess the demeanour of a witness in physical courtrooms than online, as their body language can be seen clearly. A virtual court cannot offer this level of proximity that physical courts provide.[24]

With the exponential rise in participation in virtual courts in the US, there has reportedly been a decline in the rate of ex parte orders and adjournments as virtual courtrooms are more accessible and defendants appear for all their hearings. It has also broadened exposure for lawyers, who can now compare notes with other lawyers from around the country and learn from the expertise of judges from other jurisdictions.[25]

The dawn of virtual courts will usher in a new chapter in the Indian legal system, where the power of technology is harmonised with the pursuit of justice.

The 3D digital courtroom

Given the rate at which technology is advancing, it is not far-fetched that holograms and 3D technology will be the future of courtrooms. Even if they are appearing for a hearing remotely, the demeanour, body language and other physical attributes of witnesses, litigants and other courtroom stakeholders can be easily gauged, unlike in video conferencing.[26] 3D technology can be used to create hybrid courtrooms, which bring together physical and online courtrooms. It is also possible to recreate an entire courtroom virtually using holograms. The use of holograms can also make hearings more interactive than on other digital platforms.

The Delhi High Court is already considering the deployment of 3D technology by way of holograms in courtroom proceedings. Clearly, concepts from science fiction movies are not just fantasy anymore.[27] One of the most promising courtroom applications of virtual reality will be the supplementing of arguments made in courts. Lawyers arguing a case should be allowed to make presentations or use audiovisual media to supplement their arguments or points, the way it is done in company boardrooms. That would make it easier for judges to appreciate the nuances of the case before them.

Lawyers can use 3D technology to create extremely realistic schematics of the incident in question, and this can help judges better understand and visualise the crime and the sequence of events as they happened. This is especially useful in cases where the original crime scene cannot be revisited, either because it has been destroyed or because the evidence has been tampered with.[28] The use of such tools, which are quite inexpensive, will help deepen the analysis and enable judges to look beyond the arguments presented and effectively retrace the sequence of events.

If these tools are permitted, lawyers with otherwise average communication skills would be better able to communicate their clients' positions. This would lead to a significant overall improvement in the quality of lawyering in courts, and court battles between those who can afford skilled lawyers and those who cannot would be more even. Therefore, I would argue that using technology could reduce the imbalance between the rich and the poor and lead to the justice system being fairer than it is today.

Artificial intelligence

The aim of introducing AI into the court system is to automate as many human functions as possible. Initially, AI can take over tasks performed by judicial clerks, then assist judges by analysing cases in detail and drafting potential judgments. Eventually, in certain types of cases, AI may even replace human judges entirely. This would free judges from routine or mundane disputes, allowing them to focus their expertise on complex issues that machines cannot resolve. The combined efforts of AI and the existing judiciary could significantly increase the number of cases handled and at a much faster rate. This has the potential to dramatically reduce the enormous backlog of court cases currently burdening India's legal system.

The broader goal is to train AI judges to deliver judgments within four to twelve weeks. Their decisions will be consistent across similar cases, making justice more predictable, of higher quality and delivered more swiftly than under the traditional system. This could significantly help restore public confidence in the judiciary – especially given that India's court backlog includes numerous cases of a similar nature, many of which could be handled by AI or AI-assisted courts. In some countries these ideas are already being implemented, but in India this remains a vision for the future.

The Chief Justice of India, D.Y. Chandrachud, said that technology is here to stay when introducing AI services for live transcription of constitutional bench hearings. This project followed other AI initiatives already in operation, such as the Supreme Court Portal for Assistance in Court Efficiency (SUPACE) and the Supreme Court Vidhik Anuvaad Software (SUVAS).[29] SUPACE is a composite, AI-assisted tool that reads case files, extracts relevant information, drafts case documents, collects relevant facts and/or laws, and makes them available to a judge who may be deciding a case dealing with similar facts. It is not designed to make decisions for the judges but only processes facts to produce relevant material that may be vital to them in coming to a decision. This tool produces tailor-made results for each case and helps judges navigate through cases. Not only is it a time-saving and efficient mechanism that judges can use, but it can also lead to a significant reduction in the backlog and pendency of cases in India's courts.

SUVAS is a machine-assisted translation tool trained by AI. It was launched in November 2019 by then Chief Justice, S.A. Bobde, to promote and ensure the use of regional languages in judicial proceedings by translating court orders, judgments, notifications and all other communication from English to regional languages and vice versa.

Countries such as the US have employed AI tools for research purposes and to help predict the outcome of certain cases. In the UK, AI is used to manage and organise cases and filings so there is minimal delay during hearings. China has a 'smart courts' system that allows each judge to be connected to an AI server that facilitates legal research and decision-making. It identifies precedents and principles based on data that has been previously entered, allowing judges to make speedy decisions.

Since 2014, China has been able to publish almost 140 million cases on its public portal. Algorithmic analytics allow the software to assess evidence, make a case, analyse the reasoning and recommend viable decisions. The introduction of technology in governance has allowed China to monitor judges, standardise the decision-making process and provide public services that are uniform.[30]

It is not too far-fetched to imagine India achieving something like this. It is clear that AI is the future of legal systems and that our country must adopt it as soon as possible. The existing levels of technology might only allow templatised pleadings, and that too only in simple cases such as summary suits. Cases designated for disposal as summary suits under today's procedural laws do not require any witnesses to be presented in court and are tried solely on evidentiary documents.

We need to create an online portal where lawyers or litigants can enter data in boxes provided for AI to then collate and analyse. However, if AI is expected to replace humans, the data needs to be entered in a standardised language for it to comprehend correctly. At present, AI is unable to sift through irregularities in expression, idiomatic language and other deficiencies in communication and presentation. Inputting data in a set format would alleviate this problem.

Modern commercial law firms use templates to enable the use of AI. The role of AI is to employ big data techniques to generate drafts of contracts and agreements using the input data. Lawyers then review the drafted clauses and refine them further based on the needs of their clients. The aim is not to replace lawyers but to increase their efficiency and streamline their work. This would also result in lower legal fees for litigants.

Templatised pleadings would also level the playing field for lawyers and litigants as the language used to file cases would be uniform regardless of the skills of the lawyer filing it. This would ensure fairness and efficiency in the legal process. With the judicious use of AI, a case could be concluded in six to eight months, even allowing time for appeals. Standardised templates could be secured using blockchain technology, enhancing the reliability of evidence and fortifying the digital security of case files. To achieve this, standardised authentication systems and proper procedural safeguards must be installed on online platforms.

The potential for AI to automate first-level decision-making in straightforward disputes can be explored as the majority of cases heard in our country fall in this category. Tests have demonstrated promising outcomes, indicating that AI-based systems can drastically reduce the time required for courts to resolve cases. In the beginning, AI might be best used to analyse cases and support human judges by writing out the first draft of a judgment. As the AI learns over time, it could take over judicial functions from human judges.

The first phase of using AI in courts would be in cases that require pure documentation, where the judgment is based more on data and less on nuance and interpretation. Eventually, a more efficient system capable of handling complex disputes can be built. China already has more than hundred robots in courts across the country as it actively pursues a transition to smart justice. These robots can retrieve case histories and past verdicts, reducing the workload of officials. Some of the robots even have specialisations such as commercial law or labour law.[31]

The second phase could begin once the superior judiciary is comfortable with human judges being replaced by AI at trial courts. The experiment could be extended to the courts of appeal, the high courts and even the Supreme Court. Most disputes at the trial court level should get resolved within weeks instead of the years it takes today. Even in a scenario where a case reaches the higher courts, it should not take more than two years to be resolved.

In the third phase, AI could deal with disputes that cannot be resolved by merely considering documentation. This will open up capacity for human judges to deal with more complex cases. As technology evolves, the manner of implementation of AI and AI-driven solutions will also change. The AI ecosystem can also be extended beyond the courtroom with the development of tools such as legal bots that can provide litigants with basic legal services in a cost-effective manner. The aim would be to foster a justice system in which outcomes are not solely dependent on the quality of legal representation that a litigant can afford.

In February 2023, a Colombian judge used the AI application ChatGPT to deliver a decision in court. The case pertained to insurance claims for an autistic child. The judge asked the AI bot to decide whether an autistic minor could be exempt from paying therapy fees. Agreeing with the AI's answer, he then passed his judgment, saying that according to the laws of Colombia, autistic children are exempt from paying therapy fees. The judge also stated that AI does not replace the thinking beings that judges are. It merely assists them in deciding a case speedily and in interpreting the law correctly.[32]

American courts have also implemented several AI tools to assist judges in optimising the delivery of justice. Their templatised method of conducting trials not only ensures that the law is being executed appropriately but also helps judges make faster decisions, reducing their case backlog and the probability of bad judgments. One of the AI-powered tools used in the US to aid in risk assessment is Correctional Offender Management Profiling for Alternative Solutions (COMPAS). It analyses various factors such as socio-economic background, criminal history and mental health of convicts to predict the likelihood of recidivism among them. The US Sentencing Commission also employs AI to develop and implement guidelines for sentencing to ensure that punishments are consistent and just, and in keeping with the crime.[33] In short, the US courts use AI tools to help judges make better decisions.

It is clear that the use of AI will make the legal system more effective and transparent, protecting the rights of litigants. It is a necessity for a country like India, where access to justice is compromised, lawyers are expensive, the courts overburdened and the compliance costs high. With the employment of AI and standardised templates for pleadings and contracts, courtrooms can revive the judiciary's identity as a protector of the people's rights and an administrator of justice. However, this technology might be tough to manoeuvre when it comes to completely new matters that have no precedent.

3

Revamping India's Commercial Legal System

ONE OF THE OBJECTIVES of legal reforms is to secure for every Indian the right to seek a comfortable life through honest means. That is possible only when the economy is robust and citizens can obtain a respectable level of income. This is achieved either through employment or entrepreneurship, and it is important that in the pursuit of either, one is also able to preserve one's integrity and self-respect.

But what about the economic reforms since 1991? Did the changes in government policy, the opening up of the economy to foreign investment and industrial delicensing not achieve this? Let us look at some facts and data to determine whether those widespread economic reforms have brought about the desired levels of economic prosperity and well-being, and whether they have evened out the availability of economic options for the common person and made India an easy place to do business.

India has been one of the world's fastest-growing economies over the past three decades. It has grown faster than most countries that share similar attributes, such as a large population and people with varied levels of skill. Many factors have aided India's success, including its large and young workforce hungry for success and financial independence and the exponential growth of its technology and IT sector. Between 2011 and 2019, India halved the number of people living in extreme poverty (defined by earnings of less than $2.15 per person per day).[1]

Some of the large-scale reforms over the years have been liberalising foreign direct investment, privatising sectors such as telecom and aviation, reforming tax, formalising and digitalising payment systems, and creating social security benefits. The social security benefits offered by the government include monetary benefits for poor families upon the death or disablement of their sole breadwinner, a monthly pension scheme for citizens over the age of 60, and rations for citizens living below the poverty line.[2] At the macroeconomic level, there has been government support for a better supply-side policy.[3]

Privately owned startup businesses worth more than $1 billion are known as 'unicorns', and one out of ten unicorns in the world is from India. Between 2015 and 2021, India witnessed a ninefold increase in investments and a sevenfold increase in overall funding for startups.[4] It has been reported that India is gradually transitioning from the age of unicorns to the age of decacorns, that is, companies valued at more than $10 billion.[5] At the macro level, India is currently framing policies for future-oriented industries such as green energy and green technologies that are emerging with the country's dynamic technological advancements.

The Central government has also been making a focused effort since 2014 to improve the ease of doing business in India. The country's grim ranking of 134 (2013) and 130 (2016) on the World Bank's Ease of Doing Business index had risen to a slightly more acceptable ranking of 62 (2019)[6] before the World Bank stopped publishing these rankings following alleged ethical misconduct in executing this exercise by its staff.[7] In the Economist Intelligence Unit Business Environment Rankings[8] that covers 82 countries, India stands at no. 52 globally and at no. 10 among Asian economies for the period 2023–27 (which includes projections for the future).[9] Further, in the 2024 edition of this report, India has been identified as one of the most promising markets for business growth over the next five years due to favourable ease of business policy reforms, infrastructure investments and a dynamic demographic profile.[10]

These are terrific improvements for the country. But despite our improved rankings on ease-of-doing-business lists, why does it still feel like doing any business in the country is so hard? Is there too much cronyism? But look at the flourishing startup culture today – there is no cronyism there. That is perhaps indicative of a wider distribution of economic prosperity than earlier – but is that good enough? How easy is it for someone to run a business from a small shop in a legally compliant manner?

The Indian model of economic reforms that focused primarily on policy measures has resulted in wealth remaining in the hands of a few. For close to six decades now, wealth has been concentrated in the hands of the top 1 per cent of India's population.[11] There can be no doubt that by expanding just this seemingly minuscule section of the population, the country could witness an incremental shift in the economy. It is inevitable that when the population of the wealthy increases from 1 per cent to even 1.25 per cent, a cascading effect on the rest of society shall follow.

The consequential impact of targeting growth in the numbers of the wealthy could move many from the lower class to the middle class, and others from the middle class to the wealthy segment of society. But is it not time that the economic and business environment is re-engineered to enable easy access to an honest and decent living for the general population, instead of waiting for the trickle-down effect of nurturing the wealthy? For India to become a country where an ordinary citizen could change their economic destiny much the way the US did in the postwar years, its regulatory environment for business needs a total transformation.

India's focus should go beyond the desire for international rankings to a wholesome approach towards all kinds of businesses and their differing needs, from the MSME (micro, small and medium enterprises) sector to the tech unicorns.

To do so, it will be essential to reform the laws that provide the underlying framework for business. This chapter attempts to provide the perspective needed across law and regulatory policies in various fields of activity that affect business in India. It also debates whether drastic structural change or incremental shifts would be better for bringing about reforms.

Legal reforms for business

Non-compliance and the eventual dishonouring of contracts are primarily responsible for the difficulty of doing business in India. We need to re-examine the way damages, costs and interest are awarded by Indian courts. Non-compliance should be made financially unattractive. The principles of judicial injunction – or the 'stay order' – should only be allowed in very serious situations, as injunctions are roadblocks to economic growth. Stay orders were initially devised as a means to protect the interests of all the litigants in a court dispute until its final resolution through the court process, but they have become a device in the hands of the crooked to abuse court processes.

Today, while the policy headlines make it appear that doing business in India is easier than before, in truth our infamous bureaucracy twists the simplest of policies, making it hard for businesses to operate. There is also a need for an evolved whistle-blower system in which corporate insiders could bring to light the wrongdoings of their employers, making regulatory non-compliance and wilful violation of the law risky for corporations. A robust whistle-blower policy will incentivise employees to spill the beans on these wrongdoings, intimidating business owners into complying with the law.

In areas currently covered by arbitration and insolvency laws, a speedy and result-oriented commercial dispute resolution mechanism would be an essential legal reform to improve the ease of doing business. Finally, the prohibitive upfront costs of pursuing legal remedies in our country need to be addressed through the adoption of contingency legal fees so that citizens do not hold themselves back from seeking justice simply because of the costs involved.

Sanctity of contract

I frequently come across instances that illustrate the sad state of affairs when it comes to the sanctity of contracts in India. Once, while negotiating a contract with a large Indian company on behalf of an international client, the promoter of the Indian company grew a little tired of the back and forth and said that he was willing to sign a blank sheet of paper on which I could draw up whatever agreement I felt was appropriate. We could renegotiate the contract if ever an occasion called for its enforcement. Basically, he was telling me he did not care about what was written in the contract because he knew that it would take forever to enforce the contract should the need arise. His international client would not be able to afford the delay and would eventually settle for far less than what was owed.

This example demonstrates the total lack of respect for contracts among the Indian business community. What would make Indian businessmen honour their contractual commitments? First, speedy enforcement of contracts must become the norm, and second, it must become very expensive to breach a contract. Of course, there are also benefits to be gained from building a reputation as a reliable business partner by fulfilling one's contractual commitments. This scant respect for contracts has led to a general degeneration in the Indian business environment.

India currently has a business environment in which parties to a contract continue negotiations even after the contract has been signed. Very often, these post-contract negotiations are more serious than those before the contract was agreed. What is shocking is that this is true not just among small or medium businesses but also among major corporates. It is not at all uncommon in India to come across a lack of seriousness among big companies when negotiating contracts. If an Indian businessman senses an opportunity to get away from the consequences of breaking a contract, he simply seizes it.

Companies use the weaknesses in the legal system as an arbitrage to finance their operations at much lower costs than they otherwise could. The fear of being held accountable for a prohibited action is not strong enough to deter businesses from breaching their contractual obligations. If a contracting party does not make payments at the time they are due according to the contract, the cost of the breach in India is the sum of the unpaid amount plus interest and legal fees. However, the interest awarded by Indian courts on unpaid amounts ranges between 6 and 12 per cent, whereas the interest rate on loans from banks is between 14 and 35 per cent. This means that even after paying the interest awarded on unpaid dues, it would still be a much cheaper source of funds than the regular lending market. The unpaid contractual dues are used by the breaching party to meet its ongoing cash requirements.

I had a client who had entered into an agreement with a party to sell them some goods. My client hoped to use the proceeds from the sale to make further business investments. However, the buyer failed to pay on time. Their dispute went through an arbitration process, which ended with the buyer being forced to pay the dues with interest. However, my client lost out on the profit from investments that could have been made had they been paid on time, and the 8 per cent interest awarded on the amount due was not sufficient to make up for their losses.

In most developed countries, there is a high degree of sanctity of contracts. In the UK, the penalties and damages awarded for breach of contract are much higher than in India; more significantly, the speed of enforcement of the law is much quicker too. In the US, contracts are diligently adhered to because the penalties for committing a breach and the speed of enforcement are both very high. The law for breach of contract is similar in India, but here we breach contracts with impunity and have little respect for them.

Though the underlying principles for awarding damages in the three countries are somewhat similar, there are two main differentiators. Indian courts are much slower than courts in the UK or the US, and so the threat that an enforcement proceeding holds for a breaching party is very low. In the other two countries, an enforcement proceeding is a real threat to a breaching party on account of the speed of decision-making. The second differentiator between the countries lies in the amount of compensation or financial penalties imposed for breach of contract, all of which are ridiculously low in India.

In the *Hadley v. Baxendale* case of 1854,[12] the Court of Exchequer in the UK considered the financial impact of late delivery of goods or payment and held that the damages to be awarded for breach of contract must be a sum equivalent to losses arising, or expected to arise, from the breach. Further, courts in the UK have the option of ordering payment of punitive damages in certain cases where there is sufficient cause to believe that exemplary losses were caused[13] as a result of the breach and that the general damages already awarded would be insufficient to return the party suing for damages to the position it was in before the damage occurred.

However, Indian law limits unliquidated damages to the expectations of the parties and directly arising from non-performance of the contract by the erring party, and as a general rule prefers not to impose penalties. Further, unlike in the US, punitive damages are not codified in India, and the judiciary has indicated upper limits to damages. This has a bearing not only on contractual disputes but also on tortious disputes, such as those involving environmental harm caused by businesses. Punitive damages help discourage corporate entities from harmful behaviour, as can be seen in the cases *BMW of North America v. Gore* in 1996[14] and in the case of BNP Paribas[15] having to pay a penalty of nearly $9 billion after it violated the economic sanctions imposed by the US against Iran and Cuba.

Yet, in India, punitive damages are rarely, if ever, awarded. Indian courts have recognised that laws related to punitive damages remain underdeveloped in the country but have failed to view them as a tool with which to force compliance. In a 2009 case, the Delhi High Court observed that 'India has followed the traditional concept of awarding compensatory damages to remedy the losses',[16] but indicated that there had been some inclination among the courts towards granting punitive damages. However, in the absence of codification of the law relating to punitive damages, courts will remain unwilling to impose arbitrary amounts as punitive damages.

When it comes to cases involving harm to the environment or to life, Indian courts have failed to award appropriate damages. A case in point is the Uphaar tragedy in Delhi, in which many lost their lives in a fire in a cinema hall with inadequate safety measures. The victims' insistence on recourse to criminal law could have been tempered if the damages awarded by the courts as compensation had been truly punitive in nature. However, Indian courts limit themselves to imposing general damages that are compensatory in nature, calculated in proportion to the losses incurred by the aggrieved party.

Another yardstick used by Indian courts in determining damages is the difference between the contract price and the market price of the product or service in question. This method of computation results in much lower compensation than would be awarded in the UK or the US. In those countries, in addition to general damages as awarded in India, compensation would also be given for:

i. profits forgone and costs incurred towards a third party, which would not have arisen but for the breach in question;
ii. punitive damages assessed at an amount proportionate to factors such as the harm caused, the degree of misconduct, the relative vulnerability of the aggrieved party and the advantage gained by the breaching party;
iii. damages for expectation loss, that is, the amount required to place the aggrieved party in the position they would have been in if there had been no breach;

iv. other factors such as reliance loss, lost management time, compensation for mental distress and unjust gains by the breaching party, among others.

In substantive terms, an aggrieved party would recover much larger amounts if subjected to a breach of contract in the UK or the US than in India. It is this difference that leads to deterrence of breach of contract in these countries but not in India. The suggestion, therefore, is that Section 73 of the Indian Contract Act be amended to specifically provide for these additional measures of damages, supplied with examples, to build deterrence against contemplated breach of contract. Breach of contract must be made so expensive as to pressure the parties to a contract into close to full compliance with and full performance of the contract.

Liquidated damages provided for in Section 74 of the Indian Contract Act, 1872, cover amounts specified in the contract itself as a pre-estimate of the loss arising from a breach. However, while in the UK and the US these pre-specified amounts are accepted at face value and get enforced in a brief trial, in India the courts require the aggrieved party to establish the reasonableness of the specified pre-estimate and to produce evidence to establish its reasonableness. This means the amount specified in the contract is not accepted at face value, which results in extended trials to enforce claims of liquidated damages.

As the law stands today, Section 74 of the Contract Act in India creates a dichotomy that provides for liquidated damages – which are predetermined amounts to be awarded as damages in case of breach of an agreement – but allows courts to reconsider and re-evaluate the 'actual' loss incurred by the non-breaching party. This renders such a law almost redundant, since the aggrieved party is seldom paid the full amount that has been stipulated in the contract itself and consented to by both parties at the time of signing the agreement. The suggestion, therefore, is for an amendment of Section 74 to remove the need for the claimant to establish the reasonableness of the amount specified in the contract as liquidated damages.

Damages in tort law

In the Erin Brockovich case mentioned in Chapter 1, a US court awarded such huge tortious penalties on the errant company that it created fear in the corporate world. Companies had been deterred from even considering actions that could cause harm to the environment or humans. To explain this penalty, we first need to understand what a tort is. In the simplest terms, a tort is a wrong that gives rise to legal liability but is not a breach of contract. An example would be an individual committing a 'nuisance' – that is, an act that is not a contractual breach but causes annoyance to the victim, who is entitled to peace. Other examples of tortious claims are class-action suits in the US seeking enforcement of public rights, which are not contractual.

The concept of a tort first emerged in English law and today recognises the non-contractual legal rights of individuals as well as the public in general. It can be found in countries such as the US, Canada, the UK, India, Malaysia, Singapore and Australia. The legal principles of tort have an immense impact on the rule of law, governance and public morality because they provide protection from workplace hazards such as sexual harassment and industrial negligence and can also be used to demand rights to clean air and water, among other things.

The impact of tortious suits was primarily seen in courts in the US, where massive damages were awarded in short periods of time. The system of contingency fees for lawyers in the US enabled common people to hire lawyers they could not otherwise afford to enforce their tortious rights against large corporations. As a result, large corporations in the US are more respectful of common people's rights than they are in India.

In India, while a tortious right is recognised in law, the enforcement of the law is slow and the compensation awarded by courts for contractual breaches by corporations is very low. This has led to Indian society unwillingly learning to live with tortious wrongs. People rarely, if ever, seek enforcement of their non-contractual legal rights, quietly suffering noise and air pollution and misleading advertisements that lead them to make useless purchases. The apathy about tortious wrongs is so deep that even many Indian courts don't seriously consider suits for the enforcement of tortious rights.

As a result, these suits languish in the court system for even longer than claims for the enforcement of contractual rights. This leads to lawyers advising clients against pursuing tortious claims in the courts. The only exception in India is probably the much-touted PIL system, but that is aimed more at getting the government to act on a matter rather than making corporate wrongdoers pay for the damages they have caused.

The underlying legal philosophy in the UK and the US is to award massive punitive damages for public wrongs. They do not just limit the damages to compensatory amounts, as is the case in India. In the US, the damages awarded by courts are so high that they serve to deter prospective violators, including large, wealthy corporations. India needs to take the same path and instil real fear among its rich and powerful, who currently have near-total disregard for the rights of the common people.

A few examples in the Indian context would be the failure of the Indian industry to comply with environmental laws, the sale of substandard products and services, and people causing a public nuisance with their personal or community celebrations in public spaces by crowding the roads and slowing traffic. In each of these examples, if an Indian court were to impose exemplary damages and penalties as done by courts in the US, it would foster an environment of fear of breaching legal norms, resulting in widespread compliance.

India's problem today is not that these violations are not considered transgressions of the law, but that their financial consequences are so low that the private citizen who is wronged sees no value in seeking legal remedy. The negligible financial consequences for the violator are no deterrent at all. But once the consequences become significant, the number of common citizens pursuing action to claim their rights will rise significantly. A change in the underlying principle of the awarding of damages under the law of contracts would have the result of liberating a judge's mindset from the philosophy of awarding minimal damages and directing it towards awarding exemplary damages and penalties in instances of public wrongdoing and tortious liability.

Legal fees

I had a client who won a case only after spending a few crore rupees in legal costs. They thought they would be able to recover the amount through the court as costs. However, the court awarded them costs of only ₹50,000. Given the magnitude of the client's win, I advised against challenging the judgment for costs awarded. This was not because I thought the client did not deserve to be awarded the costs, but because I had never heard of a situation in our country where a winning party was able to recover their actual expenses.

For anyone battling a legal dispute in India, a big factor to keep in mind is that the costs of lawyer fees, court fees and other expenses have to be borne upfront, often with little hope of recovering them even in the event of a win in court. A significant reason for India's failure in contractual enforcement is that the costs awarded – if any are awarded at all – are minuscule and do not sufficiently reimburse the claimants for their actual legal costs. This is in addition to the low levels of damages awarded by Indian courts, further disincentivising citizens from seeking legal redress.

The basic questions you should ask yourself before approaching an Indian court are:

i. What will I get from going to court (total damages awarded)?
ii. How much money will I have to spend (expenses in the form of lawyer fees, among other things)?
iii. How long will it take?

The answers to these questions generally discourage people from pursuing their grievances in court because there is no full reimbursement of legal fees incurred nor any form of deferred-fee option.

The provisions for awarding costs in civil litigation are primarily enshrined in the CPC under Sections 35, 35A and 35B. Section 35 stipulates the 'general costs', Section 35A the costs for 'false/vexatious claims' and Section 35B the costs for delay.[17] Section 35 of the CPC also prescribes the costs to be paid by the unsuccessful party to the winning party as a 'reasonable' (not actual) reimbursement of the legal expenses incurred by the latter.

Even though Indian courts are conferred with the discretion to determine which party is liable to pay costs and how much, the caveat binding the courts in this regard is the requirement to ascertain that costs are 'reasonable'.[18] Ideally, this should place the winning party in approximately the same position they would have been in had the trial not happened at all. But in practice, the term 'reasonable' has translated to very small amounts being awarded as costs. The Supreme Court has often pointed out that the current Indian legal system is 'wholly unsatisfactory and does not act as a deterrent to vexatious or luxury litigation'.[19] They have repeatedly called for a more realistic approach towards awarding costs, but no formal steps have been taken to remedy the situation.

Section 35A of the CPC sets a limit for the exemplary costs – which are imposed by a court on a party for abuse of the court's process or for unacceptable conduct – that can be awarded in addition to regular costs in cases where a suit or litigation is vexatious in nature (that is, a suit filed solely to harass or subdue a counterparty). This limit stands at a scanty ₹3,000. This limit was incorporated in the CPC in 1922, when perhaps the amount may have been sufficient to place the receiving party in a position of benefit. But today it is hardly sufficient to cover any costs incurred by any party, given the high fees that lawyers currently charge.

Section 35B of the CPC prescribes that the winning party be reasonably reimbursed for the costs incurred by them in attending legal proceedings when the counterparty causes frequent delays by seeking frequent adjournments or when that party fails to perform the actions or steps required to be taken at various stages of the proceedings, leading to delays. The irony is that, on the one hand, the black-letter law demands 'reasonability' in costs awarded, and on the other, that very statute sets a limit that would not even cover a litigant's transportation costs to and from the courtroom. This makes for an unfair, unjust and inequitable dispute resolution mechanism.

If India preaches costs as a restitutive concept, then there is a pressing need for the regime to completely shift to awarding realistic and actual costs that reflect present-day standards. Instead, it is discouraging genuine litigation and encouraging false and vexatious claims. If costs are calculated realistically, litigants are bound to be deterred from raising unwarranted and frivolous claims. Currently, it may even be construed that Indian courts have entirely given up on awarding any compensatory costs, considering that the award of a sum of ₹3,000 is bound to make no difference to anybody or anything.

In 2011, the Supreme Court had suggested that this amount be amended to ₹1,00,000,[20] but as of 2025 there has been no change or revision on this front. Given the current system, there is greater incentive for the unsuccessful party to deliberately delay and prolong proceedings and to make frivolous applications for frequent adjournments at the risk of a small financial penalty, since it gives them the opportunity to escape liability until actually prosecuted, which would happen at a much later stage.

This lacuna in the law, however, has not caught the imagination of our lawmakers. As early as 1921, the Calcutta High Court had extensively opined that costs should be awarded not as 'a punishment of the defeated party but as a recompense to the successful party for the expenses to which he had been subjected'.[21] This statement was made at a time when Section 35A had not even been introduced into the code. And despite similar observations having been made by several courts in the country, and even after the addition of Section 35A, the gap between the actual costs incurred by the winning party in a trial and the compensatory costs awarded to them by the courts continues to remain.

The Supreme Court observed that the provision relating to compensatory costs for false or vexatious claims or defences has become 'virtually infructuous and ineffective, on account of inflation' and requires a 'realistic revision'.[22] In another judgment, it noted that it was unfortunate that 'it has become a practice to direct parties to bear their own costs', adding that wherever costs are awarded, they are ordinarily nominal and far from a realistic estimation of the financial loss incurred by the parties in question.[23] The apex court has also said that Section 35B is seldom invoked and 'should be regularly employed, to reduce delay'.[24]

The systems in the UK and the US are far more stringent in awarding costs at the conclusion of a trial. UK courts assess costs either on a standard basis or on an indemnity basis. In the former, the courts consider an amount proportionate to the costs involved in the matter. Under the indemnity mode, the courts award an amount that most accurately takes into account the costs incurred by the receiving party during the trial. They conduct a holistic review of factors such as the conduct of the parties during the pendency of the proceedings, whether a party has succeeded and the extent of its success and the payments that have been made to make good the amount invested by the successful party.

In the US, the presiding judges are vested with the discretion to decide an amount that is reasonable and appropriate to be awarded as costs. However, unlike in India, which also in theory employs the term 'reasonable' in this respect, a more realistic amount is arrived at. In simple cases, the fee awarded may be limited to $1,000, whereas in highly complex litigation, courts have awarded much higher amounts.[25]

To have legal reimbursement be a restitutive remedy for its people in real terms, India must reconsider its fundamental laws and standards for awarding such costs. In order to transform from a system that encourages false and frivolous litigation into one that actually delivers justice, the courts must realise that costs should be awarded on a more realistic basis and the legislature must be revisited to enable this. The laws in question must be updated, and outdated rules must be weeded out of the system while ensuring that adjournment costs are made sufficiently high to deter parties from causing frequent delays in trials.[26]

A winning litigant should be compensated for their actual incurred costs, maybe on the basis of evidence submitted. This will take away one of the key disincentives for any victim of contractual breach in India seeking justice and balance the environment in favour of seeking enforcement of the law. Failure to do so will leave even winning claimants with a sense of residual injustice.

As a general rule, the losing party should be obliged to bear all the costs of the winning party. The court must provide detailed reasons if it decides to deviate from this rule. In addition to being a fair principle, this would also serve as a deterrent against frivolous litigation. The purpose of imposing such costs is undermined when courts reduce them based on the losing party's financial capacity or on other grounds that make it unfair to the winning party.

The current approach of the Indian courts not only fails to adequately compensate the winning party but also weakens the intended disincentive against baseless claims, defences and unfair delaying tactics. A strict cost-imposition standard would discourage needless litigation, ensure fair compensation, ease the burden on the judiciary and hasten the delivery of justice.

Interest

A person once approached me to defend him against a claim for unpaid dues. The complication was that the amount – which ran into hundreds of crores of rupees – was legitimately due from his company but he did not want to pay up because if he did, his company would have to borrow money from the financial markets to meet its ongoing day-to-day operational needs. He would have to pay interest on the borrowed funds at rates of 15 to 18 per cent.

However, if he delayed the payment now under dispute, then there was the possibility of the claimant accepting a lower amount in a settlement because the case would take four to five years to reach a conclusion in court. Not only that, the court would probably only add an interest rate of 8 to 10 per cent on the payable amount. Thus, refusing to pay and going to court would result in significant savings for the defendant's company – even after taking into account lawyer fees and other expenses – compared to paying up and then borrowing at high interest rates.

This example illustrates how delinquent the thinking among Indian defaulters is and brings us to another aspect of litigation arising from unpaid dues – the interest costs imposed on damages or compensation awarded to a winning claimant under Indian law. The objective of awarding these costs is to compensate the claimant for lost interest earnings because of the delay in receiving the money owed to them. On the face of it, this principle appears just and reasonable, and can be seen as an aspect of restitutive thinking.

However, it raises the questions of what rate of interest should apply and from which date it would be applicable.

The answers are provided inadequately in the CPC. Despite the understanding on this subject having evolved through different court rulings over time, execution by the judiciary has been largely inconsistent across the Indian landscape. Section 34 of the CPC provides that in a decree for payment of money, the court may order payment of an interest rate that it deems reasonable on the principal sum. The interest rate would apply for the period before the institution of the suit, and then from the date of the suit to the date of the decree (a period called 'pendente lite'). There is a third period of interest to be paid from the date of the decree until the amount is paid, called 'future interest'.

This provision also sets an indicative rate of 6 per cent on the principal sum in cases where the liability has arisen out of a commercial transaction. The law prohibits the rate from being higher than the rate at which money is lent by nationalised banks for such commercial transactions. In practice, however, courts tend to order defaulting parties to repay a lump sum inclusive of the principal amount within a stipulated time period. Only if this amount remains unpaid do the courts levy an interest rate, usually charged at 6 to 8 per cent.[27] In certain other cases, courts have imposed a pendente lite simple rate of interest at 6 per cent and a future rate of interest at 9 per cent.

This is much lower than the general interest rates for borrowing in India, which range from about 12 per cent for institutional lending from banks and financial institutions to about 35 per cent from private moneylenders. As a result, the cost of borrowing from external sources is much higher than the interest cost a court might award on delayed payments. So, if one has a short-term view like my prospective client, there is a strong financial incentive in favour of defaulting on timely payment of dues.

It is also important to consider the time taken to bring a recovery claim to conclusion, which could be up to 15 years. This means the defaulter has access to cheaper finance for all those years. This has encouraged widespread instances of wilful default in our country. India has created for itself a faulty system that tends to incentivise rather than punish breach of contract. The remedy is the award of high damages and compensation on an actuals basis.

In the UK, the interest cost awarded by courts can be as high as 8 percentage points over the base rate, which is the interest rate for business-to-business transactions fixed by the Bank of England. In addition to this interest cost award, if there is a delay in the payment of dues, a fixed sum may also be charged as a late payment fee from the defaulting party.[28] In the US, the damages awarded are so exorbitant even before any penalties are imposed that even if its legal system were to hypothetically not award interest costs, there would still be a sufficient deterrent for contracting parties to fulfil their contractual obligations.

The solution suggested for India, therefore, is as follows:

i. In each case of default, the court should determine whether the default is wilful or due to gross negligence. In either case, it should award interest that is 15 percentage points over the prime lending rate of government banks.
ii. In cases of default that occur despite the bona fides of the parties, interest could be awarded at perhaps 5 percentage points above the prime lending rate. Further, the interest from the date of decree to the date of payment could be enhanced, say to the prime lending rate plus 20 percentage points.

With these high levels of interest, the incentive to default on payments will cease, and people will be persuaded to make timely payments of contractual dues. One of the most significant beneficiaries of this structure will be the formal lenders in India, such as banks.

Forums for dispute resolution

Arbitration

How effective is arbitration as a dispute resolution process in India? In one instance, after pushing hard to succeed in an arbitration claim over a fifteen-month period, an entity had to wait another two years to recover the monies awarded, and that too as an out-of-court settlement. This was because the side that lost the arbitration challenged the award on frivolous grounds, leading to the case dragging on in courts. Finally, out of sheer exhaustion, the party that had actually won the arbitration claim decided to settle the matter out of court.

There are many such cases that demonstrate the difficulty of dispute resolution in business matters in our country. Types of disputes relevant to the business world include:

i. contractual disputes that arise from commercial dealings, debt obligations and shareholder arrangements;
ii. disputes that arise from non-compliance or violations of corporate law;
iii. corporate fraud; and
iv. white-collar crimes.

In dealing with reforming the dispute resolution mechanisms for the commercial sector, it would be necessary to provide some historical context.

In ancient India, the laws of dharma ruled. Most people had a basic understanding of dharma and the implications of its violation for themselves and their families, both in their current and future lives. When there was doubt, people knowledgeable in dharma would be consulted. A deity, a sovereign or community elders would be called in to intervene and deliver immediate justice. In the system that sought recourse to sovereign intervention, there existed a hierarchy of dispute resolution forums, with the king's court ranked the highest and the family arbitrators the lowest.[29]

A combination of ancient Indian justice delivery mechanisms and systems brought into India from outside the country resulted in the justice delivery system eventually transforming into formal courtrooms where codified laws were interpreted and enforced, and where lawyers and litigants approached judges for protection of their rights. But when courts became a formalised system of grievance redressal, it came with some consequences. A court case became an expensive, time-consuming procedure. And gradually, with a growing population and economy, courts began to get overburdened. This slowed justice delivery, which in turn had a negative impact on the development of the country.

In the search for solutions to unburden the courts, the first reaction was to lean in favour of alternative mechanisms for dispute redressal. This included administrative and quasi-judicial tribunals and mechanisms of arbitration, mediation and conciliation. Initially, arbitration had existed only as an informal option, but the need for formal codification of the practice arose very soon. The first Indian Arbitration Act was introduced in 1899, based on the English Arbitration Act of the same year. It was, however, extended only to the three presidency towns of Madras, Bombay and Calcutta. It became applicable to all of India only after the establishment of the Indian Arbitration Act of 1940.

Arbitration was introduced to:

i. unburden the formal court system;
ii. replace the judge with a person the disputing parties have confidence in to deliver justice;
iii. reduce the formalities of pleading and evidence-taking, with the objective of allowing quicker decision-making;
iv. reduce costs, which would result from a speedy and less formal process; and
v. minimise the possibility of the dispute proceeding to the higher courts.

An additional advantage of arbitration was that the disputing parties could choose to keep the proceedings before the arbitrator confidential.

However, the 1940 Act failed to achieve most of these objectives. Most arbitrations would get dragged into the formal court system on one pretext or another, and the benefits of speed and low costs were lost. Then came the early 1990s, the time when India was opening its gates to economic liberalisation and globalisation.[30] Courts had, through their various interventions, made the arbitration process redundant as parties resorted to appealing every arbitral decision that was not in their favour. The objective of reducing the burden on courts through arbitration remained unachieved. The arbitration law also needed to be aligned with international and domestic arbitral principles. Due to the inefficiencies in the law effective at the time, arbitration had become a time-consuming and expensive ordeal. There was a pressing need for new legislation that could bring balance to the world of commercial disputes and achieve the original objectives of arbitration.

In the erstwhile Arbitration Act of 1940, arbitrators were appointed based on the litigating parties' trust in them through familiarity, as it would be someone they personally knew. That was why there was never any need for them to provide in writing reasons for their arbitral awards. But as arbitration grew into a more formal mode of dispute resolution, arbitrators were often individuals who independently practised arbitration. They were usually unfamiliar with the realms of law that specific arbitration proceedings would require. This, in turn, reduced trust and confidence in arbitrators among litigants. As a result, the frequency with which arbitral awards were challenged in the courts rose.

Eventually, the Arbitration and Conciliation Act was legislated in 1996, addressing those aspects of arbitration that the previous laws had missed. It was based on the 1985 UNCITRAL Model Law on International Commercial Arbitration, which was designed to assist in reforming and modernising laws on arbitral procedure while taking into account the particular features and needs of international commercial arbitration. The act envisaged the essential principles of both domestic and international arbitration within its ambit.[31]

Arbitrators in India are now required to provide the reasons for their arbitral awards, a practice that did not exist before

1996. To provide for the timely resolution of disputes, the statute was also amended to impose a timeframe within which arbitration must be completed. However, the act still fell short of its objectives, as arbitral awards are challenged even after the reasons have been provided, delaying justice and further burdening the courts.

Other issues that plague the arbitration process in India even now include the integrity and impartiality of arbitrators, the part-time approach to arbitration by both arbitrators and lawyers, the inclination to prefer retired judges and bureaucrats as arbitrators, and the general lack of professionalism. The great failing of arbitration in its current form is also evidenced by the government challenging every significant decision by the arbitration tribunals in the courts. If even the government refuses to accept the decisions that come through the arbitration mechanism, how can private parties be expected to show any great degree of confidence in it?

Despite the many fixes to the underlying law of arbitration, the following has been the experience of arbitration among disputing parties in the Indian environment:

i. There has been some improvement in the speed of dispute resolution, with the law having been amended to impose timeframes within which domestic arbitrations are required to be completed. The focus on institutional arbitration has also been helpful, especially in international commercial arbitration, where the disputing parties are from different countries. But despite these measures, arbitrations still exceed the stipulated timeframes.
ii. Dispute resolution through arbitration has become more expensive than going through the courts because of the very high fees charged by arbitrators. Lawyers' fees also remain very high.
iii. Arbitration proceedings have become almost as formal as court proceedings, with the only exception being that courtroom etiquette is not followed at the arbitration hearings.

iv. Commercial arbitrations have become as contentious as court proceedings.
v. Almost all arbitrator decisions in India are challenged for wrongful application of law, being contrary to public policy or bias. Adding to this is the propensity of the courts to interfere with arbitration proceedings at an interim stage and to review arbitral awards.
vi. One factor that continues to be a major positive for arbitration over dispute resolution in open court is confidentiality.

Given these failings of arbitration, should the only positive – confidentiality – be enough reason for the state to continue to promote it without considering whether it addresses other important issues? We have to keep in mind the problem with arbitrators themselves. Most of them are biased, incompetent and lack integrity and professionalism.

In India, most arbitration proceedings are carried out on an ad hoc basis. This means the process of arbitration is decided mutually by the disputing parties. In ad hoc arbitration, the parties typically do not select an institution (such as a tribunal) to administer the arbitral proceedings as they consider arbitral institutions not to add much value to the process of dispute resolution. This allows them greater flexibility and autonomy to decide the trajectory their dispute resolution will take. Even with institutional arbitration, the contractual obligations clarify that in the event of any dispute between the parties and the institution, the matter would continue as ad hoc arbitration.[32]

In April 2010, the first set of rules of the London Court of International Arbitration India Rules (LCIA India Rules) was adopted by India in order to address the many lacunas in its arbitration legislation. This was done with the intention of promoting the use of arbitration through an Indian arbitral institution based on India-specific rules. However, the general sense among legal professionals is that the desired effect was not achieved.

With the enhanced Arbitration and Conciliation Act of 1996, the process of resolving disputes through arbitration became highly formal. Procedural and environmental laws were mandated to apply in a similar manner in arbitration as they did in courts, and extensive arbitration rules were enacted, further formalising the rights and duties of parties under the process. What was once a process of arriving at an amicable resolution between parties under an informal procedure now resembled a courtroom proceeding. Not only did arbitration become a time-consuming ordeal, but the persistent issue of parties challenging arbitration awards in the courts also continued.

Under the Arbitration and Conciliation Act, 1996, an application for setting aside a domestic arbitral award must be filed within three months of the date of receipt of the award or the date of disposal of a request for correction of an award. However, even before matters proceed to this stage, most disputing parties seek interim measures from the courts. They request interim protection such as an injunction during the course of the proceedings (but before the award has been enforced). The act does not stipulate any timeline for when arbitration proceedings must recommence after an interim remedy is sought. So, disputing parties never reconvened arbitration proceedings and continued to drag the matter out until the law was amended in 2015 to fix a ninety-day period from the date of an interim order for arbitral proceedings to recommence.[33]

To return to the problem of unprofessionalism in the arbitration system in India, despite the best efforts made to identify and remedy the lacunas in the law, irreparable damage has been caused to the system by the lack of professionalism of arbitrators and lawyers. This cannot be ignored. Lawyers pursue arbitration with the intention of earning a few extra bucks, placing it at the bottom of their priority list. As a result, proceedings are fixed for weekends or holidays, often without the certainty of any positive results. For these lawyers, their courtroom careers have always taken precedence over their arbitration careers. This leads to delays in the arbitration process and a continual loss of confidence in it among disputing parties.

Retired judges serving as arbitrators lack enthusiasm and motivation and have no intention of transforming their work into a serious career choice. They see arbitration work as a means to obtain a steady income after their retirement from the courts. By being incentivised to delay proceedings through the prospect of earning more sitting fees, they rob the disputing parties of access to speedy and quality justice. Arbitration has evolved into a retired people's enterprise because that is what the lawyers themselves want.

The reality of India's system is that an award pronounced by a retired judge in an arbitration proceeding is less likely to be further challenged in the courts. If challenged, it has a higher chance of being upheld. Courts naturally support their judges, and retired judges who decide arbitration matters are held in higher esteem than other arbitrators. This makes lawyers inherently gravitate towards having former judges as arbitrators. As a result, the only deciding factors in choosing an arbitrator are the individual's reputation and prestige during their time serving in the courts. However, arbitration should be an independent and individual profession that is not contingent on these factors.

The dilution of confidence in the arbitration mechanism is made clear by guidelines issued by the Indian finance ministry on arbitrations for domestic public procurement contracts.[34] The guidelines note the failure of arbitration as a mechanism to address disputes and recommend avoiding arbitration to resolve disputes in matters involving a value of more than ₹10 crore. What India needs is recognition of arbitration as a legitimate profession, not one that is overshadowed by the politics of retired judges, bored lawyers and prior courtroom drama. To achieve this, India needs to appreciate the advantages of institutional arbitration over ad hoc arbitration and accord it greater prominence. Unlike ad hoc arbitration, institutional arbitration functions on codified rules, providing clarity and certainty on a range of procedural issues. It negates the doubt and uncertainty of ad hoc arbitration when it comes to complex procedural issues. Further, the power of an arbitral institution to appoint an arbitrator whenever a party fails or refuses to appoint one expedites the constitution of an arbitral tribunal, whereas in ad hoc arbitration the appointment of the arbitrator is carried out by the courts, which may take several months and result in the parties incurring substantial legal costs.

An arbitral institution can also facilitate speedy interim relief for parties opting for an emergency arbitration process, unlike in the ad hoc process, where interim relief can only be sought from an arbitral tribunal or a court, which may take several weeks or months. Arbitral institutions are also useful in providing administrative support to the disputing parties. They can arrange venues for the hearings, facilitate fee and filing payments, and scrutinise drafts for errors, among other services. In an ad hoc arrangement, these tasks are arranged by the parties themselves or by the tribunal, making the process very cumbersome and inefficient.[35]

Learning from the Singapore International Arbitration Centre (SIAC) or the International Chamber of Commerce (ICC) about efficient administration of arbitration as a dispute resolution forum can help India bridge the gaps in its arbitration law. We can acknowledge and adopt their rules for the replacement of arbitrators and the formalities required for arbitration proceedings.[36] This will result in greater confidence in our country's dispute resolution mechanisms.

To improve public confidence in arbitration, the following additional points ought to be considered:

i. The review jurisdiction of courts must be limited to situations where a case of bias or lack of integrity, at least at the prima facie level, is made out against arbitrators.
ii. To deal with integrity issues among arbitrators, institutes that enable arbitration must track the behaviour of arbitrators and take into account feedback on their performance from the disputing parties and their lawyers. Further measures could include video-recording

arbitration proceedings and subjecting delinquent arbitrators to anti-corruption compliance, investigation and prosecution.

iii. Arbitrators must go through institutional training on matters such as substantive finance, business and professionalism.
iv. A cadre of professional arbitrators should be assembled to replace retired judges serving as arbitrators.

The solution to the challenges faced by arbitration in our nation lies in embracing institutional arbitration over ad hoc arbitration. India needs to recognise arbitration as a legitimate profession and prioritise qualifications and expertise over prestige and political influence when choosing arbitrators. Institutional arbitration offers clarity, certainty and administrative support to the disputing parties, expediting the resolution process.

Conciliation and Mediation

In business, one rarely sees a dispute being resolved through mediation. Often, one of the parties refuses to participate, leaving the other party with no option but to initiate arbitration. Sadly, this also holds true for disputes between private parties and the government. As discussed earlier, there is very little incentive for a party in breach of contract to seek early resolution of a dispute or even to act reasonably.

Conciliation, however, seems to work better if it results in a win for both parties. In essence, conciliation is a process by which disputing entities seek to amicably arrive at a resolution, permitting them to define the time, structure and substance of the proceedings for themselves. It is a concept that was earlier envisaged within the Arbitration and Conciliation Act, 1996, and is now encompassed within the definition of 'mediation' under the Mediation Act, 2023, to align with international practices. The term 'conciliation' is used interchangeably with the term 'mediation'.

Prior to the introduction of this new law, alternative dispute resolution forums were recognised under the CPC in 2002. This permitted courts to refer matters to alternative modes of dispute resolution in which the prospect of settlement existed. However, in 2010, the Supreme Court began identifying loopholes in this provision after the Afcons case.[37] Over time, other statutes – such as the Companies Act, 2013 – also envisaged alternative dispute mechanisms within their ambit by mandating the Central government to maintain a mediation and conciliation panel for settling commercial disputes.[38]

Like any other mode of dispute resolution, conciliation too is rooted in the fundamental notion that the intention of the disputing parties is to arrive at an amicable consensus to resolve their dispute. However, despite the flexible, low-cost, speedy and confidential nature of mediation and conciliation in India, they have not succeeded in yielding the expected results. Justice Satish Chandra Sharma holds that although the scope of mediation in India is steadily expanding and complex matters are falling within its domain, its success rate is fairly low.[39]

Mediation is considered by some in the legal community to be a measure that can effectively reduce the pending caseload in courts. Over 50,000 cases were settled in India through mediation between April 2021 and March 2022, according to the National Legal Services Authority. This number surged to approximately 110,000 cases between April 2022 and June 2023.[40] This might appear to be a large number, but in reality it amounts to merely 1.08 per cent of the total number of pending civil cases in India during that period.[41] As of 2023, Maharashtra had seen a meagre settlement rate of 25 per cent through mediation.[42] This is a clear indication of the low success of mediation as a forum for alternative dispute resolution and stresses the need for reform on that front.

In contrast to India, the US enjoys nearly 90 per cent success in mediation proceedings. This results in close to 95 per cent of all disputes being referred to the forum of mediation. Keeping the risk of heavy costs and long trials in the courts in mind, most civil cases are referred for mediation.[43] The high success rate in the US stems from the process giving almost complete freedom to the disputing parties to direct the trajectory of the proceedings. This makes it different from contesting a dispute in court, where the process is very formal and largely in the control of judges and lawyers.

US mediation also thrives because of the existence of full-time mediation agencies and mediators who help with the process. Mediators are chosen from the nation's current judiciary based on skills and expertise relevant to the dispute. This is one of the major differences between the American and Indian systems. In the latter, retired judges and lawyers with no expertise in the subject matter attempt to mediate disputes for some additional side income.

In the UK, the aggregate settlement rate in mediation proceedings was as high as 92 per cent as of 2023. One of the primary reasons for this high success rate is that almost 76 per cent of the mediators are recognised as 'reasonably' or 'very' experienced, with only a meagre 8 per cent deemed 'novice'.[44] For the disputing parties, it has been reported that almost 80 per cent of the expenses of a court trial are saved. With the concept of winning and losing being blurred in mediation, parties choosing this method of dispute settlement are better enabled to engage in collaborative and inventive problem-solving tactics, which can help them mutually arrive at agreements that protect the best interests of both sides.

In Western countries, disputing parties are compelled to turn to mediation or other alternative modes of dispute resolution as the damages and costs awarded by their courts are exorbitantly high. This upholds the efficiency of these alternative mechanisms. For India to achieve this efficiency in mediation, it must also push the advantages of settling cases through alternative means by getting courts to impose high damages, costs and interest. The disputing parties will then be forced to resort to mediation as their preferred mode of dispute resolution.

To tackle the lack of professionalism among its mediators and lawyers, India must establish formal training centres for mediators. These training centres could collaborate with international mediation centres to develop certification courses. Formal qualifications would incentivise prospective mediators to consider mediation as a full-time and long-term career option. The training centres could also maintain a roster of mediators with information about their specific areas of expertise so that the disputing parties could select a mediator well suited to their case.

Further, a stipulated time limit for mediation proceedings would improve the quality and popularity of this form of dispute resolution in India because disputing parties are more likely to approach this forum if they are reassured that their dispute will be resolved within a specific period of time. The timeline suggested in the new Mediation Act, 2023, is 120 days from the date of the first appearance of the parties before the mediator.[45]

Arbitration versus commercial courts

When the dispute is of high value, the integrity of the arbitrator becomes more crucial. In one case, I abandoned arbitration as a dispute resolution mechanism because I had strong suspicions about the integrity of the arbitrator appointed by the other party. That was an instance when both my client and I felt that it was safer to pursue a resolution through a court, which would be an open, public forum. Such instances make one wonder if there is an advantage in staying with the court system if a few changes could be made to it. Could commercial courts be an alternative to arbitration tribunals?

India already has a specialised system of courts to deal with commercial cases, but the major advantages of arbitration – the time limit, informality and confidentiality – need to be brought into the commercial court system through an amendment in the statute. Only then could this system become more effective than arbitration. The lack of professionalism and other shortcomings among arbitrators are not common among judges in courtrooms because of the transparency of the court system. A formal judge has a longer career than most arbitrators and is conscious of the long-term consequences of their conduct. This is the main reason for finding a higher degree of professionalism among judges.

A lot of time and effort has been spent by judges, lawyers and lawmakers to improve the environment for arbitration in India. From changes that had far-reaching consequences in the arbitration law regime to the launch of several new institutional arbitration centres, the country's legal industry has tried very hard to bring more domestic and international players to opt for arbitration within the country rather than take it abroad.[46] However, despite these measures, there still does not seem to be sufficient confidence in the system.

International arbitration centres have been set up in Mumbai, Delhi and Hyderabad, and a second liaison office of SIAC has opened in the country. India is trying quite hard to become more attractive as an arbitration hub, but there has been only limited success for arbitration as a preferred dispute resolution mechanism in the country. The problem lies in the manner of appointment of arbitrators and consequently with their conduct and impartiality. Any lawyer who has traversed the field of Indian arbitration while handling disputes regularly will be disappointed at the way arbitrators are selected and the manner in which arbitration proceedings drag on for years, taking away any benefit arbitration could have brought over the traditional dispute resolution mechanisms.

Commercial courts are not circumscribed by the limitations of arbitration when it comes to contentious issues such as fraud, which the arbitration process has trouble with. Further, if the regulation for commercial disputes is refined, the resolution of cases before commercial courts will not mean a wholly separate and time-consuming process for enforcement of awards. At present, challenges to an arbitration award take an average of 2,508 days to pass from the first hearing to the high court and Supreme Court appeals, as found by a study conducted by Bibek Debroy and Suparna Jain for NITI Aayog. The Supreme Court then takes an average of 1,421 days to dispose of such appeals.[47] This shows that, at present, arbitration awards take a very long time to get enforced.

When the Commercial Courts Act, 2015, was introduced in the Lok Sabha, then Law Minister D.V. Sadananda Gowda said the bill was an 'attempt to take our country forward so that our ranking goes up in the Ease of Doing Business Index of the world'.[48] The research by Debroy and Jain points out that the act amended both the time period mandated for pronouncement of judgment from the conclusion of arguments under the CPC and the time limits for case-management hearings in commercial disputes. After the act was brought into effect, commercial courts were notified in the cities of New Delhi and Mumbai, and e-summons, e-filing and electronic case-management mechanisms were added.

Historically, commercial courts were first discussed in the 17th Law Commission's 188th Report, which aimed to create commercial divisions in the high courts in India.[49] Here, India sought to replicate the success of commercial courts in countries such as the UK, the US and France. The Law Commission recommended the setting up of a commercial division consisting of two judges in each high court with jurisdiction over disputes of a pecuniary value of ₹1 crore or more, along with a dedicated fast-track procedure that had strict timelines for pleadings, evidence and adjudication.

In the 2009 conference of the chief justices of high courts at New Delhi, the judges broadly agreed on the need for such commercial divisions in the high courts. A bill was then introduced in Parliament later that year. Though it was passed in the Lok Sabha, it received significant opposition in the Rajya Sabha, leading to it being referred to a select committee in December that year. The committee suggested changes, leading to another round of debate in the Rajya Sabha in 2011. Unfortunately, the bill was eventually withdrawn by the government in power at the time.

In 2013, the 253rd Report of the Law Commission of India[50] made fresh recommendations for the establishment of commercial courts, again citing the need to create a positive image for India's dispute environment for foreign investors. In 2015, the law was first promulgated as an ordinance after the new bill was referred to a standing committee of the Rajya Sabha. This led to the present legal regime under the Commercial Courts Act, 2015. In 2018, further amendments were introduced, first by ordinance, expanding the scope of commercial courts in India. The amendments reduced the minimum specified value of commercial disputes from ₹1 crore to ₹3 lakh, provided for the creation of commercial courts and commercial appellate courts at the district level and enforced mandatory mediation when urgent relief is not sought. Consequently, the 2018 Amendment Act was passed and enforced.

By reducing the specified minimum value of commercial disputes to ₹3 lakh, the mandate of commercial courts now extends to nearly all disputes involving commercial agreements. The change was superficial, and much more could have been done to address the root problem of delays in the settlement of commercial disputes in the country. Regardless, a new hierarchy of courts was created. There were now commercial appellate divisions in the high courts that heard appeals from the commercial divisions of high courts as well as from commercial courts at the district judge level. Additionally, the commercial appellate division at the district judge level heard appeals in disputes decided by commercial courts at a lower level.

However, the state governments and the high courts had taken too much time in implementing the act and in establishing commercial courts. Even the designation of 'commercial court' did not match the volume of commercial cases being adjudicated, and in some states – such as Assam, which has one commercial court designated for each district – only 12 cases were being heard on average. Further, an examination of 150 cases revealed that case-management hearings were hardly being conducted, despite these being a key reform. Without tackling the larger issues surrounding courts in general, the policy has focused too much on cosmetic changes and not enough on legislative impact.[51]

Professor Sudhir Krishnaswamy and Varsha Mahadeva Aithala further echoed these views in their 2020 research paper,[52] which suggests that some aspects of our policy for commercial courts require rethinking. Did the legislature have the best motivations in mind in bringing about the reform? While the research suggests that the move to arbitration has consistently shown reduced delays in dispute resolution, that is not always a positive outcome because of the loopholes in ad hoc arbitration and the suspicions about the integrity of arbitrators. It is also worth looking into how a legislative change meant for large-value commercial disputes ends up encompassing nearly every commercial dispute in the country.

These issues point to bad policymaking. If policymaking is done right, commercial courts can be a game changer. They can reduce delays and make it easier to do business in the country. More effort is therefore needed to ensure that we do not abandon the concept of commercial courts. India will benefit from operationalising commercial courts modelled on practices in the US and other Western nations, where the judges on commercial benches are professional specialists. With increased transparency and visibility between the court systems and their lawyers and litigants, there should be little reason for the failure of commercial courts in India.

In practical terms, arbitration as a practice cannot be entirely done away with. But international entities rarely trust courts in India like they do arbitration institutions such as the SIAC. With the practice of arbitration subsisting for international disputes until India has established the credibility of its commercial courts, at least all domestic government contracts could be referred to the latter forum. Eventually, once the effectiveness of this dispute resolution forum has been proven, private entities may be confident enough to approach commercial courts to resolve their disputes.

Tribunals versus high courts

Tribunals are judicial or quasi-judicial statutory institutions set up with the primary objective of serving as a platform for the adjudication of disputes more quickly than the traditional courts. They also aim to establish expertise in specific realms of law that courts are only generically equipped to deal with. While moving towards arbitration, India also set up multiple tribunals to deal with specific disputes. Among them are the Debt Recovery Tribunal and the Board for Financial Reconstruction. Then there are tax tribunals, environmental tribunals and regulators such as the Telecom Regulatory Authority of India and the Competition Commission.

Tribunals are often manned by political appointees from the bureaucracy or retirees from the judiciary. For many of them, tribunal memberships constitute a second, post-retirement career. That is the mentality with which they approach their jobs. It also means that these individuals lack the expertise required to be a tribunal member. Therefore, the performance and efficiency of these tribunals are highly questionable.

Today, one of the key challenges India's judicial system faces[53] is the pendency of cases in the traditional courts. As of June 2021, there were 91,885 cases pending for over 30 years in different high courts of the country.[54] As of May 2021, there were 67,898 pending cases in the Supreme Court. In 2017, the Law Commission of India recognised that this burden on the courts not only leads to delays in the administration of justice but also impacts the efficiency of the judicial system in its entirety. It also noted that traditional courts often lacked the expert knowledge required for informed decision-making and adjudication.

In 1976, Articles 323A and 323B were inserted into the Constitution of India through the 42nd Amendment. Article 323A empowers the Parliament to establish administrative tribunals at both the Central and state levels for the adjudication of matters pertaining to the recruitment of public servants in India and their conditions of service. Article 323B was inserted to vest the Parliament as well as state authorities with the power to establish tribunals for specified subjects such as taxation or land reforms upon enacting a law to that effect. In 2010, the Supreme Court clarified that the subject matters under Article 323B were not to be interpreted as exclusive, and that state legislatures were empowered to create tribunals on any subject matter specified under the Seventh Schedule of the Constitution.[55]

Currently, tribunals have been created both as substitutes and subordinates to the high courts in India. They serve as substitutes because appeals against decisions of tribunals such as the Securities Appellate Tribunal are decided directly by the Supreme Court, and as subordinates such as the Appellate Board under the Copyright Act, 1957, because appeals from these tribunals are heard by the corresponding high courts. Despite the premise of exclusive expertise on which the tribunals were built, the decision-makers on their benches are primarily former district court judges or retired bank employees, individuals from generalist professions who lack the expertise necessary to serve in the position.

A look at the eligibility criteria for their selection also reveals a lot. To be appointed as a high court judge, one needs to have ten years' experience as an advocate. It is unusual for anyone under 45 to become a judge in India. But to be appointed to the National Company Law Tribunal, the minimum age is 50. How does one make sense of this arrangement, which makes most of the established partners or seniors in law firms with relevant expertise ineligible?[56]

As with arbitration, the inevitable result is that tribunals also suffer from a lack of professionalism and integrity. There is a higher conceived glory in occupying the seat of a high court judge than in assuming the position of a tribunal judge. The latter comes with fewer benefits than the post of a court judge, a shorter fixed five-year tenure and reduced constitutional protection and independence. Invariably, this does not attract the best talent and has resulted in the limited success of tribunals in India.

India might fare better with a system where expert judges are appointed to specialised branches of its high courts. I think doing away with the forum of tribunals – which is hardly achieving the objectives for which it was created – would better benefit the system. Instead, we can establish specialised branches of high courts, appointments to which should be considered a matter of pride among judges. A framework in which courts are expanded to include specialised branches with specialised judges will ensure a higher degree of professionalism than what our tribunals currently offer and revive integrity in the justice system.

In the US, tribunals are empowered to exercise only quasi-judicial functions pertaining solely to administrative actions. Their constitution prohibits judicial powers for any entity – including a tribunal – that does not act in the capacity of a court. Therefore, the decisions of these tribunals adjudicating administrative areas are subject to judicial review by the courts that have jurisdiction over them.[57] This prevents them from slipping into a situation in which their decisions are binding but are also constantly being appealed in the courts. It also carves out from the judicial system a separate branch to which the judicial powers of a court are not delegated. Therefore, the question of the integrity and professionalism of a tribunal member being equated to that of a court judge need not arise at all.

With a more organised arrangement for courts in the country, India can rid itself of the burdens that come with the tribunal structure. It can ensure that certain benches of the high courts are specialised, where judges enjoy the protections that they would have in a high court. This can reinforce the confidence litigants have in them, as disputes will be tried by qualified individuals capable of arriving at decisions that are well-informed and that protect the best interests and rights of both parties in question.

Insolvency code

As of 2021, the new Insolvency and Bankruptcy Code (IBC), 2016, regime had, in its five years of existence, helped in the debt recovery in merely 20 per cent of cases and liquidation in 29.7 per cent of cases.[58] There is no doubt that the IBC had the potential to be a major improvement over the previous insolvency laws, including the Securitisation and Reconstruction of Financial Assets and Enforcement of Security Interest Act (SARFAESI), 2002. But in a prominent insolvency case involving a real estate company, the National Company Law Tribunal, the National Company Law Appellate Tribunal and the Supreme Court of India all shied away from forcing a solution within the stipulated 180 days. No conclusion was arrived at even after the time period was extended to 270 and then 330 days.

The system simply did not believe that homebuyers were sufficiently protected under the Real Estate (Regulation and Development) Act, 2016 (RERA) to allow the real estate project they had invested in to be liquidated and entrusted to a new owner. So, the case dragged on for more than four years to general ridicule. It also called into question the conduct of the resolution professionals as the fraud perpetrated by the erstwhile promoters of the project went unaddressed. The IBC had failed the homebuyers in this case.

Most insolvency proceedings end up in unimaginable losses for the creditors. Financial institutions – that is, the secured creditors – rule the narrative once the insolvency process begins, so one has to pierce through the law and understand the realpolitik that has affected several insolvency proceedings in India over the years. Since the IBC's inception until September 2024, only 1,068 cases had been resolved, leading to a recovery of approximately ₹3.55 lakh crore by creditors.[59] Additionally, even when the market has realised that a business is ripe for restructuring, the process allows its creditors and promoters an extended run at trying to resuscitate it.

An example of this was when the Corporate Insolvency Resolution Process for the company Videocon came to its logical end in 2021. Only 4.1 per cent of the disputed value could be realised, with the creditors receiving only ₹2,962 crore out of the ₹64,838 crore they had advanced to the company.[60] In the case of the company Ruchi Soya in 2019, the lending banks took a 52 per cent loss, amounting to ₹4,350 crore, and had to sanction a loan of a further ₹3,200 crore to the company that bought the entity.[61]

However, the biggest indication of the failure of the IBC is the near-universal realisation among lawyers and judges that its promise of settlement of a dispute in 180 days is utopian. It has been achieved in only 20 per cent of cases. The rest took more than 270 days to settle under the IBC, defeating the purpose of the act and allowing the businesses' market value to plummet as the settlement process dragged on. The need for 'greater clarity of purpose' for the legislation was highlighted in the 2021 report by the Parliamentary Committee on Finance.[62]

While the wisdom of the Committee of Creditors – which is comprised of nominees of banks and institutional lenders such as financial creditors – that runs this process is unquestioned under the act, we must ask who really are the eventual beneficiaries of the legislation. The answer is the financial creditors and stakeholders such as employees and customers of the business that benefit from continuing even in a significantly reduced capacity. As a consequence, the Committee of Creditors frames a resolution scheme to keep the business or the bankrupt company going for their personal benefit but to the detriment of all other creditors.

Operational creditors – vendors and suppliers to the erstwhile business or bankrupt company – are some of the biggest losers under the IBC. These creditors are often small businesses that supply goods and services. They form the backbone of the Indian economy. The law protects the interests of the big institutions and banks over those of the small players. The recovery for operational creditors is significantly lower when compared to that of financial creditors under a resolution plan, so they face bigger debt write-offs than the banks and financial institutions. This imbalance in the law disproportionately affects smaller vendors – including MSMEs – leaving them financially vulnerable and at a clear disadvantage in the resolution process.

Thus the experience with the insolvency process is a bit of a mixed bag. Meaningful stakeholder engagement during the process of implementation of the law is clearly missing, with only financial creditors, old owners and prospective owners appearing to be engaged with the process. As a consequence, there has been media and public pressure on the government to deliver a law that is a little more fair to the operational creditors, reduces the influence of the erstwhile owners and shareholders of the bankrupt business, and prevents a windfall gain to the new owner. This has resulted in a few amendments being made to the law, but none of these have delivered the desired level of fairness.

Now, every time one demonstrates unfairness in the law, the courts and judicial forums feel the need to step in and involve themselves with the process. However, the performance of the judicial forums dealing with insolvency, commercial and arbitrable disputes in India demonstrates how mere revisions in legislation are not enough for reform. The insolvency process has become, as a consequence, more long-drawn and complicated. It is imperative that the judges who handle the cases are adequately trained in matters of business and can appreciate the nuances of the commercial world.

Currently, the problem is not merely that IBC cases are handled by untrained judges; it is also that there is an absence of a cohesive strategy that involves all the stakeholders in question. Thus, the introduction of a new law is seen as the objective of any reform, as opposed to it being the beginning of the process of reform. If the relevant ministries were to change this mindset and work in tandem with teams that periodically examined the impact of legislation, perhaps the necessary solutions could be found.

This new legislation has also brought with it new problems such as patterns of collusion and unethical practices by dispute resolution professionals. In the absence of significant investments in ensuring the quality of resolution professionals and enforcement of sufficient entry barriers, one cannot expect the legislation to work. In fact, if one were to look closely at the reasons behind the greatest failures of the IBC process, one might understand that the underlying failings lie in the very mindset of the judiciary in our country. In short, it is the abject fear within the judicial system that allows a bankruptcy to run its full course. We greatly fear the liquidation process and hence are unable to deal with the prospect of a disintegrated business in the hands of new owners. We cannot believe that this can rejuvenate a business and create value for the various stakeholders.

Historically, the liquidation process for companies in India has been long and painful, so everyone fears going down that path. In the endeavour to avoid the liquidation of a company, the deadlines for its restructuring get extended. The imposition of a strict deadline for restructuring would remove the fear of liquidation. It is the very essence of any modern insolvency law. A strict timeframe will make insolvency professionals and lenders examine the aspect of liquidation value very carefully and consider the prospect of restructuring very seriously.

Other required changes are the establishment of a mechanism for training judges to deal with IBC proceedings as well as the accreditation and rating of resolution professionals. The latter step would make them directly responsible for any wrongdoing, like public servants under the anti-corruption law.

Law of injunction

Why do injunctions or stay orders exist? In many cases, when a court is unable to complete hearings and arrive at a decision quickly, it passes orders to prohibit events that might alter the facts of the case. It is basically seeking to maintain some form of status quo until it is able to deal with the matter comprehensively, and often until delivery of its final judgment. Why should the law of injunctions be changed? Because this device is susceptible to abuse. It is not uncommon for judges to casually grant injunctions without insisting on the underlying legal tests for them to be met, and without ensuring that adequate financial and other safeguards are in place. All this slows the already slow dispute resolution process.

The abuse is usually seen when an unscrupulous party in a dispute obtains an injunction and delays the substantive hearing and thereby the final conclusion of the case. This results in significant injustice to the injuncted party, especially if the party ultimately wins the case, since the costs awarded at the end of the case are insufficient to make good the losses arising from the delay caused by the injunction. In terms of public projects, an injunction drives up costs on account of the delay in their execution, which is to the detriment of the general public.

A lot has been said and written on the impact of judicial pendency in the country, and this book has focused on its impact on business. While there is a need to reform the way the judiciary in India adjudicates business disputes, there is also a need to focus first on the casualty of pending disputes – the pause in business operations caused by injunctions.

The law relating to injunctions is contained in the Specific Relief Act, 1963. Section 37 provides for temporary injunctions and states that they will continue until a specific time or until further orders of the court concerned. Injunctions may be granted at any stage of a suit. There is no denying that this gives courts great leeway in determining the duration for which any business activity under dispute must pause.

The Supreme Court in the Gujarat Bottling Co. Ltd case[63] held that courts need to follow certain guidelines when granting temporary injunctions. They need:

i. to examine whether the applicant seeking the relief of a temporary injunction has established a prima facie case in its favour. For this, the court must attempt not to examine the merits of the case but the basic facts on which the applicant stands to contest the case.

ii. to examine the conduct of the applicant before granting the relief of injunction.
iii. to ascertain the balance of convenience – or, in other words, the balance of comparative loss caused to the applicant and the respondent in case of denial of the relief.
iv. to also examine the extent of loss caused to the applicant, and whether such loss is reparable by monetary damages or compensation. The court must undertake a similar exercise for the respondent and examine which loss would be greater and irreparable.
v. to require the party concerned to deposit an amount as security for the compensation to be paid, or to pay the compensation if, subsequently, the case is decided against the applicant.

The Supreme Court in the Gujarat Bottling case held that the party benefiting from a temporary injunction should be asked to deposit an amount as security sufficient to undo the harm caused to the opposite party in case eventual relief is not granted to the applicant.

In the Best Sellers Retail India case,[64] the court held that even when a prima facie case is made in favour of the plaintiff, the court will refuse a temporary injunction if the injury suffered on account of the refusal of the injunction is reparable through monetary compensation. There is an additional subset of temporary injunctions which are ex parte in nature, in which a temporary injunction is granted without hearing the entity against which it is passed. Such an injunction should only be passed in urgent and overwhelming cases, and lasts for a limited period of time.

While the law is sufficiently clear on the onerous requirements for the grant of temporary injunctions, it is surprising to find that in most cases a proper examination as to why a temporary injunction is being granted – despite the injury being monetary and reparable in nature – is not made. Sadly, this failing has crept into the judicial culture across the nation. Adding to this is the culture of judicial non-compliance in India.

An attempt to resolve this issue was made to a limited extent – strictly for infrastructure projects – by a 2018 amendment introduced to the Specific Relief Act.[65] The amendment reduced the discretion enjoyed by courts to adjudicate issues relating to the specific performance of contracts. It prevents courts from granting injunctions that can cause impediments or delays in the progress of completion of infrastructure projects.[66] The projects covered under this amendment are in the areas of transport, energy, water and sanitation, communications, and social and commercial infrastructure.

The 2018 Economic Survey of India pointed out that at least 52 infrastructure projects of the government were paused because of injunctions granted by courts, and that these injunctions continued for an astounding period of 4.3 years on average. This caused cost overruns to the tune of several hundred crore rupees, as these projects were debt-financed under the public–private partnership model.[67] For projects that do not involve a public element, the law on injunctions continues to apply without the amendment.

We must ask ourselves if we need to prevent businesses from getting incentivised to seek injunctions against their contractual partners to force them to come to the negotiating table. The answer, no doubt, will be a resounding yes. The present law on injunctions asks pertinent questions and imposes pertinent strictures, such as the provision of security by deposit of money by the party winning the injunction. It should be implemented in a less laissez-faire manner than it is currently being done.[68]

In the Shivashakti Sugars Ltd case,[69] the Supreme Court was cognisant of the fact that its decision could have an adverse or unexpected effect on employment, infrastructure growth, the revenue of the state, and the state of the economy.

The court held that it must avoid an outcome that has adverse effects on these factors and further declared the importance of considering the economic impact and effect of an injunction. In an interview, Justice A.K. Sikri – who was part of the bench in the case – emphasised the importance of introducing consideration of the business and economic impact in judicial decision-making and recognised the judiciary's current lack of engagement in these matters.[70]

While the 2018 amendment suggested a much-needed transition from a jurisprudence of compensation to one that considers performance and impact, the positive knock-on effects on foreign investments and investor confidence could be exponential if injunctions were not granted casually across the board. Injunctions must be granted only if the criteria detailed earlier in the chapter are fulfilled and also shown to be fulfilled by a reasoned order of the court that rejects alternatives such as monetary compensation. This would encourage courts to move faster towards resolution of disputes and keep the disputing parties engaged in the matter at hand during the evidence presentation process.

When we look at how the world views India, we must also consider the way the world views the judicial impediments to business and economic growth in India. Researchers Johannes Boehm and Ezra Oberfield (from Sciences Po and Princeton University, respectively) sought to quantify the impact of congestion and delays in the Indian judicial system on the effectiveness and productivity of domestic companies. For their study, they examined the Annual Survey of Industries for 2000–01 and 2012–13.

On the basis of their findings, they argue that businesses source inputs and organise production based on the speed of the judicial system. Therefore, where courts process cases slowly and impose impediments such as injunctions, contract enforcement is weak, and businesses may prefer to buy materials or services only from suppliers they can trust completely. Some choose to make components themselves as they are unable to trust a third party. Boehm and Oberfield state that if judicial delays were reduced to the extent found in the best-performing Indian states in this respect, industrial productivity could get a boost and grow by as much as 5 per cent.[71]

The suggestion therefore is for the State to amend the Specific Relief Act, 1963 and statutorily mandate that, for the grant of an injunction, the court has to determine whether there is going to be irreparable loss to any of the parties and consider the balance of convenience. Further, the court must secure every injuncted party against the consequences of a wrongly procured injunction.

Governance and regulation

The government claims that it has become much easier to do business in India over the last decade. In many ways this claim is true, but has the regulatory environment become good enough for honest and hardworking people to run and operate businesses with dignity, without having to compromise their integrity? Of the reforms that have helped improve ease of doing business in India, the frontrunners are the IBC, the Goods and Services Tax (GST), FDI policy changes, RERA and the facilitation of digital payment systems. However, has all this made life easier for businesses?

While one can say that it has become marginally easier for most businesses to operate in the Indian environment, the main gainers are large businesses. Large businesses have access to finance, the ear of the government, and a host of advisers to assist them with their activities. Meanwhile, small and medium-scale outfits in India continue to struggle, leaving them believing that the Indian government favours large businesses over them. But the Indian economy primarily consists of MSMEs, and how they fare has implications for how the nation perceives the idea of ease of doing business.

The other problem for Indian businesses is the general lack of alignment between regulations and reality. I recently heard an economist describe the idiocy of Indian regulations and the issue with imposing first-world regulations in a third-world context, and used this example: that of a neighbourhood dhobi, who irons garments in most urban localities in India. They often use traditional coal-fired irons and press clothes for as little as ₹5 or ₹10 per garment. Their operation is largely informal, without any licences or strict safety compliances, and one could say that this is what keeps their service affordable. Now, imagine imposing full licensing requirements and other applicable first-world safety standards on them. The cost of ironing a shirt would probably shoot up to ₹200 or ₹300, that is, a price point that is not affordable for an average Indian household.

This highlights that regulations designed for first-world countries do not translate well into third-world economies if applied without context. Imposing such standards pushes costs to unsustainable levels, makes compliance economically prohibitive and ultimately drives up prices for consumers. A mindless copying of standards adopted by first-world nations only results in India-manufactured products or services being priced beyond the common person's means, and hence not easily sellable. In the real world, businesses find ways to avoid compliance, thereby lowering production costs and keeping their products in price bands that are affordable in India. To keep products and services affordable, businesses often rely on bypassing regulation which is seen as an economic and market-driven necessity.

Notice also how the local dhobi continues to be a small business over the decades, unable to grow since they want to fly under the regulatory radar, in a world where becoming big will bring one to the notice of enforcers and regulators. So the other unanticipated outcome of these first-world regulations is that they also keep businesses small, making them fearful of growing.

However, the real issue is not the lost cost arbitrage but rather the disconnect between lawmakers and reality. India's objective should reflect its own economic conditions and not mindlessly follow models developed for first-world countries.

Hence, lawmakers must make regulations based on the ground realities of the country. The suggestion here is not to lower quality standards for India but rather to put them in context.

The MSME sector is crucial for India's growth, with a consistent contribution of 27 to 30 per cent of gross value added (GVA) as a ratio of India's overall GDP over the last three financial years.[72] Further, this sector accounted for at least 35 per cent of the manufacturing output of the country and nearly 45 per cent of exports for the same years.[73] As per the MSME registration portal established by the government, the sector employs more than 12 lakh Indians. It is important to recognise that a large majority of MSMEs try to evade the regulatory net because it does not make business sense to comply. The problem lies in their limited ability to hire professionals and advisers to help run their business.

They are expected by law to maintain books of accounts, file tax returns and comply with stringent labour laws, similar to large businesses. But most small businesses in India are run by entrepreneurs who have no formal education. The maze of incomprehensible compliance and legal requirements they have to fulfil naturally leads to non-compliance. This leads to small business owners being intimidated by petty government officials and then fleeced by local intermediaries whose services they need to meet their compliance requirements. Formal procedures are not perceived as beneficial but rather as a needless burden imposed on them for reasons they do not clearly understand.

By placing the onus on MSME owners to figure out their regulatory obligations and fulfil them, the government is placing an enormous burden on them. They are being asked to function in a way that is alien to how they work and perceive profits. Often, the costs involved in formalising a company and the risks of not doing this correctly can lead to bankruptcy. However, without an effort by the authorities to truly lower costs for this sector and consider the potential negative consequences of formalisation, the MSME sector in India is not going to realise its potential.

The suggestion is for the law to establish two or more clear standards for compliance and to allow some additional slack in compliance for MSMEs, with only large businesses being subject to a proper compliance regime. While this differentiation exists in principle in many statutes, it does not take into account practical realities when determining which businesses should be afforded such slack. The size and financial thresholds are too low and, given the rapid expansion of the economy, need frequent revision, but this does not happen.

The urban economy is intertwined with the enterprise of small-time entrepreneurs such as street-food hawkers and rickshaw drivers. The manpower for these businesses is mostly uneducated migrant labourers seeking either to supplement their agricultural income by working in the city or to depend entirely on the city's economy to fund their households back in their villages. For street vendors, the Indian government introduced the Street Vendor (Protection of Livelihood and Regulation of Street Vending) Act in 2014 in order to create a near-uniform system for their administration and regulation across states. The act grants state governments the power to frame rules for this activity.

While the state governments are under the impression that they are doing these micro businesses a favour, for these businesses it continues to be an insurmountable task to operate in a legally compliant manner. Take the example of a street-side pakora vendor. He now requires three to six licences or permits to run the business, depending on the state. Obtaining all these permits and licences after cutting through the bureaucracy is no easy task. It is the state officials who must befriend these small businesspersons and facilitate compliance, and the legal regime must place this burden on these officials so that the governance systems take the lead.

Work done by the Centre for Civil Society[74] – which focuses on libertarian solutions to problems in the Indian economy – has revealed that there are great differences among states in the implementation of the act, and that states have made little to no effort in making the new rules accessible to the individuals whom they seek to regulate through them. The procedures of registration, returns filing and appeals before the Town Vending Committee appear cumbersome and counterintuitive to street hawkers, who have lived and worked on an informal basis their entire lives. The act has not been able to bring about the required changes in the treatment or future of street hawkers and vendors in the country. Instead, the requirement to issue licences to street vendors has allowed local authorities to harass business owners or demand bribes from them for 'protection' from these rules.

The examples of the MSME sector and street vendors provide a clear picture of the changes that are being brought about and how ineffective they are, despite having the right intentions. They also demonstrate how government schemes fail or get delayed when they are needed the most because the bureaucratic architecture is not attuned to the businesses they seek to support. By placing the onus of figuring out the law and complying with the small print on people who are not educated enough to navigate the corridors of the local bodies for letters of recommendation and the online application process, the scheme has created its own bottlenecks.

Any assessment of policy requires the Central government to be the guiding authority. It needs to set up task forces to examine the needs of different states and suggest changes to keep the business environment positive. This responsibility cannot be hoisted entirely on the concerned ministries and departments. A wave of failure among small businesses can lead to an uptick in crime, as people in debt or without meaningful employment become desperate and frustrated, and are more likely to try to find loopholes in the system that they do not consider fair.

To suggest that poor policy drafting and implementation only affects those engaged in smaller businesses would be incorrect. There are similar disincentivising structures applied to bigger businesses in the form of unpredictable policy changes and arbitrary cancellation of contracts by governments. Business at the multinational level can also be deterred if policies reflect crony capitalism and if investigative agencies are seen as supporting the government's preferences for which entities can enjoy a free business environment. Recently, there have been international journalistic and research efforts showing how the Indian government's favouring of certain large business conglomerates has affected ease of doing business in the country.

When we look at the changes in policy in the telecom sector or in the governance of special economic zones, we notice that they show a pattern – one of greater regard for market players than for the market itself. If regulatory clearances at the highest levels are dependent on an enterprise's political allegiance, then we are not creating the right environment for truly competitive capitalism to flourish. In such a scenario, other institutions, such as public-sector banks, end up bending over backwards to create the right lending environment for select entities, which puts the common man's money at risk. Crony capitalism stunts market liberalisation.

The *Economist*'s Crony Capitalism Index, which can be taken with a pinch of salt because of its subjectivity, places India at rank 10 in crony capitalism on a list of 43 major economies.[75] To improve this image, India has to adopt a consensus-driven model, consulting with entrepreneurs, businesses, accountants and lawyers – both established and new, and from different scales of business – for framing business policies. This model must ensure that the authorities keep an open door for communication and an open mind to create an environment that can lead to sustainable growth. More billionaires in a country can make headlines, but for true growth, their dominance should be won on merit in the market and not on selective government policymaking.

The lack of intelligent policy governance can also be witnessed in the bureaucracy that currently impacts India's manufacturing sector. To understand the psyche of the bureaucrat the Indian manufacturing sector has to deal with, and the manner in which the bureaucracy stunts policy objectives and business growth, we need to go back to a time before the country's economic liberalisation of 1991. India was once an infamously closed economy, where we criminalised the import of a bizarre range of items to sustain our local manufacturing sector, which was too inefficient to compete internationally.

We must move away from unintelligent business design and always choose policy that creates competition and allows for businesses with new ideas to flourish and compete with the older and bigger businesses in the country. To start with, the Central government must invest in independent task forces to examine business sectors across geographies and suggest measures that keep business owners and their current business models in mind while designing policy.

To move towards a compliance regime, regulations should be brought in line with business realities, leaving room for honest profit-making by companies. Self-certification should become the norm, with state audits of compliance being by exception and violators being dealt with harshly. It will require an independent entity to study, frame and implement business-friendly regulations for India.

Whistle-blower incentivisation

In any modern economy, the need for government regulation of business operations must be balanced against freedom of operation for every business. Often, this freedom could translate into businesses flirting with the line demarcating what is lawful from what is not, but that is the very nature of entrepreneurship around the world.

Currently, the business regulatory framework in India is put together in anticipation of wrongdoing on the part of businesses. For companies, however, this overreach limits flexibility in even legitimate transactions. The Indian response has been to decriminalise laws. But it's better to put in a regulatory framework that takes into account business realities and to monitor business dealings only when there is a serious prospect of wrongdoing. The best way to do this is to have insiders spill the beans on corporate wrongdoing.

To facilitate this, the whistle-blower would need protection, both physically and economically. The law in India needs to be changed to allow for such protection and to provide financial incentives to the whistle-blower. In Frederick Schauer's seminal work *The Force of Law*,[76] he says that most law is followed due to the threat of sanction, and coercion is typical of the nature of law itself. As examples to illustrate his point, Schauer uses extra-legal sources of law, such as the mafia. He argues that even unlawful behaviour in support of mafia activity arises out of the perception of the mafia as a source of law that creates a code of behaviour for individuals. Independent actors always need to be nudged towards a favourable outcome for the collective.

For the market to function efficiently, it must avoid several outcomes that tend to distort it, such as criminal activity, the rise of monopolies, the dominance of crony capitalists, artificial scarcity and hoarding. However, market regulators cannot possibly expect to catch all illegal or anti-market activity, given their limited resources. The answer cannot be a superpower regulator with boots on the ground examining every interaction that occurs in the economy. Instead, common people need to be provided with an incentive structure that makes it possible for them to alert the formal regulators about breaches.

Whistle-blowers are essential to improving the ease of doing business as they help uncover fraud and crime that make the market anti-competitive and anti-innovation. Take the example of Hemant Kappanna, an Indian engineer who worked at General Motors (GM) in the US. Kappanna, along with a team of researchers, uncovered how Volkswagen deliberately programmed its engines to pass nitric oxide emission tests while its emissions exceeded the regulatory limit over 40 times during actual usage.[77] Kappanna was eventually fired in 2019 along with several other GM employees in a workforce reduction measure by the company. He wondered if he'd have been spared if he wasn't known as the one who had unmasked the scandal and thereby was perceived as being pro-regulation.[78]

According to a 2014 report by the Organisation for Economic Co-operation and Development (OECD), the countries with the most comprehensive whistle-blower laws are the US, Canada, Japan, Australia, South Korea, the Netherlands, New Zealand and the UK.[79] In India, not only are whistle-blowers not adequately protected, but their altruistic instincts are also inhibited by a variety of factors. Countries such as the US, South Korea, Ghana, Slovakia and Canada[80] have reward systems or laws incentivising whistle-blowers to come forward. For example, the US Commodity Futures Trading Commission recently awarded $4.5 million to a whistle-blower, raising its total payouts to $370 million since 2010. In FY 2023, the whistle-blower programme of the Securities and Exchange Commission (SEC) granted nearly $600 million in awards after receiving more than 18,000 tip-offs. Meanwhile, in the Canadian province of British Columbia, the British Columbia Securities Commission offers rewards of up to CA$250,000 for information leading to enforcement actions.[81]

Persons with knowledge of high-stakes unlawful activities in business often tend to be managerial employees or business affiliates employed or appointed by companies or individual businessmen. Concern for their own economic security is the primary consideration behind their disinclination to alert authorities when they find violations of the law by their employers. Currently, India's whistle-blower law provides only limited protection to someone who calls out a company or a business owner. The Whistle Blowers Protection Act (WPA), 2014, provides a mechanism to report illegal, unethical and illegitimate practices by public servants and public-sector undertakings.

But by virtue of being limited to government and public-sector undertakings, the WPA only provides a mechanism for whistle-blowers to tackle corruption in the government. A public servant or any other person can approach the Central or state vigilance commission, which shall mask the identity of the complainant while inquiring into his or her complaint. Additionally, disclosure of the identity of the complainant has been made a crime. The WPA was introduced after the prominent murders of some public interest and right-to-information activists.

One such individual was the engineer Satyendra Dubey, who was killed in November 2003 for bringing to public attention the corruption in the National Highway Authority of India's Golden Quadrilateral project.[82] Similarly, a deputy director of the audit wing in Karnataka's cooperative societies department by the name of S.P. Mahantesh was murdered in May 2012 after he disclosed irregularities in cooperative societies involving prominent politicians.[83] The WPA covers the Prevention of Corruption Act, 1988 (which deals with government servants).

The whistle-blower framework in the US provides protection to whistle-blowers faced with the prospect of retaliation. It does this through a host of industrial laws,[84] including legislation covering occupational safety and health, consumer financial protection, ill-effects of toxic substances and air pollution, among others. The laws serve to protect employees from retaliation by their employer when they report violations of workplace safety laws. Additionally, under the Dodd–Frank Act, an investor protection fund established by the US Congress[85] is financed entirely through monetary penalties levied on securities law violators. This fund is used to reward whistle-blowers when they voluntarily provide the SEC with credible information that leads to a successful enforcement action.

In 2023, the SEC awarded $279 million to a whistle-blower whose information led to a successful enforcement of securities regulations against violators. In 2020, $114 million was paid as a whistle-blower reward.[86] The identities of these whistle-blowers continue to be effectively protected under the law. It makes for sufficient motivation for potential whistle-blowers, who know they may stand to gain from the information they are privy to. As a result, whistle-blowing in the US after the 2023 SEC decision has led to the recovery of more than $4 billion in unlawful gains and interest made by violators.[87]

Another corporate whistle-blower protection law in the US is the Sarbanes–Oxley Act, which protects corporate whistle-blowers from retaliation by their employers. Section 806 of the act covers commodities or securities fraud, tax underpayment and other corporate fraud. Retaliatory actions such as termination of employment, disclosure of identity, harassment and change in job duties are covered as actions that constitute valid reasons for the whistle-blower to sue the employer. Employers can then be forced to pay whistle-blowers back wages, compensatory damages, damages for lost future earnings and also punitive damages.[88]

In India, the Securities and Exchange Board of India (SEBI) allows for whistle-blower incentives through the SEBI (Prohibition of Insider Trading) Regulations, 2015. The regulator introduced changes in 2018 that mandated all publicly listed companies to have an internal whistle-blower policy. However, the suggested policy did not lead to a significant change in the environment for whistle-blowers. Any suspected violations would be internally addressed, allowing companies to stifle whistle-blower voices and complaints without employing an independent review.

SEBI continues to adopt a policy of incremental improvement or tinkering to make its whistle-blower system work. In 2019, it introduced a mechanism for whistle-blowers to approach it directly to report complaints of violations of SEBI regulations.[89] SEBI has also attempted to expand the policy over time to include a wider variety of corporate frauds, accounting irregularities and insider trading. In 2021, the regulator increased the award for whistle-blowers from ₹1 crore to ₹10 crore in an attempt to encourage more whistle-blowers to come forward with information on market violations.[90]

But even though the law on whistle-blower incentivisation for insider trading has been improved since its introduction, it has significant shortcomings when compared to its international counterparts. First, the comprehensive protection from retaliation offered in other countries has not been properly replicated or adopted in India. Second, the cap of 10 per cent of the total amount involved in the violation for the reward for the whistle-blower means the financial incentive for whistle-blowing remains very low, especially when compared to what other jurisdictions such as the US provide.

Additionally, while SEBI is free to assign the amount awardable to the whistle-blower, a higher predetermined minimum percentage of the amount involved and removal of the cap introduced for whistle-blower incentives may be necessary to encourage more people to come forward. Penalties could also be considered in cases where individuals attempt to mislead authorities or wilfully fail to report misconduct despite having a duty to do so. The establishment of knowledge of wrongdoing in a court of law can rely on various forms of evidence, including documentation, witness testimonies and circumstantial proof.

With robust whistle-blower protection and incentivisation, the country can aim for a more efficient market. Of particular importance is the impact whistle-blowing would have on disclosure obligations. The underlying principle in mandating public disclosure of information for listed companies is that the public should be aware of the full truth of their status and should be able to trust the price at which their stocks are traded on the market. Most developed economies follow this principle, and failure to make adequate disclosures results in massive fines for companies. A consequence of this is that when a public company's shares are sought to be purchased in a developed economy, the acquirer would not need to conduct extensive due diligence on the affairs of the target company, since all the risks and potential upsides are already factored into the share price.

The situation in India is very different. Many public companies avoid full disclosure of price-sensitive information. Consequently, detailed due diligence must be conducted when someone wishes to acquire a significant number of shares in a company. The exercise often results in the prospective buyer asking the targeted company to publish certain facts in the public domain and make stock-market filings before deciding to invest. This shows that shares of a listed public company in India do not always reflect the company's true value.

The Indian corporate culture of partial or inadequate disclosure of information to the general public, to shareholders and to market regulators impairs the market and undermines people's trust in it. Historically, private and public listed companies in India have kept their disclosures to a bare minimum, and any disclosures made are often misleading. The companies' rationale is that additional information will unduly benefit their competitors. Each individual corporate actor's miserly behaviour regarding disclosures has encouraged a culture of non-disclosure across Indian industries.

The key to ease of doing business lies in ensuring that the fundamentals of the market-based economy are strong. Competition along with fair play is a central feature of a thriving economy, and investor protection is a significant aspect of such fair play. For a long time, institutional and foreign investors have been demanding greater disclosures and a better regulatory regime in India to tackle information asymmetry in the market. In 2014, responding to such demands, SEBI amended a clause in the equity listing agreement, which is the agreement between a company and the stock exchanges for listing the company's shares. It now requires board-level oversight for disclosure and communications. Further changes were made on matters regarding disclosure or material subsidiaries.[91]

Under the SEBI (Listing Obligations and Disclosure Requirements) Regulations, 2015 (SEBI LODR), a material subsidiary is defined as one whose turnover or net worth exceeds 10 per cent of the consolidated turnover or net worth of the listed entity and its subsidiaries, as per the immediately preceding accounting year.[92] In 2018, the SEBI LODR Regulations were amended to introduce a specific requirement regarding unlisted material subsidiaries. As per the amendment, at least one independent director of the listed entity must be appointed to the board of such an unlisted material subsidiary. For this purpose, a subsidiary is considered material if its net worth or turnover exceeds 20 per cent of the consolidated net worth or turnover of the listed entity and its subsidiaries, based on the preceding financial year.[93] Further, in 2025, an additional provision was introduced for high-value debt-listed entities, prescribing a similar 20 per cent threshold to determine materiality. Under this provision, a subsidiary is deemed material if its net worth or turnover exceeds 20 per cent of the consolidated net worth or turnover of the listed entity and its subsidiaries, as per the previous financial year.[94]

In 2015, an American business consultancy firm called FTI Consulting rated companies on their mandatory and voluntary disclosures on an index that mapped quarterly financial information, annual reports, shareholding information, board and management information, and analyst transcripts. It was revealed that updated analyst transcripts and public information regarding analyst engagements were not disclosed by a majority of the BSE 100 companies. The firms scored a low median voluntary disclosure score of only 3.5 out of 6, with a third of the BSE 100 companies scoring less than 3 out of 6. These low scores indicated the historical trend of non-disclosure among Indian corporations and the need for a better regulatory and market framework in the country.

With the introduction of SEBI regulations for listing obligations and disclosure requirements in 2015, a significant stride was made towards ensuring minimum standards of public disclosure by listed companies. Among the regulations is a requirement that listed companies submit an annual informational memorandum to inform investors of any information that SEBI might consider relevant. The introduction of this memorandum was prompted by the lack of information in Indian corporate annual reports, which also do not always provide the information in an investor-friendly manner.[95] Owing to these changes brought in over the last decade,[96] annual compliances for listed companies now include disclosure of related-party transactions and changes in key management personnel.

These steps improved India's score on the World Bank's business extent of disclosure index to 8 in 2021. The index is scored from 0 to 10 in increasing order of disclosure. India's score was just 6 in 2013, while other Asian economies such as China, Singapore, Indonesia, Malaysia and Thailand all scored a perfect 10.[97] This is despite most of these countries having the same issues as India, such as the need for higher GDP growth to close the gap between their economies and the developed Western economies.

Internationally, a recent prompt for a relook at the corporate disclosure regime to ensure better compliance came when the US Securities and Exchange Commission announced charges against the tech giant Facebook (now Meta) for making misleading disclosures in its periodic filings about the risks pertaining to misuse of its user data by third parties.[98] Facebook's user data had been used by a third party to provide services to political parties in the 2016 US elections. However, Facebook did not disclose this categorically until 2018, which led to a fall in its share price. Facebook paid $100 million to settle charges brought against it for not altering the risk-factor disclosure in its filings despite being aware of the data leak.

In India, risk-factor disclosure by companies is characterised by the provision of a variety of delayed and inadequate information. While offer documents typically list a variety of risk factors, the current regulatory environment does not adequately force companies to distinguish between hypothetical and real risks. Despite this latest round of improvements, much needs to be done in India to ensure a clear and internationally recognised disclosure regime that attracts more well-founded investments and increases trust in Indian companies.

As the recent Infosys whistle-blower saga shows, when companies hide information to boost profits, violating disclosure guidelines in the process, it leads to a significant erosion of public and investor trust in the company as well as in the regulatory environment.[99] But until the market regulator and the government's think tank abandon the practice of reactive regulation, we will see only tweaks to previous policies. As long as we continue to play catch-up both in regulation-making and implementation, the market cannot realise its true potential. For investors from across the world to choose to invest in Indian companies with confidence in the coming decades, SEBI and the corporate affairs ministry must set high disclosure standards that do not suffer from ambiguity.

4

Harmonising Indian Law with the Indian Sense of Justice

SHOULD THE LAWS OF a country be in alignment with the cultural character of its people? What role would the cultural instinct of the people have in matters of law? Would it not be simpler for people to just follow the existing laws and pay a penalty if they don't? And would such alignment of the law mean going back to the rule of law indigenous to the country? Indigenous to the country as of what point in time? How far must one go back then? And which indigenous laws must be considered? Those that apply to the largest constituent of the population? Must the law in India, for example, inculcate within itself the Hindu sense of dharma?[1]

Ideas in jurisprudence

The reason the law of a nation must endeavour to align with its people's cultural character or collective social instinct is to give it moral legitimacy in the eyes of the public. This will help generate genuine respect for the law among them and a willingness on their part to comply with it. When a law has social acceptability among the majority of the people, compliance will follow because the people *feel* the need to follow it. They will view compliance as being in their long-term interest, whether individual or social. This in turn will help create a law-abiding society.

A law that lacks moral legitimacy results in people complying not out of trust and a sense of need but simply out of fear of the consequences of non-compliance. They do not see compliance with such a law as being in their social or individual interest. Thus, whenever they feel they can escape these consequences, they don't follow the law. This results in a society that has little respect for the law and, in some situations, completely rejects it. If non-compliance becomes rampant, in jurisprudential terms it is referred to as a 'dead law'. So any law in a democratic system must have social resonance to make it a living system for society. If most of the population is inclined to comply with the law, knowledge of the law also becomes widespread, and the law is no longer a stranger to most.

Let us consider the Indian situation in this context:

i. There is general non-compliance with the law, though one could put that down to a complete failure of enforcement.
ii. There is non-compliance on account of a lack of awareness of the law. Examples of this would be a street food vendor not having the requisite permits and licences, or a driver or domestic help buying an illegal tenement since that is all they can afford.
iii. There is non-compliance rooted in the hope of getting away undetected. Examples of this would be homeowners deviating from building bylaws, vehicle and factory owners disregarding environmental laws and measures for groundwater preservation, or air pollution regulation.
iv. There is also non-compliance because the regulations lack sufficient moral credibility and/or authority. This is when the law is not in accordance with the will of the people. Examples include the wearing of helmets by those riding pillion seats, the ban on the use of plastic bags, bursting firecrackers during Diwali, compliance with building bylaws, etc.

The fundamental reasons that persuade the population to comply with the law are twofold: individual benefit (that is, people agree with the law) and the fear of punishment. However, widespread non-compliance suggests that the current enforcement system doesn't inspire any fear. Consequently, this leads to individuals pursuing immediate short-term goals at the expense of adhering to laws that are seen as overly complex and inconvenient, ultimately reflecting the lack of public confidence in the law.

Evolution of law in India

Fundamentally, the law derives from the public consciousness of right and wrong.[2] Therefore, it is a reflection of the public's views on morality. Public morality, in turn, derives from the propriety accorded to actions and behaviours by society, imposed by force or by custom. Historically in India, the laws were broadly consistent with the principles derived from native Indian philosophies. Even though the subcontinent was subdivided into many kingdoms with ever-shifting borders, the laws were fairly uniform across these realms as they were based on the then-dominant scriptures and scriptural commentaries, that is, dharmic[3] principles.

Of course, the concepts underlying dharmic principles were not as black and white as the laws of today are. They varied from person to person, from community to community, and indeed from one context and circumstance to another. In today's world, we might think of these principles as fluid, since they shifted based on the context in which they were applied. For most of ancient Indian history, including the periods that are thought of as mythological, there is no clear articulation of the principles of dharma. This is probably because they remained unwritten down through the ages. At any point in these eras, multiple layers of dharmic principles had to be considered when deciding how a particular dispute might be settled.

Sometimes these principles would conflict, resulting in a *dharma-sankat* or a dharmic problem. This could be resolved by an individual deciding to follow one principle over the others after accepting that the consequences of that decision would have to be owned by them – not just in their present life but probably in their next too. The concept of the *dharma-sankat* remained a popular philosophical tool, as is evidenced by Mahatma Gandhi's usage of the term in his book *My Experiments with Truth*. He uses it to explain his hesitation when deciding a name for the organisation he founded in 1894 to fight discrimination against Indians in the Natal province in South Africa.[4]

Gandhi's hesitation stemmed from the fear that naming it 'Natal Indian Congress' would emphasise ethnic or national origin, undermining his vision of uniting all groups around a shared cause for justice and equality. He wanted to avoid positioning the organisation as representing only Indians in South Africa as he envisioned it playing a broader role in advocating for all marginalised communities. A specific name tied to the Indian community would limit its appeal to other oppressed groups. Hence, his *dharma-sankat*.

It was around 1500 BCE to 1200 BCE[5] that certain general principles of dharma came to be articulated and written down. Until then, the principles of dharma were in practice through unwritten traditions rooted in social customs, rituals, teachings and moral practices. These principles were passed down through the generations and were deeply embedded in the culture, religion and social structures of early Indian societies. It was only much after the Upanishads, Ramayana, Mahabharata and the Puranas that our rishis articulated certain key principles of dharma in writing. These were collected in the dharma Sutras and the Manu Smriti.[6] One might even imagine these texts as having been compiled for the period of Kali Yuga, a period when it became difficult to grasp the principles of dharma from the unwritten, and when true knowledge would be lost to mankind.[7]

During those eras, the community sought decisions from its wise men, in particular the Brahmins, who were said to have a deep, academic and layered understanding, as well as an intuitive grasp of principles of dharma applicable in specific instances. Their views would be sought and followed, but this worked more like a system of arbitration.

In many instances, the advice of the local devata would be sought to deal with and settle differences.[8] One continuing example of this practice can be found in the Goludevata traditions, thought of as the ultimate arbiter of disputes among the Kumaonis. Dr Meera Baindur, a professor of humanities and social sciences and an avid researcher of Indian philosophy, describes how the Goludevata's actions are viewed by the ordinary people of the region, who view the process of justice through the incidents that take place in the lives of the petitioners after the written prayer is hung in the temple.

Any untoward incident is seen as a part of Goludev's justice for lying or being morally culpable. For instance, a family member could fall sick or cattle may die. However, any favourable outcome is seen as Goludev's justice for being morally correct.[9] Often, these adjudicatory devatas would 'possess' the body of specific individuals and express their views and decisions through them.[10] This advice was adhered to out of fear of incurring the deity's wrath. Many communities in rural India still follow traditions that are along the lines of this Goludevata system.

In certain Indian kingdoms with well-structured governments, an administrator would often play the role of a judicial officer. In the imperial Chola kingdom, while small disputes were resolved at the village level, the *thandal*, or judicial officer, decided more complex judicial disputes at a higher court of appeal. This court consisted of the *thandal*, public notaries and local judicial officers, called *nyayaththaar*.[11] Kautilya's *Arthashastra* also makes reference to the Mauryan system of justice around the period 322 BCE to 298 BCE, describing administrative units called *sthaniya*, *dronamukha*, *khrvatika* and *sangrahana* (similar to our modern districts, tehsils and collective units such as parganas). Kautilya mentions that there were courts in each *sangrahana* and also at the intersection of districts (*janapadasandhishu*). These courts each comprised three judges (*dhramastha*) and an equal number of ministers (*amatya*).

But generally, it would be fair to assume that there was no single institutionalised judicial system that applied uniformly throughout the territory and nation of India. Some of this changed with the arrival of rulers from the Middle East, and subsequently from Europe. The new rulers brought to India religious principles based on Islamic[12] and Biblical scriptures[13], and other governance behaviours and rules based on their own tribal and cultural roots. These new thought processes revolved around the Ten Commandments of the Jews and the ideas of justice and fair play that evolved in the Middle East and Central Asia over the next few centuries.

Christianity came to India first around 50 CE, when Christian evangelists arrived on the coast of Kerala with the Saint Thomas Christians. While certain Semitic ideas were introduced into India, they might not have found their way into the legal system. However, when Christianity was reintroduced into India by the Portuguese around the 15th century, leading to mission stations in Cochin and Goa, and eventually to the Christianisation of almost the entire population of Goa by the 1700s on account of Portuguese rule, Christian or Semitic principles were firmly introduced into the Indian legal landscape.

Early Islam came to India during the lifetime of Prophet Mohammed himself, with a local ruler in Kerala adopting Islam. This resulted in some Islamic ideas being introduced into the legal system in Kerala. A few centuries later, during the pre-Mughal era in northern India, several Muslim rulers established short-lived dynasties and introduced Islamic law in the region.

Delhi was ruled by the Delhi Sultanate after Qutubuddin Aibak founded a kingdom covering much of north India in the 1200s. Then, during the Mughal era (1526–1857), various parts of India saw the introduction of Islamic law in certain sections of society. Towards the end of the 17th century, about 150 million people and an area of 3.2 million square kilometres were under Mughal rule. This area stretched from

Kabul to Bengal, Odisha and parts of the Deccan. During this period, both the mystic/Sufi tradition and Ulema-based Islam spread widely. While Akbar's reign saw the restriction of the powers of the court Ulema and several other Islamic practices, his great-grandson Aurangzeb reimposed the *jizya* on non-Muslims and prohibited the construction of Hindu temples in 1669.[14]

While the Middle Ages did see all-pervasive sovereignties in the subcontinent, they did not dominate the landscape as the modern Indian state does. So, while the old law (before the advent of people from the Middle East and Europe) generally continued to apply to the larger population on the subcontinent, the ruling communities were governed by the legal principles they had brought from back home. And the natives who worked closely with these new rulers adopted some of the legal principles the new rulers applied to themselves.[15] In the absence of statistical and other empirical evidence, we have to speculate that native laws were influenced only marginally by the rulers from the Middle East.

Since the 11th-century invasions by the Turks and subsequently the Mughals, the local laws were significantly influenced by Islamic law that had its origins in the Koran.[16] However, these laws largely applied to the Muslim populations, and the native Hindus continued to govern themselves by applying dharmic principles. In situations of conflict between Islamic and dharmic law, it is likely that the law of the rulers prevailed – to the extent they had the ability to enforce it.

However, European rule, for reasons not relevant to this discussion, attempted to 'civilise' the natives in every way possible, including by seeking to force their home-grown legal principles on all of India. They tried to achieve this by ridiculing native ideas, the structure of Indian society at the time and even its legal principles, and subsequently through spreading European cultural and religious ideas among the natives.

However, European rule only had limited success in its quest to build a European hegemony in India. It led to various native Indian communities being allowed to continue with their old legal principles in specific situations involving civil law, though European criminal law came to be applied uniformly throughout the lands ruled by the Europeans. Hence, key laws such as the Indian Penal Code, the criminal and civil procedural codes, Evidence Law and the Law of Contracts were enacted and enforced by the English on all populations and territories controlled by them. However, personal laws, including those relating to inheritance and marriage, continued to be dominated by native ideas and laws.

The present legal framework in India is based primarily on English and European principles.[17] The origins of English and European law, in turn, derive from their sense of morality, which is based on Biblical values including the Ten Commandments, the teachings in the Old and New Testaments, and the evolution of jurisprudence based on these sources.[18]

Colonial and post-colonial judicial systems

Legal imperialism is a consequence of colonialism. It has left a deep impact on the legal frameworks of colonised nations. The influence of the legal systems of the colonial powers on the indigenous societal structures of the colonised regions was not merely a consequence of colonisation but a deliberate strategy by these powers to ensure control, exploitation and cultural dominance of these lands and their peoples. The colonisers didn't just introduce their own legal frameworks; they often forcibly displaced the native legal systems.[19]

These foreign systems often had little to no relevance to local nuances, leading to systemic inefficiencies and widespread discontent among the native populations. The dislodging of indigenous legal traditions by the imposed systems led to severe marginalisation of the native legal systems, reducing them to mere customary practices that no longer had any formal recognition or validity.[20]

Many colonised regions were subject to the simultaneous operation of indigenous and colonial legal systems. While the colonial laws were predominant, the customary laws were still informally adhered to by the native populace. This dual system often led to contradictions and ambiguities in legal proceedings and interpretations of the law.[21] The dichotomy in the system often favoured those aligning with the colonial powers, creating disparities in access to justice. While the colonisers and their allies benefited from the privileges of the colonial legal system, the indigenous populace was often left to navigate the complexities of two conflicting legal systems.[22]

It was fairly clear that the colonial legal systems were tailored to protect the economic interests of the colonisers. This often involved the usurping of local resources, the control of trade by the colonisers and the manipulation of labour laws to exploit the indigenous populations.[23] By imposing their legal systems on the lands they controlled, colonisers also attempted to redefine cultural narratives. Laws that undermined local traditions and practices were introduced, facilitating a slow erosion of native cultural identities.[24]

The post-colonial era witnessed the once-colonised nations grappling with the remnants of colonial legal structures. For many of these nations, the inherent imbalances and biases of these systems continue to affect their socio-legal dynamics.[25] The intertwining of colonial legalities within native systems has made legal reforms in post-colonial societies a challenging task. Efforts to decolonise legal systems often encounter resistance even as they try to rectify centuries of alien legal norms that had been imposed upon them.[26]

One strategic principle asserted by the imperial powers marked the era of colonial domination: the presumption of knowledge of the law on the part of the people. This principle assumed that colonised individuals were familiar with and understood the European legal frameworks imposed on them.[27] By embedding this assumption in their legal frameworks, the colonial authorities sought not only to solidify their control over the nations they had colonised but also to offer a veneer of legitimacy to their dominance.[28] This resulted in the gradual sidelining of indigenous legal traditions in favour of European laws, eroding the cultural and legal identities of the colonised territories.[29]

Yet, this imposition has not gone unchallenged. Colonised communities are pushing back and reaffirming the significance and validity of their indigenous legal systems.[30] Some territories have adopted an approach of legal pluralism, which allows their people to engage with European laws while concurrently preserving and practising their local legal traditions.[31] Intellectual currents, such as decolonisation of knowledge, have emerged to critique and challenge the Eurocentric biases inherent in the colonial legal structures.[32] On the ground, this resistance has manifested in various forms – ranging from civil disobedience and boycotts to more organised forms of protest.[33]

In the context of reforming Indian laws, my suggestion for the resolution of this conflict is to redefine certain basic aspects of Indian law to make them consistent with what is naturally acceptable to the native Indian population. This will ensure that people are not branded criminals merely as a result of instinctive, culturally guided actions on their part.

By following the common law system imposed upon us by our colonial subjugators in the interest of stability, India has continually missed great opportunities to revive its civilisational wisdom. Further, by not examining how the Indian sense of justice may have been lost as a result of invaders bringing their own systems of administration-oriented laws, the country's legal framework has subjected common Indians to perpetual confusion as they attempt to navigate a foreign-imposed set of laws in their own country.

Indianisation of our laws

Why do we even need to consider this historical context? The reason for its relevance in India is that most citizens of our country have little understanding of the laws that govern them. However, they understand the cultural and religious values that have been passed down to them through the ages. Since it is quite easy for them to comply with these cultural and religious values, if the nation's laws reflected these values, it would be easy for them to comply with the laws. The imposition of laws inconsistent with the natural values of the people results not just in laws being actively breached, but also in unintentional violations where people are not even aware of such laws.

Multiple instances of this show up in Bollywood movies, often glamorised, and in daily life when, say, a street vendor might believe that he or she has set up an honest micro-business while in fact they have violated some law or licensing requirement. To get a sense of this disconnect, consider insider trading in the Indian stock market and piracy of intellectual property. India would never have had a tech revolution if software piracy had not been the norm, and a bunch of our people would be dead but for reverse-engineered drugs.

Now the question may be asked – if one goes by outdated cultural and scriptural values, how does one deal with the changes in the modern world? In fact, who decides what is outdated? And when a law that does not naturally flow from our culture or tradition is enacted, what should be the role of the state in educating the population about it?

The pathway to Indianisation of the legal system requires one to examine how the Indian sense of justice can be reintroduced in our laws, study the impact of legal imperialism on India as a colonial and then a post-colonial country, and analyse the impact of all these factors on legal compliance.

Next, one would need to focus on certain structural changes required to bring the Indian system of justice closer to the Indian instinct of justice. We need to move away from the common law, a precedent-heavy system we have inherited from our colonial oppressors, and test the principles of presumption of knowledge of law on the part of citizens and of burden of proof for efficacy in the Indian context. We must also discuss the right of individuals to impart private justice versus the right of law enforcement agencies to impart justice.

Implications for compliance and enforcement

For any law to be a living law, the general citizenry needs to comprehend its broad principles, if not the nuances, and then buy into them. Otherwise a law could be born dead, as in the case of the recent changes attempted in the farm laws, which were perceived by certain farmer communities as laws that would leave them vulnerable to big companies; the Citizenship Act, which sought to provide a quick path to citizenship to one category of persons and not others, based on the religion-based partition of India in 1947; and the amendments to the Motor Vehicle law, which imposed harsh penalties for violations of traffic rules. For the buy-in to happen, the Indian government will have to take forward the common sense of morality among the citizenry and articulate or infuse it into the law.[34] Once this connection exists, the population can then operate based on its own sense of morality, with the law now codifying it.

Morality derives from people's religious leanings and their spiritual sense.[35] In the Indian context, for the majority of the people, regardless of the formal religion they follow, the general sense of morality would derive from a mix of the underlying Indian traditional religious systems (termed 'Hinduism' in law), with influences from the Semitic religious systems (principally Christianity and Islam) and from the atheistic principles that have come to the fore in India since Independence.

There can be no doubt that most Indians, in their desire for justice, will be in agreement with the following notions:

i. Justice must be delivered, even if it conflicts with the law as framed.
ii. Procedural delays in the delivery of justice are unacceptable.
iii. A judge must determine the truth, regardless of how the prosecution or plaintiff/defendant present their cases.
iv. There must be accountability for wrong judicial decisions and for anyone misleading the legal process.
v. Compensation and penalties must be proportionate to the breach or offence.

vi. The common man must not be expected to know and understand all the laws.

Even in other parts of the world, compliance is more easily achieved with laws aligned with the citizenry's sense of fairness and morality. This is because the law then resonates with the people's notions of what is right and wrong so that appreciation of the law of their land comes naturally to them, since they fear a breach of the law will have karmic implications or bring them punishment at the hands of God. The suggestions here have been made keeping in mind the need to have buy-in from the larger population for the law so that compliance follows naturally. When this is the case, violators are aware they are committing a wrong when they do so and hence have *mens rea* and are justifiably prosecuted and punished.

However, the obstacle to such a change lies in the Indian elite. Unfortunately, this includes most lawyers, judges, academics, journalists, bureaucrats and others who are inclined to believe that it is better to let loose one hundred criminals rather than have a single innocent person convicted. While a significant number of the people of the country support the idea of swift justice for heinous crimes like murder and rape – which can carry capital punishment – only a minuscule segment of the Indian elite has reservations about taking a life or implementing an execution – even if it is obvious to most that it is just and fair – without due process. But an overwhelming or powerful section of the population does not truly care about an extended trial for those accused of heinous crimes, and dismissal of their views would contradict the principles of democracy.

While one can quite confidently suppose that the general public does not desire the execution of an innocent person, there is little support among them for an inefficient due process – that is, the idea of letting a hundred criminals loose so as not to have an innocent condemned. It is unbelievable that there are instances when judges acquit some accused persons even if they are completely convinced of their guilt, merely because the prosecution has done a poor job. This situation is simply unacceptable to the vast majority of the Indian population. The trick, therefore, lies in designing a legal system that convicts almost all criminals, if not all of them, while at the same time providing maximum protection for the innocent against any miscarriage of justice.

The idea of letting a hundred criminals get away with their crimes as long as the process does not end up convicting an innocent person is the basis on which the existing system in India is designed. It derives from the Anglo-Saxon idea that the State should not take any active part in depriving a person of life and liberty when it cannot give life, which is in the hands of God. Hence, God is left to deal with the hundred criminals let loose.

To add some context, the blind justification of the due-process path would be understandable if there were no better alternative, but the claim that there is no way other than to follow the existing due process because a tiny minority believes that this is unacceptable is flawed. What happens to the principles of democracy in such a scenario? The elite feel that the 'commoners' do not understand the law and that only they possess the capacity to comprehend it and decide how justice should be administered. This attitude goes against the very concept of universal franchise.

In the natural course of things, common folk place their trust in public intellectuals, many of whom belong to the elite class. However, this trust is often abused by this minuscule section, which imposes its views on the vast majority of the people. Their justification for this is not very different from that of the British Raj – which is that they are simply endeavouring to civilise the uncivilised, ignorant and prejudiced majority. It is simply illogical for a small minority of intellectuals and the elite to believe that they can and should dictate the destiny of a population of over 1.3 billion.

It is said that the proof of the pudding lies in the eating – so is the existing system serving to achieve this goal? In the current system, how can one be certain of someone's guilt or innocence even after a trial, considering that witnesses can be influenced or bribed? Or consider this: the poor cannot defend themselves adequately and suffer the consequences of being poor; that is, they can be convicted unfairly or become victims of under-trial imprisonment. So, the lofty objective of ensuring that no innocent person is convicted often fails in the case of the poor and those who are improperly defended. Hence, should we not go with the hope of achieving maximum convictions of the guilty, while accepting that humans cannot design a system that is foolproof against the conviction of every poor innocent person? Having said this, we need to build a robust legal mechanism that will serve to nail the guilty and simultaneously seek to secure the innocent against bad faith or negligence on the part of the police and/or the prosecution.

At this point, we might need to delve into how laws came into existence in the first place. An educated guess would be that they likely originated in a primitive form during the days of cavemen when certain actions were allowed while others were not. Regardless of their geographical location, there must have been some understanding among the people of the world of the basic principles of right and wrong. There are some universal expectations across societies, such as promises should be kept and integrity should matter, which reflect the genesis of the basic idea of fairness, based on culture and not religion. Furthermore, the concept of fairness may have varied across civilisations and communities, depending on factors such as geography, society, upbringing and indoctrination, but the idea of fairness itself is universal. It is important to remember that law is a means to an end and not an end in itself. Its purpose is to maintain order, ensure justice, and protect the rights and freedoms of individuals. Indians find it challenging when compliance with a process prescribed in law becomes a goal in itself, rather than a tool for the delivery of justice.

A large portion of our population still lives in rural areas and follows traditional practices. Their understanding of justice may be different from that of people residing in urban areas, urban areas being more Anglicised. While it is important to have a legal framework that upholds basic human rights and principles of justice, the framework should also be flexible enough to accommodate the diverse cultural and social contexts of the country.

The process of indigenising laws involves aligning them with the instinctive sense of justice prevalent among the people, but it does not mean compromising on fundamental rights or principles of fairness. Rather, we have to recognise and incorporate the values and customs that resonate with Indian society. It requires a deeper understanding of the Indian context and an acknowledgment of the unique challenges and aspirations of our people. Aligning Indian laws with Indian instincts would involve a comprehensive review of the existing laws to identify areas where they may be disconnected from societal values and expectations.

The objective should be to create a legal system that is not only effective and efficient but also in tune with the values of the people it serves. It should inspire confidence and trust while also addressing the concerns and aspirations of all sections of society. Such a system will not only enhance access to justice for citizens but also foster a sense of ownership and pride among them.

In Indian mythology, and even in the modern Indian psyche, taking a life for a justifiable reason has widespread public endorsement. For example, the act of Ram killing Ravan was widely perceived as fair. As mentioned earlier, there are dialogues in Bollywood movies in defence of vigilante actions, citing the Ramayana example, which demonstrates the widespread public sentiment in this matter.

Hence, indigenisation of laws will be a complex and ongoing process that requires continuous dialogue, engagement and introspection. It will be a journey towards creating a legal system that reflects the spirit of India and upholds the values and aspirations of its people. Only through such alignment can the Indian legal system truly serve as a pillar of democracy and ensure justice for all. In this chapter, I suggest some changes that can bring the spirit of the law closer to the spirit of the Indian people. It is an approach that prioritises efficiency and certainty in the law and closes the loopholes often used by criminals to escape accountability. Here, the aim is to suggest structural, conceptual and cultural changes that are needed to bring about a better legal regime for the common man.

Shifting from common law to civil law

Law students across the country are often met with a myriad set of daunting rules – of precedent, *stare decisis* and *per incuriam*. These rules determine the hierarchy of precedents set by courts and also ensure that the law is in a constant state of flux, being shaped and reshaped by judges. These are edifices of common law and give the collective category of judges the right to influence the law every time a bench in a competent court has the will to do so. Common law consists of a set of legal principles which form the basis of English law. India is a country that applies common law just like the US, Australia, the UK, India, Singapore, Malaysia and others.

Some of the basic distinguishing features of common law include the following:

i. *It is judicial precedent/case law-based.* The law has come into existence bottom up, that is, on account of a common set of legal principles that evolved through court decisions over a period of time. As a consequence, in a case bearing similar facts or circumstances as one already heard by the same or a higher court, the judge is obliged to follow the decision of those courts in those earlier cases. This holds even when the judge believes that justice would actually be delivered with a different decision. In such a situation, either the judge has to distinguish the case they are hearing from the earlier case – that is, establish that the facts and/or circumstances of the earlier case were different – or deliver a judgment in line with the decision in the earlier case, even if they disagree with it.
ii. *It is an adversarial system.* The judge acts as a referee between lawyers appearing for the different sides in a dispute or a criminal prosecution. Lawyers ask questions, deal with evidence production and present arguments based on evidence gathered by them. Judges rely principally on the arguments presented before them. While they do have a somewhat residual power to inquire into the matter before them, they seldom exercise this power.

As a consequence, justice often becomes very dependent on the lawyers hired by litigants, and in most cases the litigant with the better lawyer (usually the more expensive lawyer) wins. In criminal cases, the accused are often defended by better lawyers, and in India the prosecution is led by lawyers who might not be the best. As a consequence, a very large number of accused who are prosecuted (not to mention those who are let off even without prosecution for various reasons) get acquitted, and conviction levels are abysmally low.

The basic features of civil law are as follows:

i. *Judicial precedent is not binding in civil law.* Law is formulated on a top-down basis, that is, the sovereign frames the rules of justice and the courts apply the rules. As a consequence, a judge inquires into the facts of a case and takes decisions based on statute, but applies his or her own sense to arrive at decisions that will deliver justice. Here, a judge in a case may come to a conclusion different from a decision in an earlier case where the facts and circumstances were similar. Judges are not compelled to follow earlier decisions with which they disagree. So, every decision delivered by a judge is not binding on third parties. Therefore, there is an incentive in civil law systems for more clearly defined statutes since they must work as operational guidelines for all judges who encounter the legislation.

ii. *It is an inquisitorial system.* It is the judge's job to establish the facts, apply the law and, in criminal cases, bring the formal charges. Judges demand evidence and find facts. They are the ones who ask questions of the witnesses, and not the lawyers. The lawyers write the pleadings, assist the judge in investigations by providing favourable evidence and finally present arguments based on the evidence gathered by the judge. As a result, the role of the lawyer in the civil law system is limited when compared with the role of the lawyer in the common law system.

As a consequence, the outcome of a case is less dependent on the capability of the lawyers representing the litigants than it is in the common law system. So, the amount paid as legal fees by a litigant, or the affordability of lawyers, can be expected to have a lesser impact on the eventual outcome of a case than in the other system.

Here are some points elaborating on the background to this, though their basis is anecdotal, describing the features most Indians would like to see in their justice system:

i. Delivery of justice should be prioritised over sticking to precedent.
ii. A judge should take full responsibility in determining the facts of a case and applying the law, and not just be a neutral umpire between two sides of the argument.
iii. The identity of the lawyer and the fees paid to them should have lesser implications for the eventual outcome of a case.
iv. The accused, in a criminal case, should be obliged to present a case of innocence instead of just poking holes in the prosecution's case.

On account of our English or common law legacy, our courts are obliged to stick to precedent, relying principally on cases presented by lawyers. Our judges are obliged to act as neutral umpires/arbiters and not take on an inquisitorial role. This leads to a very real problem, as this system allows the accused in criminal cases to get away by demonstrating fault lines in the prosecution's case.

These seemingly unresolvable characteristics of our legal system owe to the common law principles the English left behind for us, and which we have continued to adopt and apply post-Independence to this very day. The quick comparison of common law and civil law presented here illustrates that these seemingly unresolvable characteristics of the law need not be as daunting as they are today if India were to apply the civil law system. However, it would appear that our establishment has no clue that an alternative system of law exists. The establishment has never debated this aspect.

Most of continental Europe, Japan, China and other countries outside of the Commonwealth apply the civil law system, which allows flexibility for a court to decide cases based on its sense of justice on a case-by-case basis without being bound by precedent. It also allows a judge to be inquisitorial and make inquiries that go beyond what is presented in court to determine the truth. From this one might assert that the civil law system is indeed a worthwhile alternative to consider for India.

Historical perspectives

The origins of the common law system can be traced back to the 1160s when the King's Bench was instituted in England by Henry II. It comprised a circuit of judges known as the Assizes who were duty-bound to extend the customary law of the Normans throughout the realm, making it 'common' for all. The decisions that came from this system became the norm and were followed by judges in subsequent trials, though the judges did have the liberty to expand or contract the principles expressed in these prior decisions.

In the late 1500s, lawyers' arguments were included in court proceedings, and precedents or prior rulings were considered paramount. Then in the mid-1700s, Chief Justice Lord Mansfield (1705–93) penned a set of views on the formation of new laws, which were commended as valid principles. William Blackstone (1723–80), who succeeded him as an eminent jurist, authored the four-volume *Commentaries on the Laws of England*, which became the most popular treatise on common law soon after. He wrote that common law is 'superior to legislation', that is, judges have the right to interpret legislation and that their interpretation of legislation would be final. For the last ten years of his life, Blackstone served as a justice in the Court of King's Bench and thereby influenced the court's views as well. Binding precedent took a firm hold on the legal system of England in the 19th century as common law strengthened its grip over almost all recorded disputes in courtrooms, including property disputes and cases dealing with personal injury, free speech and even abortion.[36]

Article 141 of the Indian Constitution – an example of recognition of the principles of common law in their absolute form – states that the 'law declared by the Supreme Court shall be binding on all courts within the territory of India'. This provision clearly indicates the intention of the framers of the Constitution. They envisaged a legal system under which any law declared by the Supreme Court or a hierarchically larger bench would be binding on smaller or equivalent benches. The 'law' referred to under this provision is the legal principle that emanates from a judgment or an interpretation of statutes.[37] The high courts bind smaller courts within their jurisdiction and hold persuasive value over other benches in other regions, while the Supreme Court binds all courts in India. A purposive interpretation of this provision would settle that the expression 'all the courts' means all courts except the Supreme Court. This forms the basis of the common law system in India.

The principle of *stare decisis*, that is, to stand by things decided,[38] which is firmly entrenched under the English legal system, has been embodied in Article 141 and upholds the common law principle of precedent. So, the reasoning behind a decision, the *ratio decidendi*, will lie in the binding power of the Supreme Court and not in the facts of the case under consideration. The notion of *stare decisis* rests on the firm understanding that a decision is binding once it has been made formally. Any ancillary observations or explanations flowing logically from the matter shall not hold the same binding power.[39]

Civil law dates to 450 BCE, when a system for dispute resolution in ancient Rome was first put into writing and known as the Law of the Twelve Tables. It was the earliest attempt at creating a general code consolidating the existing ways of handling public and private disputes into a set of written laws. Prior to the Law of the Twelve Tables, dispute resolution was largely customary and hinged on the royal laws, which made it ambiguous and inconsistent for uniform imposition in all circumstances.[40]

The Twelve Tables were authored by ten commissioners called *decemvirs,* after complaints that judgments by courts were delivered on the basis of unwritten customs that could be accessed only by a limited group of practitioners called *patricians*. The resulting ten tables (and an additional two) were formally posted on bronze tablets, certifying certain applicable principles such as the validity of slavery in return for unpaid debt.[41]

The civil law tradition originated in continental Europe. It seeped into the Spanish and Portuguese systems, and it saw further adoption in the 18th and 19th centuries by countries that sought to reform their legal systems, such as Russia and Japan. The aim behind the propagation of civil law may have been to aid these nations in accelerating their economic gains and political power vis-à-vis the Western European nation-states.[42]

Unlike in the case of common law, the role of judicial precedent is not binding in nature in civil law. Civil law systems are based primarily on substantive and procedural laws that judges apply in their decision-making. It means that judges have greater freedom to interpret the law as fitting to the circumstances and to decide cases after appropriate application of the law. This subjectivity permitted to them in the interpretation of statutes allows them to apply their judicial minds in hearing a dispute and in determining which law would apply to it. Under common law, this freedom is lacking, as the role of judges is limited to following precedents that display coherence with the applicable laws and circumstances of the fresh cases before them. By allowing judges inquisitorial powers, including the authority to request documents and testimony, civil law systems empower them to make better decisions.

India's struggles with judicial precedent or case law

In most cases, judges in the lower courts follow and apply judicial precedent without much reluctance. However, judges in the higher courts, that is, the high courts and the Supreme Court, are reluctant to do so when they disagree with the precedent. It is often observed that superior judges get irritated when asked to detach from their personal sense of justice and follow precedent regardless.

Judges in India are not instinctively inclined towards this common law constraint on their ambitions to deliver justice. While there certainly exists among them the intention to be bound by the contours of common law principles, their desire to guard the rights of the people and ensure fair play in the specific circumstances of a case drives them to find means of avoiding the precedent. As a result, in their enthusiasm to deliver what they believe is justice, Indian courts tend to sidestep established principles and precedent, in turn violating the most fundamental principle of common law. It is not uncommon for judges in India to disregard previous decisions or refuse to acknowledge their relevance if they believe those decisions do not align with their personal views and understanding of the law, or their legal beliefs regarding the matter at hand.

But what is wrong if this situation continues and leads to better judgments, especially if one is advocating the civil law system for India? The problem is that while this works in a limited sense and in specific disputes, it does a disservice to the overall justice delivery system in the country. Judicial behaviour that is mandated to follow a precedent-based system but diverges from it distorts the much-valued aspect of predictability in the law. Predictability means that parties to disputes can anticipate judicial outcomes without having to go through the dispute resolution process in court in the form of a trial. Predictability in law helps avoid needless litigation and the overburdening of courts.

While Indian courts mostly rely on precedent, there is an increasing number of cases in the higher courts resisting precedent, putting the legal system in danger of unpredictability. However, if the Indian inclination is leaning in favour of delivering justice specific to the circumstances of a case rather than following precedent, the better approach might be to align the legal framework with this inclination and adopt the civil law system.

Then judges can apply the law to the facts of a case in the manner that they believe will deliver justice. This will align the legal system with their legal instincts and make the law more predictable than it might be at present. It has been said that the hallmark of an efficient system is its predictability. In a lecture delivered in 2011, Lord Jonathan Hugh Mance, former deputy president of the UK Supreme Court, provided a pertinent example of the hesitation in common law to accept legislative supremacy. Using an example of Mauritian legislation and its history before the court,[43] he said that 'the infinite circumstances affecting human existence fit uneasily within straitjackets' and that 'governmental suspicion of judicial discretion' can lead to potential injustice. Mance discussed the legislation passed in Mauritius withdrawing bail in all serious drug cases. The result, he said, was long periods of detainment due to delays in criminal trials. The courts in Mauritius struck down the legislation for being inconsistent with their constitution.[44] While some would see this as an instance of courts coming to the rescue of citizens, someone affected by drug-related crimes would paint the courts as the villain for stopping a popular government's efforts to put an end to the constant release on bail of drug offenders during trial.

Lord Alexander John Reid, a prominent British judge who was popularly referred to as the 'Law Lord', had remarked in *The Judge as Law Maker*[45] that 'There was a time when it was thought indecent to suggest that judges make law – they only declare it ... but we do not believe in fairy tales any more.' Therefore, all common law systems do allow judges to make and remake law endlessly, and reinterpret law, thereby limiting legislative innovation.

It also suggests that judges may pause legal disputes while they reflect on decisions, but their judgments can change over time, potentially leading to inconsistencies. In doing so, they either have to sidestep a precedent by distinguishing it on the basis of different facts or by overruling past precedent.

The increasing inclination of courts in India to indulge in rule-making themselves would amount to 'legislating' the law rather than interpreting it.[46] In *Vishaka v. State of Rajasthan*,[47] the Supreme Court prescribed some laws pertaining to sexual discrimination at the workplace in the absence of a codified law on the subject. In another case, *Suraz India Trust v. Union of India*,[48] the Supreme Court was tasked with reconsidering two of its judgments. As a result, the apex court effectively went on to amend constitutional provisions – a power originally vested with the Indian Parliament under the Constitution.

This judgment gave the judiciary the ability to appoint and transfer judges, arming the courts with a power that was not expressly vested in it under the law at that time. Judges are crossing the line of separation of powers between the judiciary and legislature more regularly, almost as though in protest against the principles of common law. This behaviour is contrary to the constitutional principle of separation of powers.

Former chief justice of India S.H. Kapadia observed that in 'many PILs, the courts freely decree rules of conduct for government and public authorities which are akin to legislation. Such exercises have little judicial function in them. In such matters, I am of the opinion that the courts should be circumspect in understanding the thin line between law and governance'.[49]

The judge's personal sense of justice usually outweighs the principles of common law in the courtroom, leaving the legal system in a convoluted grey area that does not entirely conform to the common law ideology but does not entirely digress from it either. Some aspects of the civil law system can be identified in this trend, but there are many features in this trend that violate that system too. Given this situation, it would be better to transition to a civil law system so that judges are not bound by earlier court decisions and can deliver justice in accordance with a few broad, codified rules and legal principles. This would also be very close to the dharmic system of justice, where the broad principles are enshrined and codified in the scriptures, and specific justice is delivered in accordance with the factual circumstances of a case.

However, this is not dharmic jingoism at play. The civil law system is working well in every country that has adopted it, that is, the European countries, Japan, China, and others. It would work in India too, since not only does the majority of our population, but also our judges, value the delivery of justice in every individual case based on codified legal principles and rules, while being unbound by past decisions.

The compounding of problems by adversarial courts

Adversarial courts in the common law system are involved with the determination of facts during the adjudication process. In this process, two parties compete, each to prove its account and to argue a case against the other, and the judge takes on the role of a referee to ensure that the principles of fairness and legal rules are adhered to. The aim is to ascertain the truth by means of the open competition between the disputing parties.

The parties must also determine the witnesses crucial to the dispute, along with the nature of the evidence that is to be collected and presented in court. The court simply oversees the process of collecting this evidence and the arguments revolving around it. As a result, a lot depends on the quality of lawyering deployed by a litigant. The better lawyer often means a greater likelihood of a win, which does not necessarily mean a greater likelihood of justice. As a result, those with deeper pockets have an advantage in this system.

In criminal proceedings, the prosecution is duty-bound to prove its case beyond a reasonable doubt. There are very limited offences, such as those involving dowry death, gang rape and money laundering acts, where the accused have to prove their innocence if bail is sought. Presentation of evidence and arguments is vital when it comes to proving a case against the counterparty, and the judge acts in the role of an umpire. The lawyers in the common law system are tasked with submitting filings and making presentations before the judge to persuade the court on points of law and fact. This leads to low-quality investigations and a high rate of acquittals compared to convictions.

Even in civil cases, the burden on the plaintiff is relatively heavy, especially in cases against the State, where the presumption is that it can do no wrong. This inequality is compounded by the fact that a lot of information is available only to the State, which feels no obligation to disclose it to the general public. So it assumes no duty towards the prosecution to deliver important documentation.[50]

This approach, however, does not necessarily work for the Indian masses. Most citizens would like to seek a full and final determination of facts and the law from courts, not just a decision based on which side presented its case better.

The alternative is the inquisitorial system, part of the civil law approach. Here the judges are not bystanders who oversee and adjudge cases passively but are active participants in the case, conducting thorough investigations, collecting all possible evidence and playing an active role in determining which witnesses are to be summoned and heard.[51]

In criminal cases, the aim is generally to conduct official inquiries and pre-trial interrogations and investigations to completely avoid bringing an innocent person into the courtroom.[52] This is done to ascertain the truth so that the courts can be entirely avoided with regard to these persons.

Inquisitorial courts that emerge from the civil law system make little use of judicial precedent. This gives judges the leeway to decide cases independently and on the basis of their own understanding of the law. Unlike in the adversarial system, the judges in the inquisitorial system also provide references for all material utilised in a trial, which gives them an active role in the hearing. These ideas stem from the principles of judicial autonomy.[53]

Under the adversarial system, judges pronounce judgments based on the findings and evidence presented by litigants and from the examination and cross-examination of the parties to a trial. However, under the inquisitorial system, judges actively question and hear the parties directly rather than basing their decisions solely on the arguments presented by lawyers. The emphasis is on applying the law, as the burden of proof is shared between both parties to convince the judge of the facts of the case. Thus, lawyers in the adversarial system have a much more active role than in the inquisitorial system, as their work has the biggest influence on the decision of the court. Lawyers in the inquisitorial system are merely advisers.

It is clear that under the adversarial court system, the performance and skill of a lawyer are of utmost importance. If a lawyer makes weak arguments in court, their client is more likely to lose under the pressure of the counterparty and be proven guilty. This is an unfair system, where access to justice for a party is primarily reliant on the lawyers representing it. To the Indian mind, judicial treatment of litigants should not be based solely on the affordability of lawyers, because that approach strays from the very objective of achieving justice for all, as envisaged in the Indian Constitution.

Justice is intended for all, and the justice system must deliver it equally to all. If the justice system must deliver justice equally to all, it is only prudent for India to move to an inquisitorial system in which the judge is the investigator, relying on the interpretation of applicable law and not on precedents. India needs a more structured system where justice is predictable and certain. The Indian mind expects a judge to determine the facts of a case and deliver justice no matter how a case is pleaded or presented by a lawyer. This thought has greater alignment with civil law principles than with the common law approach. So why should India not align its legal system in a way that is not only consistent with the general mindset of its people but also enjoys widespread acceptance across the world?

What if India switches from common law to civil law?

A switch to the civil law system would require the realignment of various administrative structures of governance so that the change delivers the desired results to the people. This includes the manner in which the police investigate a case and the way the prosecution functions.

The immediate consequences of the switch would be the following:

i. Judges would be bound only by the language of statutes and not by prior interpretations of them. It would become easier for citizens and their advisers to evaluate the facts of a specific case in the context of the statute that applies to it and anticipate the direction the judgment would take. Naturally, it would also be easier to predict the outcome of a case as people would no longer have to wonder about which prior judgment might appeal to a judge and which one the judge may want to avoid.
ii. Since courts would no longer be able to sit back and act as umpires, judges would become responsible for determining all the relevant facts of a case and applying the law to it. Justice would become less dependent on the skill of lawyers.

Only judges and not lawyers would be responsible for any miscarriage of justice. So, one can be hopeful that litigants complaining that their lawyer was not up to the mark or did a poor job of presenting their case will be more or less a thing of the past.

To implement such a change in the legal system, there would need to be amendments to the Indian Constitution, a complete overhaul of procedural laws and specific changes in various substantive laws. Thereafter, it would take a few years for judges and lawyers to change their mindset, move away from common law and function according to the system of civil law. Thus, among the legal reforms suggested in this book, this would be the most extensive legislative exercise.

Presumption of knowledge of the law

Presumption of knowledge of the law is a legal principle associated with the concept of burden of proof. Briefly, this presumption means that every citizen is considered to be fully aware of the law, and the lack of knowledge of the law is no defence for a citizen in the legal context.

It stems from the idea that laws, once codified and made public, are accessible to all citizens. To explain this, we can again use the example of the street food vendor. He is typically a poor individual trying to make an honest living through small-time entrepreneurship. However, he is often unaware of the licences and permits needed to set up such a business. If he goes ahead and begins operations anyway, the authorities subject him to penalties because the presumption is that he is aware of the legal requirements and has acted in wilful violation of them. So the cops, the municipal and other authorities extort money from him or subject him to penalties and confiscate his belongings, all for trying to set up an honest, small-time business. This is an outcome of the imperial law that independent India seems to love.

Another example is that of a farmer in rural India who finds a buried treasure on his land. He digs it up and tries to sell it. He is immediately arrested since the law deems that buried treasure belongs to the State and the farmer must be aware of the law. Both these examples demonstrate an imperial law being put into action. It does not take into account whether the farmer might be unaware of his violation of the law. Should such imperial laws continue to be applied in independent India?

My suggestion is that we rid ourselves of this imperial concept of presumption of knowledge of the law. This knowledge and its wilful violation must be established against an individual before they can be prosecuted for breaking the law. The corollary is that the government must be burdened with informing its citizens of the law. It cannot be allowed to shirk its responsibilities and prosecute its citizens for its own failure to disseminate vital information.

An associated concept is the burden of proof. Within the historically shifting legal landscape of the Indian subcontinent, this concept has crystallised over time. This principle requires that in a legal dispute the litigants are to present concrete evidence to support their claims. This 'burden' consists of two pivotal facets:

i. Making fact based assertions: A party's claim, accusation or defence needs to be substantiated. Simply making a claim will not be enough; one is required to provide concrete evidence to bolster their claim as well.
ii. Presumption of knowledge of the law: Ignorance of the law is no longer a viable defence. While one may be excused for not knowing a specific fact, not knowing the law is not a valid excuse for its violation. Every individual, by default is expected to be aware of the prevailing laws once they are codified and made public.

Principles such as presumption of knowledge of the law legitimised colonial rule and helped maintain power imbalances benefiting the colonisers. These principles helped the colonisers in the following ways:

They were instrumental in establishing the authority of the rulers: By introducing an alien legal system and then assuming that everyone, including the colonised, was aware of it, colonisers effectively asserted their legal and moral authority over their colonised territories. The colonised were expected to follow the coloniser's culture and systems.

They created a facade of fairness: On paper, the presumption that everyone knows the law conveys an image of an egalitarian system. But in reality, the swift introduction of foreign legal systems left the native populations in colonised lands such as India unaware of and often defenceless against laws they genuinely did not understand. They were forced into a system that strayed completely from the customary practices that they considered their law. The imposition of a new system bound them within new walls, giving them no time to acclimatise.

They undermined indigenous legal systems: Colonisers not only imposed their own rules, but by presuming that all the people knew and understood the law, they subverted indigenous legal systems that local communities had followed for generations. Colonisers in India commented on the country's lack of legal principles and the limited observance of the rule of law – using these misleading remarks as an excuse to force upon us their foreign ideas and imperialist self-interests. Their intention was to misrepresent India's culture and laws, both within the country and abroad. Former Supreme Court judge, Justice (Retd.) Abdul Nazeer pointed out in a lecture delivered in 2021 that the coloniser's incorrect views of the ancient Indian legal system may have been made out of 'ignorance, imperialist self-interest, or a contempt for Indian culture and civilization'.[54]

Presumption of knowledge of the law among the common people helped maintain power imbalances benefiting the coloniser: The native populations, unfamiliar with the complexities of the foreign legal structure, often found themselves legally disadvantaged, and this solidified the power dynamics in favour of the colonisers.

They created economic dependencies: By instituting laws that favoured colonial enterprises, local economies were manipulated into becoming heavily dependent on the colonisers. In particular, the laws on land and resource ownership were tweaked to ensure that valuable resources like minerals, crops and labour were easily accessible to the colonisers and at their ready disposal. This led to the erosion of indigenous practices.

Even to this day, India has been unable to find an escape from the colonial psyche that has replaced its own legal philosophies. Justice Nazeer also said in a speech that great lawyers and judges are not born but are made through proper education and strong legal traditions. He mentioned Manu, Kautilya, Katyayana, Brihaspati, Narada and Yagyavalkya as the legal giants of ancient India. 'The continued neglect of their great knowledge and adherence to the colonial legal system is detrimental to the goals of our Constitution and against our national interest,' concluded the retired judge.[55]

India needs to release itself from these colonial traps because a nation's traditional legal practices often reflect the cultural values of its society, but the imposition of foreign legal systems by the colonisers effectively erodes its indigenous practices, leading to the slow disintegration of its cultural values as well. In colonised India, this overt preference for colonial legal systems over indigenous systems sent a clear message that the latter were inferior. This not only led to a loss of cultural heritage for the country but also instilled in its people a sense of cultural inferiority.

Many post-colonial societies still grapple with the remnants of these colonial legal systems. They are often conflicted between their traditional legal values and those imposed during colonial times, leading to legal ambiguities and social tensions. The laws set in place by the colonisers continue to shape property rights, trade relations and economic policies in colonised countries, sometimes disadvantaging local enterprises. The erosion of cultural identity due to the dominance of colonial legal systems has left a lasting impact on indigenous societies. This is why the quest to rediscover and reclaim indigenous identities often becomes central in post-colonial narratives.

I suggest the following solutions to do away with this toxic law in India:

i. Amending the law to revise the legal presumption that every person in India has knowledge of the law. Such a presumption should apply on an irrevocable basis only in the case of laws that have widespread acceptance in society and are identified as such in a statutory list. As for laws not on this list, including court rulings, there could be two other categories:
    a. where such a presumption is useful but refutable with evidence of lack of knowledge of the law on the part of the accused; and
    b. consisting of the residual unlisted laws where no such presumption can be attributed, in which case the prosecution or plaintiff, as the case may be, will have

to establish that the violator had actual knowledge of the law.

ii. For every law where the government would like the presumption to exist, there must be a legal obligation on the government to provide widespread publicity and training in the law to the population. Failure to provide this will result in the presumption being negated.

Essentially, the prosecution must be obliged to establish that the government had made sufficient efforts to ensure that most citizens could not claim ignorance of the law. This will give the people ownership of their laws, and the laws will appear less like impositions by the country's elite.

Revisiting the Blackstone Principle

The Blackstone Principle, named after the English jurist William Blackstone, emphasises the importance of minimising false convictions in the criminal justice system, even if it means potentially allowing guilty individuals to go free. Blackstone's famous quote – 'It is better that ten guilty persons escape than that one innocent suffer' – became a cornerstone of legal thinking in Anglo-Saxon jurisdictions.[56] While initially well-intentioned, the principle's impracticality has given rise to several problems.

Also stemming from Blackstone's Principle is the concept of 'beyond a reasonable doubt' in criminal law, which puts a high burden of proof on the prosecution.[57] While it was created to ensure that no accused would be wrongly convicted, in practice this principle has led to a wave of criminals evading punishment, causing turmoil in society. Manipulating the prosecution to take advantage of weak cases has become a common tactic for criminals to escape conviction. Overburdened courts and a predilection for granting bail have made it easier for criminals to roam free, as the standard of proof beyond all doubt is very difficult to achieve.[58]

This phenomenon of extrajudicial killings is often linked to the application of the Blackstone Principle. While initially well-intentioned, the principle's impracticality has become a tool for the police and politicians alike in countries like India for personal gain and extortion. Sometimes covertly sanctioned by the government, extrajudicial killings are murders carried out for financial incentives or personal vendettas.[59]

During the insurgency in Punjab, the state police was backed by the government in neutralising terrorists, leading to numerous extrajudicial killings. While some people in society supported these actions, viewing them as necessary for dealing with terrorists swiftly, innocent lives were also lost. Some of the policemen involved in the extrajudicial killings faced trial and conviction for their crimes.

The Blackstone Principle has also given rise to contrasting judgments and outcomes. In the US, the trial of the former athlete and actor O.J. Simpson highlighted the paradoxical nature of the principle. Simpson was acquitted of the double murder of his ex-wife and her friend in a criminal trial but was later found liable for their wrongful deaths in a civil trial.[60] Due to the higher burden of proof in the criminal trial, the acquittal differed sharply from the outcome in the civil trial, which used a lower standard. The variance in proof standards allowed for different verdicts based on the same facts. Such situations underscore the absurdities that can arise from the application of this principle.

In India, the continuation of the Blackstone Principle has meant that litigants in civil cases can hide facts and misrepresent the truth without facing consequences. To ensure honesty and fairness in court proceedings, there should be zero tolerance for untruths or acts of perjury, and violators should face immediate and effective penalties for making false or misleading statements. In the US, lawyers can be debarred for these misdeeds. But in a country grappling with the complexities of its legal system, the focus appears to be heavily tilted towards the rights of the accused whenever there is a heated debate on how to ensure a balance between the rights of criminals and the rights of victims. This often leaves the rights of the victims in the shadows.

This skewed perspective is often attributed to the elitist view that advocates enjoyment of all human rights for the accused until proven guilty, even in the case of heinous crimes like murder. However, the majority of common people on the streets hold a different view. They seek retribution when they are victims of grave offences and feel that the perspective of the country's elite, who represent a minority, should not override the will of the majority in a democracy.

Therefore, a shift towards an inquisitorial court system will address the shortcomings of the Blackstone Principle, since it will empower judges to actively seek the truth and go beyond the arguments presented by the opposing lawyers. Under this system, judges who possess superior legal knowledge will have to take into account all relevant information, even if the lawyers and litigants are unaware of certain laws or fail to disclose crucial facts. The need for the onus to be equal for both parties to prove themselves right will arise when there is an active judge, as provided for under the civil law system, who will ensure that the innocent are protected.

Some might argue that democratic principles should not always prevail over what is morally right, but in taking the morally right route, the challenge lies in determining who gets to decide what is right or wrong. Granting this decision solely to the elite would be unfair. Once a society embraces universal adult franchise, it should not differentiate between the approach to punishment harboured by one section of society and another's on the basis of their class or status.

The shift that I propose here will not just align the law with the mindset of the majority of the Indian people but will also result in greater confidence among them that justice will be consistently delivered.

Victims' rights versus wrongdoers' rights

The system should ensure that victims of crime and their families find a sense of justice while respecting the rights of the accused. The legal system should deliver a sense of retributive satisfaction to the victims of crime and create a deterrent for potential criminals. A lenient attitude may inadvertently encourage non-criminals to take the path of criminality. The balance between ensuring justice for the victims and protecting the accused is a delicate one. Former Supreme Court judge Justice Krishna Iyer once said, 'The criminal law in India is not victim-oriented and the suffering of the victim, often immeasurable, is entirely overlooked in misplaced sympathy for the criminal.'[61]

The Indian legal system follows a disturbing trend – one in which the general concern (among the elite and opinion makers) is not directed towards the victim but flows to the support of the accused in the majority of cases. Ashok Kumar, a former police officer with a career spanning three decades, has noticed that the victim is 'not the major concern of any of the wings of the criminal justice system'. On the contrary, the accused get all the privileges. 'It is well evident that criminal law in India is not at all victim-oriented,' says the ex-cop. 'The victims are usually overlooked in misplaced sympathy for the criminal.'[62]

The accused is treated like a privileged entity as the law demands that the burden of proof should be on the aggrieved to prove the accused guilty and not on the accused to prove his innocence. Even if the accused are found guilty, in India powerful criminals often enjoy a comfortable life in jail. Some are even caught running large-scale extortion rackets during their time of incarceration.[63] A stronger victim protection plan will deter criminals from committing offences under the presumption that they will not be held liable for them or that the courts and the system will favour them. Currently, victims of heinous crimes are apprehensive of cooperating with the court or testifying before it because it is often the case that the police refuse to file a first information report or that investigations are not conducted appropriately. There is then little chance of the accused being prosecuted. Men, women and others who report sexual violence are even more vulnerable and often face extreme pressure or threats from the accused, but the system does little to deter such behaviour.[64]

It is not that our courts are ignorant; they have identified the need to protect the rights of victims. However, protection has not been provided to them during the trial process. Justice Krishna Iyer noted in *Rattan Singh v. State of Punjab*,[65] 'In truth, victim restitution is still the vanishing point of our criminal law. This is the system's shortcoming, which lawmakers must address.' It was also held in *Nirmal Singh Kahlon v. State of Punjab*[66] that the right to a fair trial and investigation extends to both the victim and the accused under Article 21 of the Indian Constitution.

In the US, the Crime Victims' Rights Act[67] grants certain safeguards and rights to victims of crime. These rights include protection from the accused, timely notice of court proceedings, the right to attend public court proceedings, the ability to be heard during various legal processes, the right to confer with the government's attorney, entitlement to full and timely restitution, proceedings free from unreasonable delays and the right to be treated with fairness and respect for their privacy and dignity.[68] Similarly, the Code of Practice for Victims of Crime in England and Wales (Victims' Code) is a statutory government document providing victims with the information, services and support that they are entitled to receive from the criminal justice agencies, including the police and the Crown Prosecution Service.

The UK Victims' Code provides the following:

i. Information and support: Victims have the right to be informed about the progress of their case and the key stages in the criminal justice process. They are entitled to receive information about the support services available to them.
ii. Special measures: Victims may be eligible for special measures to assist them in giving evidence, such as screens or video links, to make the process less intimidating.
iii. Victim personal statement: Victims have the right to make a 'victim personal statement' to express the impact of the crime on them, which is considered during sentencing.

iv. Attendance at court: Victims have the right to attend court and to be kept informed about the trial process.
v. Compensation: Victims are informed about the facility through which they can seek compensation for their injuries or losses through the Criminal Injuries Compensation Scheme.
vi. Restitution: Where possible, the court can order the offender to pay restitution to the victim for losses or damages incurred.
vii. Review of decision not to prosecute: Victims have the right to request a review of a decision not to prosecute.
viii. Victim liaison officers: Victims may have access to a victim liaison officer who can provide support and keep them informed about their case.
ix. Youth justice: Special considerations are made for young victims, including the provision of age-appropriate information and support.
x. Equality and diversity: The Code emphasises that services must be delivered without discrimination, taking into account the diverse needs of victims.[69]

The Victims' Code aims to ensure that victims are treated with respect, dignity and sensitivity throughout their interaction with the UK criminal justice system. It is designed to empower victims by providing them with information about their rights and the support services available to them.

There is a pressing need for a victim-oriented justice delivery system in India. The most essential function of society must be to deliver justice to every aggrieved individual in a codified manner, as it is in some overseas jurisdictions. Even though Article 21 of the Indian Constitution provides for the protection of victims of crime, the administrators of justice such as the police and the courts are not treating it as important at all. That curbs the people's access to justice and narrows the scope of laws in the country, which now appear to protect only accused individuals.

Theories of punishment

Christianity preaches that since God created man, only he has the power to take his life. This belief is based on the notion that a person has only one life and that no other person should have the right to interfere with it or cut it short. Theological and ethical principles from Christian teachings have influenced the development of most of the world's legal and penal systems. For example, the concept of retribution, the idea that punishment should be proportionate to the offence committed, can be traced back to Judeo-Christian principles found in the Old Testament. The phrase 'an eye for an eye, a tooth for a tooth' reflects this idea of proportionate punishment.

Similarly, Christianity has contributed to the development of deterrence theory by emphasising the consequences of sinful actions. Fear of divine punishment, as well as the idea of earthly consequences for wrongdoing, has influenced the notion that punishment should act as a deterrent to potential offenders. Further, even the concept of rehabilitation of offenders has been influenced by the Christian principles of forgiveness and redemption, and its teachings on the possibility of personal transformation. The concepts of humanitarianism in the treatment of offenders as well as those of mercy or clemency have been similarly drawn from Christian ethics.

With its emphasis on compassion, mercy and the inherent value of every individual, Christianity has led to more humane and compassionate approaches to punishment. This includes advocating for the fair and just treatment of prisoners and a focus on rehabilitation rather than solely punitive measures. Colonial India adopted these theories of punishment, including the reformative theory of punishment, which advocates the moral transformation of criminals so they can become better citizens of the country. This theory relies on the notion that a criminal does not cease to be human simply because they have committed a crime.

Good actions are considered 'prescribed' and unacceptable actions 'proscribed'. A proscribed act could also be known as a 'wrong', and public reason directs the caging of such misdemeanours. Sovereign law construes an action that attracts this social disapprobation as an 'offence', which must legally be subjected to 'just and fair' judicial investigation and duly evidenced and established as a 'crime'. A crime, which is a proven offence, impels caustic consequences in the form of 'punishments'. The dilemma with imposing punishment lies in whether it should be intended to inflict pain, to constitute castigation or penalty, or to prevent the punished persons or others from committing the crimes in question, enabling them to realise their mistakes and reform their behaviour to undo the injustice they have caused. While the punishment of a criminal is the protection a society needs from mischievous and undesirable actions, and for the conversion of tainted convicts into law-abiding citizens, the tools adopted to impose this punishment often come under question. There are four major theories of punishment: the deterrent theory, the preventive theory, the reformative theory and the retributive theory.

The Indian judicial system generally decrees life imprisonment at 14 years, after which remission is given to a large number of prisoners upon their application. Section 433-A of the Code of Criminal Procedure, 1973, provides that in cases where life imprisonment has been awarded, a perpetrator cannot be released before serving a minimum of 14 years. Indian courts seldom rule beyond that threshold. The National Crime Records Bureau reported an average of 82 murders every day as of 2021, and these are only the reported cases.[70] Thus, it can be said that 14 years of imprisonment does serve as a deterrent as the lawmakers might have intended it to be.

The US sentences proven criminals to 200 years in federal prison for heinous crimes as applicable under their law.[71] This is what would constitute a true life sentence. A criminal who has once been sentenced to life imprisonment will probably never see the outside world again. But in India, criminals are being released after 14 years in prison and the possibility of their becoming repeat offenders reduces the deterrent effect of life imprisonment and fails to prevent the commission of gross crimes in the country.

The main aim of the preventive theory is to remove the criminal from society so that they can be transformed morally and be prevented from committing further crimes.[72] To achieve this, fear of punishment is induced through the sentence of life imprisonment or death. This also disincentivises potential criminals in society and instils a sense of fear among them, reducing the overall rate of crime. Ideally, this should work as a preventive measure in the matter of frequently committed misdeeds, as isolation from society and moral training should deter the convicted from repeating their actions.

Detention and confinement are considered effective ways to remove criminals from society. Housed thus for the period of moral training and transformation, they can be reintegrated into society once the punishment has been served. The goal of the punishment is not to avenge the crime but to prevent it in the long term. However, for this goal to be achieved, the offender must be imprisoned for as long as it takes for them to be transformed. But this approach cannot work if procedures such as investigations are delayed and the accused is not detained proactively. In India, the usual life-prison term of 14 years is not sufficient to induce this sense of isolation and deterrence in the minds of criminals and potential offenders. We still witness intense brutality and heinous criminality daily. It is a well-acknowledged fact that the complete eradication of crime is almost impossible to achieve, but we can envisage a society that is better regulated and monitored by adopting appropriate methods for the prevention of crime.

The retributive theory of punishment is the one that most Indian minds align with. It is rooted in the firm belief that criminals must be punished for their wrongdoings. It does not concern itself deeply with the moral transformation of the criminal as much as it does with the nature of the punishment being proportionate to the offence. It justifies punishment as moral justness for an evil voluntarily done[73] and advocates for legal sanctions grounded in vengeance and retaliation for acts of an immoral and heinous nature.

The theory is based on three primary notions: first, that offenders or individuals who commit crimes are morally liable to suffer punishment proportionate to their crime; second, that it is morally justifiable for a legitimate entity delivering punishment to pronounce a deserving punishment; and third, that it would be deemed immoral to intentionally punish innocents or to inflict a disproportionate punishment on them (for example, if their case could not be proved). Retributive theory is the path where criminal law and morality converge for India.

Reformative theory is based on the notion that a wrongdoer does not cease to be a person even after they have committed a crime. It advocates the need for moral training and character building of the wrongdoer rather than penal actions against them, attempting to transform the perpetrator during their period of confinement. Therefore, detainment is viewed not as a torturous punishment but as a journey of self-awareness and moral conversion. Gauging and addressing the mental state of the convict and their family is paramount to the process. Deterrence through punishment is discouraged.[74]

Imperatively, retribution appears to be the violent, incompatible solution as compared to the reformative approach. It may also be believed that a society that moves towards civilisation loses the need for retributivism in its desire for revenge as this feeds into the animal instincts of a nation. This seems a prudent perspective when an onlooker assesses a society. But when one is subject to a heinous crime or wrongdoing of a gross nature, it is hardly the case that one would seek the moral transformation of the convict. While the idea of a reformative society is highly appealing, the majority still seeks retribution. They seek heavy punishment of the guilty as vengeance for the wrong they have suffered at their hands.

In Hinduism, the belief is that man has multiple lives and that the karma from one's previous life affects the next. Unlike Christianity, Hinduism does not rest on the concept of one life gifted by the Almighty. A criminal, like any other member of society, also has multiple lives, and in this current life they must be punished for their misdeeds. The notion is that punishment in this life does not mean the end of everything for them. India as a democracy must cater to the majority, which seeks the retaliation that the retribution theory of punishment provides. The public desire for a system with harsh punishment for gross crimes outweighs the elitist tilt towards reformation, as the Indian psyche has no qualms about having hardened criminals sentenced to death.

Law of contempt

After Independence, the new nation of India soon recognised that the legal system inherited from the British Empire needed a fresh perspective. The laws, which had been designed for and by the British so that they could govern Indians, were no longer relevant to the sentiments of the nation.

One of the laws that drew significant scrutiny was the Contempt of Courts Act, particularly when it came to criminal contempt. It was clear that while civil contempt played a vital role in enforcing court decisions, the powers bestowed upon judges in matters of criminal contempt were far-reaching and needed re-evaluation. To explain these concepts, civil contempt means wilful disobedience of any judgment, decree, direction, order, writ or other processes of a court or wilful breach of an undertaking given to a court.[75] On the other hand, criminal contempt essentially means the publication of any matter or the doing of any other act whatsoever which scandalises or lowers the authority or dignity of the court, prejudices or interferes with any judicial proceeding, or interferes with or obstructs the administration of justice in any other manner.[76]

Criminal contempt is often associated with challenging the authority of the court, but it extends beyond mere disobedience of court orders. It encompasses acts that are perceived as lowering the dignity of the court, such as general criticism, allegations of corruption against the court or attribution of motives to a judge.

The interpretation of what constitutes scandalising the court or lowering its authority has become a subject of debate. What might have scandalised or lowered the court's dignity in the past may not hold in the present. Accusing a judge of bias or corruption, for example, could be seen as undermining the authority of the court in terms of the general belief in its impartiality. The contempt law is based on the idea that judges, unlike members of the general public, cannot defend themselves against serious allegations that could not only tarnish their reputation but also interfere with the independence of the judiciary. To safeguard the authority of the judiciary, the law treats any statement that challenges the court's dignity as an act of contempt. The language of the law itself left room for ambiguity and broad interpretation, raising concerns about the potential misuse of power by the courts.

It is important to distinguish between criticism directed at individual judges and criticism directed at the authority of the court as an institution. Remarks made about a judge should be dealt with in accordance with defamation laws rather than by invoking contempt charges. Unfortunately, this distinction is often blurred, stifling freedom of expression. The absence of a truth defence in contempt cases further fuels the debate, raising concerns about fairness in dealing with genuine criticism and about adhering to the principles of natural justice.

As India moved forward, it became increasingly evident that the authority of the court did not lie solely in the judges themselves but also in the principles of justice and fairness that they upheld. It was crucial to foster an environment where legitimate criticism and public scrutiny of courts are encouraged, as they play a vital role in holding the judiciary accountable. While attempts to influence the judiciary needed to be addressed, the term 'interference in the administration of justice' applied to criticism of judges was too broad.

India needs to embark on a journey to reassess and revise its contempt-of-court laws. The goal should be to strike a delicate balance between preserving the authority of the judiciary and safeguarding the fundamental right of citizens to express their opinions freely. Clarity and specificity are key, ensuring that the contours of contempt are well-defined and immune to misuse. Transparency, accountability and adherence to the principles of justice are vital to this transformation.

India must embrace the opportunity to create a legal system that truly reflects the aspirations and values of its people. The re-evaluation and reform of laws, such as the one on contempt of court, will mark a pivotal moment in the nation's legal history. Steps towards fortifying the foundations of a robust and democratic judicial system – one that upholds the principles of justice, fairness and freedom, reflecting the nation's own journey, which must be progressive, inclusive and true to the spirit of its people – are essential.

Critics argued that this law, which is designed to protect judges from baseless accusations, often stifled legitimate criticism and hindered freedom of expression. The absence of the truth defence in contempt cases further fuels the debate, raising concerns about fairness in dealing with genuine criticism and about adhering to the principles of natural justice. The absence of a truth defence in contempt proceedings implies that even with demonstrable hard evidence of judicial corruption, an accusation against a judge as such constitutes contempt. Consequently, the veracity of corruption and the substantiating evidence are deemed irrelevant, potentially resulting in punitive action against the accuser.

British judges, by contrast, display a different approach. They seldom react adversely to criticism in the media and rarely invoke the contempt law. This divergence in approach between the Indian and British judiciary must ignite a debate on the appropriateness of arming the Indian judiciary with such a draconian law, where truth holds no weight and judges seemingly assume the role of prosecutor, judge, jury and executioner.

The times are changing, public patience with those in ivory towers is thinning, and the judges ought to change. The general public generally feels that judges should venture out and express their views and opinions on various matters. This evolving sentiment perhaps led to what was a historic event – the unprecedented press conference held by four senior judges of the Supreme Court of India in January 2018. Their actions defied the unwritten code that judges do not address the media and caused shockwaves throughout the legal fraternity. The press conference highlighted the internal challenges plaguing the country's highest court, exposing the rifts there and generating intense debate within the judicial system.[77]

Former chief justice of India K.G. Balakrishnan expressed his dismay at the event, calling it 'painful and unfortunate'. He feared that it could erode public faith in the judiciary. Former Delhi High Court judge, Justice R.S. Sodhi, even went so far as to call for the impeachment of the four judges, asserting that they should no longer sit on the bench and deliver verdicts. However, this did not happen. In fact, one of the judges who had addressed the press conference went on to become the next chief justice of India. His name is Ranjan Gogoi, and he later found himself entangled in allegations of sexual harassment.

The way these accusations by a member of staff of the Supreme Court were handled raised eyebrows and ignited a fierce debate about the limitations of the contempt-of-court law. The Supreme Court took suo-motu cognisance and a three-judge bench headed by a now former chief justice of India was constituted. After initially absolving Gogoi and penalising the accuser, the court subsequently reversed the penalties imposed on the accuser.

Critics argued that judges, like any ordinary persons, should be subject to the principles of natural justice and the defence of truth. They questioned the need for a law that seemed to muzzle the truth, disallowing a valid defence against contempt charges. They also highlighted the discrepancies and contradictions in the judiciary's response to the allegations against Gogoi, emphasising the importance of a fair and unbiased investigation into the matter.

After this incident, lawyer Prashant Bhushan faced charges of contempt for some remarks he had made criticising the Supreme Court and the Chief Justice of India. However, the judge overseeing the case ultimately handed down a symbolic one-rupee fine, prompting questions about the efficacy and purpose of such legal proceedings. The very notion of a judge sitting in judgment over allegations made against him seemed paradoxical, casting doubts on the fairness and impartiality of the system.

In the same case, the Supreme Court observed that there were two requirements for satisfying a defence of truth under contempt proceedings – that the defence is in the public interest, and that the defence is bona fide. However, this has also been contested, because truth might be considered an aggravation of contempt. If a statement is derogatory to the court and its reputation, any statement of the truth could further scandalise and bring the administration of justice into disrepute.[78] Hence, the law continues to protect those on the Bench from public debate, regardless of the truth.

Today, given the climate of discontent and growing disillusionment with the judiciary, people's faith in it has begun to waver. Society yearns for a more transparent, accountable and inclusive judicial system that embraces the principles of natural justice and the principle of truth as a valid defence when giving the citizen the right to criticise or question the motivations of a court or a judge. The call for reform echoes through the halls of justice, as the need to bridge the gap between theory and reality has become increasingly apparent.

It is time that the judiciary began to treat itself as a service provider and not as a wielder of sovereign authority. It must open itself to criticism, and truth must be considered a valid defence. It goes without saying that the law, however, must protect the judiciary from falsehood and malicious criticism.

5

Constitutional Reforms

CONSTITUTIONAL REFORMS GENERALLY SPRING from political ideas. In India, the debate on such reforms is usually between those who seek a Western-style democracy and those who wish for a greater degree of 'Indianisation' of the country and its systems of law and governance. In this chapter, let us look at the kind of changes that could be made to our Constitution to improve the rule of law in the country and strengthen the people's faith in the Indian justice system, which is increasingly seen as one that favours the powerful and wealthy, inefficient and untrustworthy. constitutional reforms should be transformative changes and not simple tweaks that bring about incremental changes. The suggestions in this chapter are about recalibrating the scales of justice to reflect the needs of the people. They should be aimed at improving the very quality of justice itself, making it more consistent and predictable.

The first proposal for change is to introduce a transparent performance review mechanism and to align job incentives for judges with the quality and speed of justice delivered by them. The aim of this change would be to make the judiciary see itself as a service provider instead of a sovereign enforcer of the law and dispenser of justice. The latter concepts are imperial ideas from the English court system. While, by assuming sovereign immunity, the Indian judiciary allows its judges to work with independence, it does not hold them accountable to anyone for their actions, deeds or misdeeds. This allows judges to often mask or defend their lack of professionalism and avoid taking responsibility for their mistakes.

The second idea is to restructure the Supreme Court, splitting it into a constitutional court and a final court of appeals. Our apex court has become burdened with cases that it would not have been expected to handle at the time our Constitution was framed. This distracts it from its primary role of dealing with cases of constitutional importance. A restructuring would allow it to have a division dedicated to dealing with these important cases.

The third suggestion would be to rethink the ambit of Article 136 (a constitutional provision that enables litigants to challenge any order of a high court or other court or tribunal in the Supreme Court) and Article 142 (which enables the Supreme Court to complete justice by delving into areas that fill gaps in legislation and go beyond statute to deliver justice) of the Constitution. The former results in a massive workload for the court, and the latter is interpreted to bestow the Supreme Court with unchecked and unfettered power, which at times is interpreted to mean that the court has legislative powers too.

The fourth proposal is to divest the Supreme Court and high courts of their jurisdiction for PILs. This can be handled by specialised tribunals, which would unburden the higher courts while still allowing for an avenue for the public to seek relief in an open public platform (like in courts) in these tribunals.

Most lawyers currently practising in the Supreme Court and the high courts lament the falling standards of judges at these superior courts. Thus, the fifth suggestion is to upgrade the existing process for the appointment of judges in the constitutional courts. Instead of the government the appointing the judges to the higher courts, or the collegium system in which a panel of the most senior judges of these courts appoints new judges and transfers incumbent judges between courts, we move to a process that is inspired by the one in the US and give primacy to the parliament and its committees.

The sixth and final suggestion is to extend the tenure of judges. A long tenure or a lifetime tenure for judges in the superior courts will help settle their apprehensions about their post-retirement prospects, utility and status. This stems from frequent complaints from across the political and social spectrum about judges who are approaching retirement age. There is a perceived loss of independence and impartiality among these judges as they are at a stage when worries about their future relevance lead them to work with one eye on post-retirement engagements. A system of lifetime tenure for judges would eventually help resolve this issue.

Judicial accountability

Any human resources professional will tell you that performance reviews are great for maintaining professionalism, quality and efficiency in an organisation. There is no reason why this approach could not be applied to our judges too. Is there a current performance review system for Indian judges, and does it deliver value to the litigant and in general to the Indian nation? If the answer to either of these questions is no, then we need to consider an effective performance review mechanism for judges.

In the days of administration by royalty, justice was delivered by the sovereign (or by officials appointed by the sovereign). There are anecdotal stories of the king or his ministers mingling with commoners in disguise to get direct feedback from them on the functioning of their governance systems. In the medieval period itself, sovereigns in India had begun to segregate their judicial professionals from those who ran their administration until English rule took over and went on to clearly articulate ideas of segregating a professional cadre of judges from the sovereign.

In those days, the only time a judge's performance would be reviewed was when their rulings were appealed. Even after Independence, India continued with this British system of very little review of the judiciary's performance. In fact, independent India went on to assert and defend this concept of an untethered judiciary, using for its defence the importance of independence of the judiciary from the Parliament, the state assemblies and the Central and state governments.

Of course, the argument for independence of the judiciary is sound. After all, the superior courts (the high courts and the Supreme Court) are called in to challenge acts of legislation and the deeds and misdeeds of the government. Further, courts also have the jurisdiction to deal with disputes involving governments and the behaviour of government officials. So, to give individual judges the courage to deal with such cases impartially, they need to be granted professional independence. The government should not have a say in the career advancement of judges so that they can operate neutrally.

But the problem increasingly manifesting itself is that many judges are not as impartial as they ought to be. Thus, the absence of performance reviews for judges is perceived as part of the reason for the failure to deliver the desired levels of independence in the judiciary. Further, other problems have crept into the system, among them the massive backlog of cases in our courts, the low number of judges, the poor judicial infrastructure, the falling levels of professionalism at both the bar and the bench, the frequent adjournments, questions about judicial integrity and the poor quality of judgments that are frequently overturned in appeals. These problems may be linked to the absence of a performance review system for judges. This has resulted in long delays in deciding cases, inconsistency of outcomes in similar cases and unpredictable justice delivery. Ultimately, it has reduced the level of confidence among the people in the judicial system and the rule of law.

In 2001, a pioneering journalistic effort at performance review of the judiciary was attempted by an Indian magazine, which asked 50 senior counsels to evaluate the judges of the Delhi High Court on criteria including integrity, punctuality and knowledge of the law. Unfortunately, after the report was published, the editor of the magazine was slapped with contempt proceedings. It was held that the article made libellous remarks about the judges and that the statements were an attack on their honesty, integrity and judicial competence.[1] Eventually, the editor had to tender an unconditional apology to the court. This unease with judicial performance review is not unique to India.

It also brings to mind the judicially rejected National Judicial Appointments Commission (NJAC) Act, 2014, which specified 'ability, merit and any other criteria of suitability as may be specified by regulations' as relevant for the appointment of judges to constitutional courts. During the arguments in the NJAC case in the Supreme Court, then attorney general Mukul Rohatgi brought up various failings of the collegium system and cited instances of judges belittling the authority of the court with their conduct.[2] While the government of the time used these facts to claim that the collegium was not a good system, they can also be used to show why judges must demonstrate a higher level of professionalism.

It is entirely possible that a truly unbiased system of performance review for judges would improve the level of judicial professionalism in the country. But how can this be achieved without doing away with the independence of the judiciary? The suggestion is to allow for a performance review with no role for the executive or legislative arms of the nation, that is, the government and the Parliament or state assemblies. That retains judicial independence while still allowing for judicial review.

This can be done in the following ways:

i. Peer review: Inputs on a judge's behaviour, technical and legal skills, general professionalism and integrity from other judges at the court where they work.
ii. Review by judges in the higher judiciary: An informal mechanism for this already exists. The challenge would lie in reviewing the performance of judges of the Supreme Court.
iii. Self-assessment: Periodical gathering of this feedback on various metrics relevant to what a legal professional might

want to see in a high-quality judge can be considered as part of the evaluation.

iv. Feedback from lawyers: This feedback should be gathered periodically at various stages of a dispute or case. This will avoid biased feedback based on the outcome of the case.

v. Feedback from litigants: Similar to gathering periodic feedback from lawyers, the suggestion is to gather feedback on the judges, but this time from the actual consumers of the nation's service of administering the law and delivering justice.

Pointing to the need for courts to create a litigant-friendly environment, former chief justice of India N.V. Ramana quoted his American counterpart Warren Burger, who had said, 'The notion that ordinary people want black-robed judges, well-dressed lawyers and fine courtrooms as settings to resolve their disputes is incorrect. People with problems, like people with pain, want relief, and they want it as quickly and as inexpensively as possible.'[3] If this sentiment is given adequate weight when determining our nation's policies, a system sensitive to the needs of ordinary Indians must be created, one that takes into consideration the opinions of litigants and their feedback on the time they spent in the country's courts.

The idea of litigant-focused judicial performance review is also seen in other parts of the world. The American Bar Association introduced its Guidelines for the Evaluation of Judicial Performance in 1985, which were updated 20 years later, that is, in 2005, and in the interim have inspired similar guidelines across the world. Besides outlining criteria for assessing judicial performance, it also includes methodological and administrative guidelines.[4] These guidelines have been used to implement judicial performance review across several US states. For example, in New Jersey, questionnaires on several performance standards regarding the legal ability and comportment of judges are filled in anonymously by advocates.[5] A judicial evaluation commission then assesses this feedback and also reviews video footage of courtroom proceedings where necessary.

The International Framework for Court Excellence is a quality-management system developed by the International Consortium for Court Excellence (ICCE). Created using inputs from judicially trained advisers from several parts of the world, it provides guidelines to help courts worldwide improve their performance. The latest (third) edition of the framework, published in 2020, has proposed a continuous improvement methodology to be adopted by courts.[6] Through a self-assessment process, it places the onus on the judges and other judicial staff to collect information about their own performance.

Under this framework, specific weight is assigned to parameters like court leadership, strategic court management, court workforce, court processes, user engagement, affordability and accessibility of services. It also takes into account public trust and confidence in the court. Such a self-assessment methodology could be a first step for courts moving towards a system that would ultimately involve the public in the overall process of evaluation of courts as well as individual judges.

The Supreme Court of Victoria in Australia followed the ICCE framework to implement a programme that allows feedback from all court users on the performance of judges in the state. Various organisations related to the country's judiciary – including the attorney general's office and the Australian Government Productivity Commission (AGPC) – conduct regular, independent performance reviews, evaluating metrics such as efficiency and equity and factors such as 'perception of court integrity'. The AGPC's report is submitted annually to the relevant minister. Other courts in Australia publish their own annual reports, which include details on the progress of pendency, advancements in technology and litigant access or support.

In England and Wales, the judiciary has created a mechanism for senior judges to conduct appraisals of junior judiciary members on the basis of their decisions, legal knowledge and workload management.[7] The American system has been using performance assessment methodologies for several decades to assess both courts and individual judges. Under the Civil Justice Reform Act, 1990, the director of the administrative office of a court must prepare biannual reports providing pendency statistics for each judge at the court and specifically mention the number of cases pending for more than three years. This information is made public, which allows citizens to develop informed opinions on the state of their nation's judiciary.

A recent working paper by researchers from Cross Disciplinary Knowledge Data Research or the XKDR Forum, a research organisation in Mumbai, suggests a framework for litigant-centred performance review in the context of contract enforcement in India.[8] The paper states that by gathering information on a large scale from cause lists, orders and case lifecycles, one can obtain real-time information to evaluate issues of judicial performance on metrics such as consistency. This is relevant only in the matter of past cases for which such data is available. The paper also notes that perception surveys of stakeholders in the judicial process – including litigants – could be used to evaluate court performance. The suggested metrics[9] that can be gauged from the information thus collected directly from litigants include:

i. Judicial independence: Perceived adherence by judges to procedure and the rule of law, and fairness and impartiality in their judgments.
ii. Judicial predictability: Perceived clarity during the various stages of each case regarding the process of the court, as well as certainty regarding substantial hearings on hearing days at the court.
iii. Cost of litigation: Perceived convenience in assessing the opportunity cost of engaging in litigation and the user-friendliness of courts.

In 2022, two interlocking studies based on samples from the district courts of two Indian states[10] concluded that access to justice, quality of judicial activity and public trust are the three broad dimensions of judicial performance. Further, it suggested that judicial policymakers such as the collegium and the government must devise ways to incentivise good judicial performance and also adequately disincentivise bad judicial performance that falls below a certain threshold.

However, it is not sufficient to only consider litigants' reviews of the performance of judges. The review process must be holistic, and stakeholders such as lawyers and other judges should be able to assess the judges too. Lawyers who have argued before the judges being evaluated must provide periodic reviews on them and their work as determined by the framework laid down by the XKDR Forum. This would include the conduct of the judges, their consideration of arguments and precedents, and their analysis of the law to decide trials in a fair and just manner.

Judges from the higher courts hearing appeals can evaluate the quality of the judgments passed by the lower-court judges and also their ability to interpret arguments to arrive at informed decisions free of bias and personal views. Similarly, judges from the lower courts may assess the performance of higher-court judges based on their ability to bifurcate questions of law and fact to pronounce their judgments. Subsequent to such periodic scoring by the stakeholders of the courtroom, a final score indicative of the ability of individual judges could be computed. This score would be a true indication of the integrity and abilities of a judge because it takes into account not just their decision-making abilities but also their conduct and ethics. Such a scoring system would incentivise judges to display efficiency and sincerity.

In order to make the judicial system efficient, training programmes and incentive schemes could be offered to judges to make them better qualified to provide their service of justice. A robust framework can be developed for compiling the specific questionnaire for their evaluation by stakeholders, which could contain binary questions as well as scoring on a scale to assess the quality of judicial performance. This review can be conducted at various stages of a case. For example, for appeals, information can be gathered at the pre-admission as well as the final hearing stages. Several studies in the field have confirmed that, irrespective of the order or format in which such information is sought, it is possible for a court's performance to be assessed on parameters of independence, efficiency, predictability and accessibility.[11]

The collective feedback from various quarters on the performance of judges can be analysed using carefully chosen, neutral individuals or a certain level of AI. The resulting evaluation can be shared with the judge, along with suggestions for improvement. The outcome of this performance review should have a bearing on the judge's remuneration and their tenure in the judiciary. The hope is that a properly implemented performance review system across different levels of the judiciary will result in judges becoming more responsive to the needs of the litigant. They will be compelled to assume the role of a service provider delivering justice to the people, rather than that of an official wielding sovereign authority and delivering justice at their pleasure and convenience. This change in attitude will benefit the people of India enormously.

Bifurcation of the Supreme Court

At present, the Supreme Court is bogged down with PILs and constant appeals from the lower courts. As a consequence, it is unable to devote time and resources to deal with its principal task of settling questions of constitutional interpretation and the law. To get a perspective on this issue, let's first look at the hierarchy of courts in India and how they were meant to operate. At the absolute top is the Supreme Court, the highest court of the land. Below the Supreme Court are the high courts, which are the top courts in the state or territory over which they have jurisdiction. Below each high court are the district courts and sessions courts, which are the highest courts in each district of every state. The district courts have jurisdiction over civil cases while the sessions courts handle criminal cases of their respective districts.

There are a host of other lower courts below this level, as well as tribunals and other quasi-judicial authorities established under specific statutes to deal with certain kinds of cases. Appeals from these tribunals are heard at either a high court or the Supreme Court, depending on the case. These quasi-judicial bodies were established to reduce the workload of the high courts. Let us now look at the functions of the high courts and the Supreme Court. The high courts were established primarily to handle appeals of judgments delivered in cases of private disputes at a lower court. They are also a court of first instance for challenging the constitutionality of both legislation and state administrative action. The high courts were designed to be the final court of appeal in every state to deal with these kinds of disputes, barring a few exceptions, including cases under Article 136 of the Constitution that involve questions of law and legal interpretation, which would require an appeal before the Supreme Court.

The functions of the Supreme Court are to be a forum for challenging decisions made by the high courts and certain tribunals, to rule on petitions for protection and enforcement of the fundamental rights of the people, to hear disputes between states and to provide a view on constitutional issues upon reference from the President of India.

According to recent statistics, the number of pending cases in the Supreme Court has been increasing each year. From 70,852 cases in 2022, it rose to 79,636 cases in 2023 and to 82,308 as of May 2024.[12] The extraordinarily large number is the result of litigants persuading their lawyers to challenge decisions made by high courts in the Supreme Court. This has resulted in the Supreme Court becoming burdened with a huge number of petitions seeking special leave to appeal judgments of the lower courts under Article 136 of the Constitution. Consequently, the apex court is now struggling to deal with cases of constitutional importance that could have far-reaching consequences for the country. Concluding those primary cases would go a long way in resolving disputes of various kinds that remain pending in the lower courts for lack of constitutional or legal interpretational clarity. Hence there is a suggestion to split the court into one that deals purely with legal and constitutional interpretations, like most supreme courts do in most parts of the democratised world, and another, a court of appeals, to deal with appeals and petitions under Article 136 of the Constitution.

Despite having the largest population in the world,[13] the strength of the Supreme Court is 34 (as of 2019).[14] The Constitution originally envisaged a Supreme Court with only a chief justice and seven other justices but left the power to expand the number of judges to Parliament, which exercised its power to expand the strength of the court in nearly every decade after Independence. The number of judges in the Supreme Court increased to 11 in 1956, 14 in 1960, 18 in 1978, 26 in 1986, 31 in 2009 and then to the present number a decade later.[15] To provide a global context for these numbers, the number of judges serving in supreme courts in the US is 9, while the UK has 12. Canada also has only 9 serving justices, and Japan and South Korea have 15 each.[16] While the number of Supreme Court judges in India is considerably larger by these global standards, it still remains insufficient as long as our apex court continues to function as just another court of appeals.

All apex courts worldwide have similar duties of constitutional adjudication or interpretation. However, the judicial pendency problem at our Supreme Court indicates that India's apex court is not a supreme court when compared to similar courts in the rest of the world – that is, a court that is purely an interpreter of the law. We need to recognise the seriousness of the problem of our highest court having slowly transformed into a quasi-administrator. India does need a court of appeal at the top, but there is also a crying need for a separate court to interpret the Constitution and settle matters on the interpretation of statutes.

In 2022, the then Chief Justice of India responded to a PIL by stating that even doubling the strength of the Supreme Court or the high courts would not be an adequate solution to their high pendency of cases.[17] According to recent data, the current pendency of cases is rising across courts, with over four and a half crore cases pending.[18]

A similar upward trend is noticed overall in the rest of the judiciary, as pendency across courts in India grew by 2.8 per cent annually. As of 2022, the courts have a record backlog of 4.7 crore cases across different levels of the judiciary.[19] Even if no new cases were to be filed, the Supreme Court would take nearly a year and a half to conclude its pending cases. The high courts would need three years to clear their backlogs.[20]

A contributing factor to this pendency in the Supreme Court is the expanded jurisdiction of the court. The Supreme Court has been willing to hear cases of all categories, especially those relating to Article 136. This article essentially grants extraordinary jurisdiction to the Supreme Court to consider special leave petitions in cases where a direct appeal is not admissible. By virtually eviscerating the difference between the treatment of special leave petitions and the treatment of appeals, the apex court spends an inordinate amount of time hearing cases that have already traversed two judicial forums. Most of these cases do not lead to amendments to the concerned laws.

The Supreme Court is also the first forum for appeal for tribunals such as the National Company Law Appellate Tribunal and the National Consumer Disputes Redressal Commission. The appeals arising from these cases add to the workload of the apex court. This kind of expansion of jurisdiction has made the Supreme Court of India act more as an administrative court rather than one that only hears cases presenting substantive questions of the law.

In the Supreme Court, judges normally sit in benches of two or three. Presently, each bench sits through oral hearings of at least forty cases a day. Earlier, high court orders were considered final, with appeals allowed only in cases with substantive questions of law that could be considered under the Supreme Court's remit. However, due to judicial laxity, the Supreme Court has strayed from its original purpose, which was limited to interpreting the law. This has contributed to the growing backlog of pending cases. This lax judicial behaviour perseveres with little sensitivity to the existing backlog of cases, many of which are more than a decade old. Former Chief Justice of India Uday Umesh Lalit made efforts to reduce the number of long-pending cases in the Supreme Court during his tenure,[21] but many such attempts have only resulted in incremental change and not in any long-term, institutional transformation. Recently, concerns have also been raised about the declining global reputation of India's Supreme Court when it comes to the persuasive value that its judgments provide to courts in other jurisdictions. In a study conducted by Article 14, an India-based independent research organisation, it was discovered that judgments by the Supreme Court of India were cited less often in other jurisdictions in the period from 2014 to 2019 than in the preceding five years.[22]

To address these issues, there is a wide, sweeping reform that has always been available, and it is now being increasingly discussed. This idea is the bifurcation of the court. In recent public debates, such as those initiated by former Vice President of India Venkaiah Naidu,[23] the reform has been presented as a regionalist solution to the inaccessibility of the Supreme Court, with certain commentators demanding the creation of regional benches of the Supreme Court. However, this requirement has become largely redundant with the transition of the Supreme Court to a virtual court after the COVID-19 pandemic. The judges have now also become more accepting of virtual hearings and online filings. However, to save the standing and credibility of the Supreme Court as a forum for the interpretation of law, bifurcation should still be attempted.

A permanent bifurcation into a constitutional court and an apex court of appeals must ensure that the two courts have similar standing in the hierarchy of courts. The Supreme Court would then be able to develop different institutional cultures appropriate to each of the two courts. The constitutional court would only be eligible to hear questions of law, and its structure would resemble the current system of constitution benches, while the court of appeals would primarily address the demand for second appeals. But to ensure that appeals to the Supreme Court do not become a common practice, the latter court would hear only certain appeals. The court of appeals should be vested with the power to hold judges of the lower courts liable for wrongful interpretation of law or wrong precedents, judgments of subpar quality and other forms of negligence that diminish the service of justice.

A comparison of the Supreme Court of India with other apex courts globally

A study conducted by the *Supreme Court Observer* presents a fresh perspective on the need for bifurcation of our Supreme Court and modification of its culture.[24] The Supreme Court hears oral arguments daily throughout the year. This pattern is also observed in neighbouring countries such as Bangladesh. However, the top courts in Australia, Singapore and the US only hear oral arguments during certain periods of the year. For example, Australia's apex court hears arguments for only two weeks in a month. The study highlights the stark contrast between the schedules of apex courts in other countries and that of India.[25] The gruelling schedule of oral hearings at the Supreme Court of India burdens the cognitive and intellectual capacities of its judges. Therefore, a bifurcated court would be able to specialise and handle this workload better.

Limiting Article 136 and Article 142

The unanticipated application of articles 136 and 142 of the Constitution by legal practitioners has warped the Supreme Court's calendar. To understand the issue, let us look at each of these articles in turn. Article 136 gives the court the power to directly entertain petitions seeking permission to appeal against any order by any court or tribunal in the country and is generally operationalised to challenge high court orders. Advocates focus on the 'peculiar' facts of their cases to raise them to the apex court level, conveniently overlooking the fact that it is only in exceptional circumstances that Supreme Court jurisdiction should be invoked even under Article 136. The Supreme Court has analysed the ambit of the provision and concluded that the apex court is not a regular forum of appeal for such cases and that the provision does not confer the right to such an appeal to any litigant. The article only confers a discretionary right on the Supreme Court to hear special leave petitions when the demands of justice need to be satisfied.[26] It has been clarified that the Supreme Court must exercise its power under Article 136 only in exceptional circumstances, when a case of public importance arises or to determine questions of law.[27] But certain lawyers are able to frame appeals of lower court decisions in terms of the principles that govern Article 136 jurisdiction and are met with only feeble resistance from the Supreme Court. This results in the top court taking on a very large volume of cases, far exceeding what might have been anticipated when the Constitution was framed.

Instead of using the Article to leave a window for exceptional cases involving the most important issues or consequences, the justice system has effectively ignored the spirit of the

Constitution by converting all high court appeals into special leave petitions, taking advantage of the complaisant petition admission culture at the Supreme Court. When this institutional practice deems all petitions as special, clearly none is tested to determine if it is special. Even in dismissing the most frivolous of petitions under Article 136, judges and officials have to spend time considering the plea, which affects the court's efficiency.

My suggestion is for Article 136 in its present form to be reworded to clearly underline the extraordinary factual situation or consequences as well as the grave legal error committed by the high court that would call for a petition to be heard by the Supreme Court. While courts, including the Supreme Court, have guarded their review jurisdiction from expanding over the years, the most extraordinary jurisdiction of the apex court has been expanded without due consideration of the consequences. The Supreme Court's own words have guided my suggestions. In the 1988 case of *P.N. Kumar v. Municipal Corporation of Delhi*[28], Justice E.S. Venkataramaiah remarked that the Supreme Court has 'no time today even to dispose of cases which have to be decided by it alone and by no other authority' because a large number of cases were pending for as long as 15 years. Justice Venkataramaiah added that even if no new cases were filed in the Supreme Court, with the present number of judges it 'may take more than 15 years to dispose of all the pending cases'.

Looking at Article 142 now, we find that it was initially thought of as a special provision to be used in exceptional situations for allowing the court to go beyond what was envisaged by legislation to deliver what might be thought of as complete justice in the eyes of the court. Over the years, the court has used Article 142 for a variety of purposes, and not always with the requisite insight or expertise. For example, in matrimonial disputes where the Supreme Court felt that greater justice would be delivered by shortening the long-drawn divorce proceedings, it would bypass such proceedings in the lower courts and deliver divorce decrees through its own orders.

Article 142 allows the court to 'pass such decree or make such order as is necessary for doing complete justice in any cause or matter pending before it'. This means a decree passed by the court using its powers under Article 142 is enforceable as law.

Article 142 was adopted as Draft Article 118 during the Constituent Assembly Debates on 27 May 1949. The Article was also peculiar because its use was not debated by the otherwise vibrant Constituent Assembly when it was adopted. Perhaps this itself indicates that Article 142 may not have been intended to become a source of power for the Supreme Court to grant itself law-making authority.[29]

In 1989, this power was used to bring relief to persons affected by the Union Carbide gas leak in Bhopal.[30] In this case, the Supreme Court opined that 'prohibitions or limitations or provisions contained in ordinary laws cannot, ipso facto, act as prohibitions or limitations on the constitutional powers under Article 142'. The apex court took an ultra-expansive view, saying that even if a statutory scheme existed and 'complete justice' made different demands from the executive, it would impose them. While the court was presented with a worthy cause, the action of the court may have stifled legislative developments that could have in due course created a framework for torts that cause large-scale devastation. With the rising numbers in PILs, special leave petitions and curative petitions that the apex court keeps entertaining, the functional purpose of the Supreme Court has been forgotten.

Moreover, in order to achieve complete justice, the court often introduces new laws to solve issues brought before it. While well-intended, it harms the larger public and the constitutional mandate of segregation of powers because the court's decisions are not open to judicial review. Very often, orders are passed with little attention to the root cause of the issue. The apex court tries to provide a quick fix without taking into account any repercussions it may have in the larger sense (say, with respect to enforcement) and hence affecting the greater public good. This in turn stifles the process of democracy because the court is overstepping its role.

In 2014, the Supreme Court famously used this power to cancel all coal blocks granted by the government from the year 1993 and imposed a penalty per tonne of mined coal.[31] In 2016, it invoked this power again to ban the sale of alcohol within 500 metres of all highways[32] in an attempt to curb road accidents. The court's swift moves on a complex policy question caused losses of livelihood to hundreds of liquor vendors across the country. The order was then modified to limit its scope to areas with low population densities and hilly terrains.[33] The apex court also used this power in 2019 to direct the formation of a trust for the construction of the Ram Mandir in the Ayodhya case[34] and in 2022 to order the release of one of the assassins of former Prime Minister Rajiv Gandhi. Two other instances showcase the sheer unpredictability of the use of Article 142: instituting the Justice Mukul Mudgal Committee to probe the IPL league spot-fixing scandal and taking steps to restore the marble of the Taj Mahal.

Unfortunately, the consequences of the top judicial body's increasing inclination to venture into legislative-cum-executive innovation stifle the growth of the legislative mandate and the necessary public process required for the formation of policies agreeable to the stakeholders involved. For example, in the case of the highway liquor ban, many months passed before the Supreme Court modified its order. By then, several small-time liquor vendors – who were already operating in a difficult regulatory environment – had to sell their businesses and land in order to mitigate their losses. The court is therefore the least accountable organ of the state when it comes to executing innovative ideas or pushing underdeveloped ones. This case should have made the apex court look into the role of Article 142, which was never intended to allow judicial minds to supplant legislative thought and thereby adversely affect the lives of ordinary citizens.

This kind of use of Article 142 has resulted in widespread allegations that the Supreme Court is eroding the principle of segregation of the executive, legislature and judiciary as envisaged in our Constitution. It is increasingly commonplace to see the court frame law and policy, probably owing to the ordinary Indian and civil society holding the legislative bodies in low regard as to their calibre, commitment and trustworthiness.

The consequences of this unintended expansion of the Supreme Court's jurisdiction have greatly increased the workload of the court in a manner unanticipated when the Constitution was drafted. In the eyes of many lawyers and public commentators, this unbridled authority to wield constitutional power has distracted the apex court's judges from dealing with everyday cases that are of immense importance to litigants. Instead, the judges are becoming more engaged in broader issues of administration and public interest, thereby adding to factors behind the slow pace of justice delivery in the country.

Judges who overstep their jurisdiction often justify it by saying that it serves the public interest to ensure complete justice. With each new generation of judges pushing this overreach even further, it will eventually lead to the constitutional segregation of powers being discredited by the so-called guardians of the Constitution. That would expose India to the risk of executive authoritarianism. So, unless we truly believe that our legislature is failing in its citizen-centric duties and that there is no hope of reversing this situation, we should do away with Article 142 in its current form. The power of the Supreme Court to grant relief in individual cases should remain, but its orders in these cases would not be enforceable as law.

Article 142 fails to contribute to the furthering of democracy in India by making the public dependent on the Supreme Court for quicker solutions than can be sought from any other institution. Decisions by benches of the Supreme Court that are passed without taking into account any consequences only work to the detriment of the apex court's own reputation. Placing the judicial elite above all other classes of citizens does a great disservice to the nation.

Public interest litigation tribunals

Public interest litigation is a much-loved and highly popular tool that demonstrates the effects of Article 142 of the Constitution on justice delivery. This Article has become a constitutional tool in the hands of our constitutional courts, even though it has not been infused with this power in the Constitution itself. It has come into existence through the court's own interpretation of the Constitution. The first such litigation was in 1979, when Hussainara Khatoon brought the inhuman conditions of undertrial prisoners to the notice of the Supreme Court. The landmark ruling of the court held that every citizen had a fundamental right to a speedy trial. It emphasised the importance of effective administration of justice and equality. This ruling resulted in new jurisprudence that has given judges of the Supreme Court and the high courts all-pervasive authority to deliver 'full justice' beyond the written letter of the law. It can be compared to the concept of 'equitable relief' in English law. In short, it is an expansion of the courts' jurisdiction by interpretation and not by legislation.

However, the Indian constitutional courts and democracy functioned quite well between 1950 – when the Constitution was legislated – and 1979, when the outcome of the Khatoon case expanded the Indian courts' jurisdiction. If the judiciary and the democracy were working satisfactorily until then, was there a need for this expansion of the jurisdiction of the superior courts? It has only served to slow them down while distorting democracy. India is probably the only Western-style democracy where the court wields this level of authority and power while being accountable to no one but the judges themselves. An international client of ours, commenting on the tool of PIL in the famous 2G telecom licence-cancellation judgment, once said to me: 'In other countries, we have regular coup d'états, but in your country PILs are like coup d'états, they have constitutional authority and are executed by the courts.'

Some might see PIL as one of the significant Indian contributions to global public-law jurisprudence. This experiment – which relaxed the requirement of locus standi and expanded the Supreme Court's jurisdiction over governance in India – has been emulated in other jurisdictions such as Pakistan and Nepal. The Supreme Court itself acknowledged the influence of PIL jurisprudence outside India in a judgment delivered in 2010. However, only recently have some scholars begun to explore the real and potential negative impacts of PIL. Various theories have been put forth to explain why the Supreme Court pushed to establish PIL jurisprudence after the Emergency declared by Indira Gandhi in 1976. During that time, fundamental rights were suspended in order to control the public and curb protests against alleged corruption in the Congress Party.

Despite this, the economic costs of disparate and activist PIL jurisprudence have received little judicial attention. The impact of PIL on a country's democratic systems can be better understood through the concept of separation of powers between the judiciary, legislature and executive. Modern democratic governments derive some of their legitimacy from this division, which finds its origins in the ancient Roman Republic. Article 50 of our Constitution places the responsibility for this separation of powers on the State. Article 50 mandates the State to take steps to 'separate the judiciary from the executive in the public services of the State'. During the Constituent Assembly Debates, Professor K.T. Shah advocated for the insertion of a stronger provision titled Article 40A that declared 'complete separation of powers'. However, K. Hanumanthaiah argued for functioning in harmony instead of in mutually exclusive silos.

Dr B.R. Ambedkar sided with Hanumanthaiah because they both disagreed with the idea that the executive should be entirely separate from the legislature. However, Dr Ambedkar was clear that the executive should be separated from the judiciary. The resulting absence of a clear separation of powers becomes more evident on reading Article 142 of the Constitution. The debate on the separation of powers continued in the newly appointed Supreme Court. In the *Re: Delhi Laws* case of 1951,[35] then Chief Justice of India H.J. Kania noted the lack of express separation of powers but stated that when a legislature has been given powers to pass laws as its primary duty, the implication is that other bodies such as the judiciary are not 'intended to discharge legislative functions'. The primary task of judicial review – to 'strike down' erring legislation – has become lost in translation as judges routinely haul up government departments, secretaries and even public-sector companies in the misguided optimism that they can steer the ship, thereby stepping into the realm of the executive and sometimes into the realm of the legislature too.

What is actually in the hands of the judiciary when it comes to interfering in legislative and executive action is 'judicial review', which even votaries of separation of powers do not oppose. Undoubtedly, it is the prerogative of constitutional courts to examine legislation on the anvil of fundamental rights, which must be given liberal and consistent interpretation to ensure the permeation of liberty across Indian legal, political and social life. But in order to examine legislation, there would be little disagreement on the proposition that the rules of locus standi – which restrict the opportunity to challenge legislation only to those directly affected – should also not stand in the way.

Legislation must be open to judicial challenge by its direct, incidental or potential subjects, as well as by conscientious objectors. However, my agreement with a liberal interpretation of the locus requirement would end here. What has occurred in the name of representative petitions through PIL tells a different and deeply problematic story. All executive policy is open to debate in appellate courts, leading to the Supreme Court finding itself stuck trying to determine the 'right' path rather than the constitutional path. The apex court's problems stem from its lack of administrative expertise, which the Constitution has entrusted to the executive branch of the state.

In August 2018, then Attorney General K.K. Venugopal implored the judges to examine the budgetary impact of the Supreme Court's PIL-based orders on the telecom, mining and coal sectors. The Attorney General was unforgiving in citing several examples of the thousands who had lost their jobs as a result of the Supreme Court's decision to ban the sale of liquor vends located near national highways. The bench was unmoved, reminding the government of unused funds in welfare projects instead. This combative approach towards fund allocation is far from the judiciary's mandate, even though the judiciary has a role in ensuring the realisation of positive as well as negative rights for the citizens. While concern for efficiency in welfare projects, fairness in spectrum allocation and environmental safety in mining is appropriate, PIL jurisprudence makes the original forum for complaints against violations in this context the final arbiter of facts as well as of the efficacy of policy.

As several Supreme Court judges would admit, the court simply does not have the level of expertise to make quick decisions on a wide variety of issues. However, it regularly does take snap decisions to impose interim directions and exercise a supervisory mandate in PIL jurisprudence. This mechanism produces irregular results, is arbitrary in its interference and delays action such as the development of industry and infrastructure and the policy mandate of an elected government. Enthusiastic judges often rely on Article 142 to act as a shield against valid questions raised about the court overstepping its mandate.

In January 2020, there was widespread discontent in the national capital over the inaction of both the Central and state governments on the issue of air pollution in the metropolis. A two-judge bench of the Supreme Court held several hearings on the matter and made a snap decision[36] to install smog towers on a pilot basis. The suggestion had come from the Delhi State government and the Central Pollution Control Board, and the Supreme Court increased the pace of installation of smog towers in the city. The unsurprising result was that there was no major reduction of pollution in the areas surrounding the smog towers. While the executive could be blamed for ineffective policymaking and expenditure, the approval of the exercise by the Supreme Court allowed for a peculiar division of accountability. Now neither the executive nor the judiciary could be exclusively held accountable for the money spent, the land allocated or the time spent in installing the towers. This example shows the limits of Article 142. While equity-based jurisprudence is essential to fill legislative gaps, the Supreme Court has merely become another inefficient administrator. In 2014, the ban on the sale of alcohol on national highways and the cancellation of coal blocks allocated since 1993 stemmed from the Supreme Court's assertive use of its powers under Article 142.

If the citizens are disappointed by an elected government's actions, the internal mechanism of elections will boot the government out. However, large fund allocations and infrastructure projects worth millions are completely at the mercy of the snap opinion of a two-judge bench with no context. While the aggrieved parties in this regard may have approached the Supreme Court themselves, PIL jurisprudence masks the identity of the actual forces behind any litigation. There are several examples of industrial competitors funding litigants and lawyers to approach courts with sponsored PILs that are malicious or have vested interests. A PIL should serve the public good, and therefore the court has to first assess whether a case truly aligns with this goal before entertaining it.

It is often very hard to determine whether a PIL is filed with similarly dubious intentions at the time of filing. Therefore, the court should first identify the public interest sought to be protected and then determine if it would be worthwhile protecting that public interest even if the proceedings were brought about by vested interests. Then, it should impose huge costs on the petitioner and the identified sponsor whenever the existence of malice or vested interest is proven. The sponsor of such petitions must be duly penalised, and the penalties should include a percentage of the sponsor's business revenue.

PILs are a drain on the Supreme Court's resources as well as on the public exchequer that funds the judiciary. In all PILs, because the public-spirited petitioner is not always an expert, fact-finding becomes a necessary exercise, prompting governmental authorities to file several successive status reports before any judicial action can be taken. In this process, our apex court spends countless hours and days awaiting and supervising the information necessary for adjudication. This has led to an unwarranted expansion of judicial review into affirmative and positive fund allocation, policy recommendations and the stopping or starting of industrial or commercial activity.

A certain elitism has crept into jurisprudence involving PILs. It carries the assumption that the ordinary citizens of our country are not suited to engage with issues of public importance through democratic and electoral means, and that solutions must be devised in the high chamber of judicial opinion by a handful of individuals. This group of individuals cannot, despite its best efforts, be as diverse in opinion and background as India's populace or its elected leaders. It is an elitism that allows the Indian judiciary to disregard executive policy.

Even though executive policy may lead to less-than-desirable outcomes, the feedback loop between the executive and the people is central to the growth of the country. Effectively, by stepping into the shoes of the executive, the Supreme Court interrupts this feedback loop. This often infuriates the public and its elected leaders, but criticism of the Supreme Court does not have any effect because there is no authority that can hold the apex court accountable for its decisions or misjudgments. Hence the spate of decisions from it that do not deliver the intended outcomes or deliver unacceptable though unanticipated outcomes has and will result in the judiciary slowly losing its credibility. Thus, the guardian of the Constitution, entrusted with ensuring that it is followed, is seen as the one disregarding it by overstepping its judicial boundaries, that is, disregarding the philosophy of segregation of authority as enshrined in the Constitution. Some critics might even call this the subversion of basic constitutional principles by the final arbiters of the Constitution. It has resulted in the judiciary slowly losing its credibility.

More people are approaching the Supreme Court through PILs than ever before. According to data compiled by the *Supreme Court Observer*, there has been a massive increase in the number of PILs in the last decade.[37] There were 70,835 filed in 2019. Not all of these cases are orally heard, but an overwhelming majority of them are letter petitions, which are heard at least once. Several among these have multiple hearings over many years. Additionally, the Supreme Court allows judges to pick issues of their choice to start suo motu PILs. Of the total number of such petitions started over the last three decades, more than half have been filed in the last five years.

Several high courts have also been weighed down by PILs. This has often resulted in non-experts reviewing government policies and issuing interim bans that lead to delays and losses. One such example is the notice against mechanised mining of riverbed material issued in 2022 by the Uttarakhand High Court in response to a PIL.[38] It has led to several industries being affected by proceedings in which they have not been included.

In the pre-PIL era, the Indian executive and legislature were headed by governments formed by a single political party. However, coalition politics ruled the roost from the 1990s until the monumental resurgence in 2014 of politics based on the concept of a single party and one leader. During the period of coalition governments, the fear of disturbing the coalition's balance kept the executive from adequately tackling the judiciary's incursion into matters of policy. But from

2014, India has had a stronger executive backed by a large parliamentary majority. The result has been constant efforts by the executive to reclaim constitutional authority, including the process of selecting judges.

This would be the natural course of action for a strong government unhappy with the constant tinkering of its policy, but the executive has taken this route not because of the risk of the court declaring its actions unconstitutional, but because it is aware of the waning of political and executive power over the years due to an activist Supreme Court. If the apex court had not tried to actively address matters beyond its remit, the assault from the executive may not have taken its current form. An example is the court's attempt to police the agricultural legislation introduced by the government in 2020, when three controversial farm laws were passed with the aim of liberalising the agricultural markets.

The new laws sought to allow farmers to sell their produce outside government-regulated markets, thereby facilitating private contracts and promoting deregulated trade. However, farmers feared that this would weaken the 'minimum support price' system and leave them vulnerable to exploitation by big corporations. In response to a challenge to the constitutionality of the new laws, the Supreme Court appointed a committee to suggest changes to this legislation. Neither the composition of this committee nor its final report was appreciated by the country's citizens or their elected government. Eventually, the new farm legislation was repealed, the court's efforts leading to a denial of democratic conversation on the progression of India's agricultural sector.

The Supreme Court's involvement reflected its role in balancing legal reform with public concerns, with judicial time wasted in such efforts. The judges' motives for intervention in cases like these have also been skewed. Instead of providing a suitable interpretation of legislation, it has attempted to create innovative technocratic solutions to what are essentially democratic problems that require democratic solutions. However, citizens do need a forum where remedies can be sought for administrative failures. That is why I suggest the creation of 'PIL tribunals' to provide citizens with such a forum. The constitutional courts shall preserve their powers to interfere in determining questions of law but shall not indulge in matters that do not. The culture of judicial policymaking would then come to an end.

There is an urgent need to delegate the complicated exercise of fact-based adjudication to specialised tribunals that will hear PILs. This will allow the courts to focus on their primary duty of handling regular cases. To ensure that the judiciary is no longer able to exceed its remit, these tribunals should be helmed not by judges but by appropriate persons drawn from outside the judiciary. I don't mean a bureaucrat, as the bureaucracy in its current form cannot adequately criticise its own policies. Certain professionals and experts, adequately trained and qualified, could be chosen to run these tribunals in a manner that does not replicate India's bureaucratic pace and attitude.

These tribunals should first seek to establish facts and hear expert opinions before proceeding to mandate solutions, putting back into judicial discourse the need for evidentiary rigour. Too often, courts have started prescribing solutions without fully understanding the nature of the problems before them. A PIL petitioner easily achieves publicity without exercising any rigour in describing the nature of the problem that they seek the judiciary to resolve. The PIL tribunals should frame appropriate rules for evidentiary rigour and adopt a participative approach to adjudication. The bureaucracy's limitations should be understood before action is proposed.

The PIL tribunals should hold powers similar to the relief of mandamus issued by a writ court. Additionally, the tribunals should do what writ courts struggle to do because of their workload by ensuring that the social and economic costs are seriously considered before any final decision is made. This would prevent shortsighted judicial policymaking that leads to economic stalling. The higher courts would not lose their authority in this process, but such authority would be supervisory because their role would be to receive direct appeals from the tribunals. However, in such appeals, the higher courts must first decide if a judicial review is even necessary and then ensure that the appeal focuses solely on questions of law and does not ask for a re-examination of the facts. This prevents turning the appeal into an original hearing and will expedite the process. The big difference from the current situation would be that the burden of factual determination will not concern the courts, and they will have the benefit of reasoned orders, along with the estimated economic costs of the prayers sought in the petitions before them. The culture of judicial policymaking will then come to an end, both for executive accountability for badly drafted policy to take centre stage and for Supreme Court judges to shed the assumption that they are supremely aware of all aspects of a public dispute that has not reached the court through any affected party. After all, not for nothing has it been famously said about our beloved Supreme Court that it is supreme but not infallible.

Appointment of judges

A high-visibility aspect of the Indian judiciary is the process of appointment of judges to the superior courts. In many ways this is a political tug-of-war between the courts on one side and the Parliament and government on the other. It has a direct bearing on the quality of judges who get appointed and thereby the quality of justice that is delivered. It is difficult to predict the method that will be adopted for appointing judges to India's superior courts in the future because of the current impasse between the collegium system of appointment and the stillborn NJAC, which tried to address the lack of involvement of the citizens in the selection of judges by involving public representatives who hold political power.

But lack of confidence in the political class is not enough reason to continue with a system that has a non-elected body making decisions. Any thought driven by this lack of confidence is proof of the lack of confidence of India's elite in democracy and public mandates. However, an unelected and unaccountable body (or, in other words, accountable only to the personal conscience of its constituents) appointing judges doesn't really address the broader question of whether a hand in judicial appointments should be extended to all Indian citizens, regardless of whether they support the current ruling dispensation or not.

To create a system that is truly representative of everyone who can be impacted by judicial rulings, the appointment process needs to ensure that public and political representatives get the opportunity to pose critical questions about a prospective judge's ideological leanings, functional orientations and work experience. While the process for appointing judges to India's Supreme Court has been aiming for greater transparency and an independent judiciary, we are still a long way from an ideal system. Currently, we are caught in a tense standoff between the judiciary and the executive, with each side trying to wield control over the process, leading to a status quo that leaves the future highly unpredictable.

History of judicial appointments to superior courts

Before Independence, the appointment of judges to the Federal Court of India (which later became the Supreme Court) was primarily based on the recommendations of the British government. There was no formal process, and appointments were often influenced by political considerations. After 1947, the process of judicial appointments underwent significant changes. The Constituent Assembly worked hard to create an independent judiciary and laid the foundation for the process of appointing judges. In its report dated 21 May 1947, an ad hoc committee of the Supreme Court advised that it was not expedient to leave the power of appointing judges of the Supreme Court to the unfettered discretion of the President.

The key provisions regarding judicial appointments are found in Article 124 and Article 217 of our Constitution. Article 124(2) states that the President of India shall appoint judges to the Supreme Court after consultation with other judges of the apex court and the high courts as he deems necessary. This provision established the system of consultation as an essential aspect of judicial appointments. Article 217 states that the President shall appoint judges to high courts after consultation with the chief justice of India, the Governor of the concerned state and the chief justice of the high court to which the appointment is being made. The term 'consultation' has been a subject of constant re-interpretation and controversy. In the initial years after Independence, the consultative process was not well defined, and the executive had significant control over appointments. But over time the judiciary asserted its role in the appointment process to ensure the independence and transparency of the courts.

Voices of discontent among the political leaders grew. A.G. Noorani – an Indian scholar who was also a lawyer and a political commentator – writes of an early correspondence[39] between Sardar Vallabhbhai Patel and Pandit Jawaharlal Nehru in Volume 10 of *Sardar Patel's Correspondence*. In a letter dated 23 January 1950, Prime Minister Jawaharlal Nehru complains to Vallabhbhai Patel about the then Chief Justice of India H.J. Kania regarding a matter pertaining to a judge of the Madras High Court by the name of Justice Bashir Ahmed, and suggests that Kania must resign. Patel's reply is illuminating of the real realpolitik of judge–executive interactions.

Patel writes that he is fully conscious of Kania's faults but thinks that he has 'been able to manage him'. 'This is the only time when he has pressed his views to this extent,' Patel continues, 'otherwise, in the past he has generally deferred to my views or, indeed, to your views whenever you had any occasion to discuss matters with him.' He goes on to acknowledge Kania's tendency to be sensitive about 'certain points' and 'become petty-minded' in his persistence. 'But that, unfortunately, is a trait not uncommon with some heads of the judiciary who feel that they have the sole monopoly of upholding its independence, integrity and purity,' Patel concludes.

Has the Indian political landscape changed much from the time of this correspondence? I doubt that there has been any evolution in our collective political thinking.

The Three Judges Cases

The interpretation of this consultation process was clarified through a series of landmark judgments passed by the Supreme Court in 1982, 1993 and 1998. These judgments – which came to be known as the 'Three Judges Cases' – established the doctrine of judicial primacy in appointments to the judiciary. In the first Judges Case *(S.P. Gupta v. Union of India,* 1982),[40] the Supreme Court ruled that the chief justice of India's opinion should take precedence in the appointment and transfer of judges, but it didn't lay out a specific consultation process.

The second Judges Case was the *Supreme Court Advocates-on-Record Association v. Union of India* case of 1993.[41] The judgment in the case expanded on the first ruling and stated that the chief justice of India should consult with a collegium of four of the Supreme Court's most senior judges for appointing and transferring judges. This case established the collegium system, which became the dominant method for judicial appointments. The third Judges Case (*In Re: Special Reference 1*, 1998)[42] further fine-tuned the collegium system, asserting that the Chief Justice of India should consult a collegium composed of the Chief Justice and four senior most judges of the Supreme Court for appointments and transfers of judges.

The NJAC controversy

In 2014, the Indian Parliament attempted to replace the collegium system with the NJAC Act, which would have established a new body consisting of the Chief Justice of India, two of the senior most judges of the Supreme Court, the Union Minister of Law and Justice, and two other individuals chosen by a committee. However, in 2015, the Supreme Court declared the Act and the constitutional amendment that birthed it unconstitutional.[43] The court instead reinstated the collegium system as the appropriate method to be followed for judicial appointments, emphasising the paramount importance of judicial independence.

A decade later, the collegium system is still the primary process for appointing judges to the Supreme Court and the high courts. The President of India makes the final appointments based on the recommendations of the collegium. However, a critical omission in this appointment process is that crucial questions, which ought to be answered by the prospective judges before they embark on their judicial journey, are never posed to them.

In the US, judges at the Supreme Court, appeals courts and district courts are nominated by the President, but the appointments must be confirmed by the Senate Judiciary Committee, which holds confirmation hearings for each nominee before their appointment. These hearings give citizens an opportunity – through their representatives in the Senate – to question the nominees about any previous controversies concerning them. Once appointed, the judges hold the post for life.

If a similar system is adopted in India, it could resolve many misunderstandings about judicial appointees. A bipartisan parliamentary committee could conduct this process, similar to practices already employed in fields such as defence and technology. This committee could have the power to reject an appointment in extraordinary situations such as when a background check uncovers facts about the prospective appointee that disqualify them. This would only require a simple majority vote.

Such a system would increase public trust in the judiciary and minimise the chances of candidates with questionable integrity assuming office. Moreover, it would demand that judges act in a way consistent with their testimonies before the parliamentary committee. If these hearings were televised and streamed, they would not only bring to public knowledge the scrutiny of individual appointees but also showcase the strength of the judiciary and the harmonious balance of power between the various departments of the nation. This level of public scrutiny of the process would also lead to a higher quality of judges at the superior courts. They are likely to be more knowledgeable and to have balanced, non-partisan viewpoints, which would make them consistent in their legal views and approach, and professional in their behaviour and conduct.

Extended tenures for judges

The matter of post-retirement positions for judges has been much debated in political, academic and public intellectual circles because of complaints about the quality of justice delivered and the neutrality of judicial decisions made by judges approaching retirement age. Former Attorney General K.K. Venugopal spoke about the benefits of raising the retirement age for judges at nearly every judge's farewell ceremony held between 2017 and 2022. But his repeated calls to keep experienced judicial minds in the game have fallen on deaf ears.

A more radical solution to the issue is lifetime tenures for judges. As mentioned earlier, this system already exists in the US but remains unexplored in India. However, life tenure for Supreme Court judges could solve several problems, including the ever-present threat to the independence of the Indian judiciary. Some countries grant life tenure to judges while still imposing a mandatory retirement age. For instance, in New Zealand, judges can be called to preside over cases even after they've retired. Another way to do this is by imposing term limits of a specific number of years, as observed in South Africa (twelve years), Mexico (fifteen years) and Switzerland (six years).

The US Constitution allows judges to serve 'during good behaviour', which is interpreted as a tenure for life or until voluntary retirement (or impeachment). Alexander Hamilton, one of the founding fathers of the American Constitution, argued that this provision ensured that the judiciary would be insulated from political pressure. This measure, along with the provisions for protection of judicial salaries and for judges' removal only through impeachment, ensures that judges can exercise their judicial minds free from political objectives. Further, the scholar Tom Ginsburg has suggested that the American system allowed judges to hold their positions for life to the detriment of certainty in the appointment of new judges. The fact that life expectancy has been increasing over the past few centuries has meant that while the average tenure of a US Supreme Court judge was 14.19 years from 1789 to 1970, it has increased to 25.3 years from 1970 to the present.

While the life-tenure system has its challenges, it could be crucial for safeguarding the ideals of the Indian judiciary. The current retirement age in India is much lower than in many other countries – Supreme Court judges retire at 65 and high court judges at 62. This means that 10 to 15 years of a judge's productive life remain untapped. It is a grave loss to the nation, and hence the retirement age for judges needs revisiting. Indian judges wanting to continue working after the age of 65 face a number of restrictions. Retired Supreme Court judges cannot practise law before any court in the country under Article 124(7) of the Constitution, which forbids them to 'plead or act in any court or before any authority within the territory of India'.

This leads some retired Supreme Court judges to work as arbitrators on domestic and international arbitration tribunals, typically for high-value commercial disputes. Others may be appointed to chair committees established by the Supreme Court as part of the judicial process in certain disputes. Examples of this would be the appointment of a retired Supreme Court judge to supervise the drafting of the Constitution of the All-India Football Federation[44] in 2023, and the appointment of another to head the Committee on Prison Reforms in 2018.[45]

However, a much more common way for retired judges of the Supreme Court and the high courts to re-engage with the law is by being appointed to tribunals by the government.

The appointment process for such tribunals inevitably gives significant power to the Central government to decide the fate of judges who wish to continue their professional journey post-retirement. Bodies such as the National Human Rights Commission, the National Green Tribunal and the Press Council of India have retired Supreme Court judges as their chairpersons.

A report in 2016 by the Vidhi Centre for Legal Policy highlighted that seventy of the last hundred judges to retire from the Supreme Court accepted post-retirement governmental appointments.[46] Twenty of these judges took up permanent tribunal appointments, while the remaining were divided between ad hoc commissions and committees. Thirty had been appointed within one year of their retirement, and seven were appointed even before their retirement.[47] A majority of these appointments were made by the Central government, highlighting the persistent concerns about judicial independence.

Only 43 per cent of these appointments had any judicial involvement, such as membership in a selection committee that includes the chief justice of India or a high court chief justice. However, there is a systemic concern about legislation that embeds retired judges in such bodies, with 56 per cent of post-retirement posts being required by law to be filled by retired judges, creating a demand for judicial talent. A 2021 study by *ThePrint* confirmed that the pattern had changed little, with 71 per cent of the last 103 judges retiring from the Supreme Court taking up governmental assignments.[48]

Another relevant factor is that a Supreme Court judge's salary dips significantly after retirement, halving from approximately ₹30 lakh per annum to a pension of ₹15 lakh per annum.[49] After recent efforts by former Supreme Court Chief Justice N.V. Ramana, government support in the form of a domestic worker and a chauffeur was extended to judges after their retirement, in addition to lifetime coverage of expenses for a secretarial assistant. Other supporting financial emoluments increased too. However, Arun Jaitley's radical suggestion that judges should be provided a pension equal to their last-drawn pay has not been taken into consideration.

However, even a pension that is equal to the last-drawn pay does not address the ambition of judges with active judicial minds waiting to be put to good use. It also does not properly address interference and influence by the executive resulting from judges having taken on post-retirement positions. It should be obvious to neutral observers that as long as posts are being handed out by the political executive to judges, it will affect their decisions or observations on the government in power.

There is also the issue of judges taking up post-retirement political appointments that have no judicial flavour, such as a Rajya Sabha seat or governorship of a state. These appointments are questionable and could be said to erode trust in the judiciary as they generally benefit politicians in power, such as chief ministers. In principle, while judges should have the freedom to lead a political life if they choose to after retiring from office, public perception of the judiciary – and especially of Supreme Court justices – must be prioritised over such independent ambitions.

For all these reasons, it is time that life tenure for judges be considered a viable alternative to secure full judicial independence, instead of making incremental shifts by raising the retirement age by a couple of years or more, as suggested by the ex-attorney general. Having said this, increasing judges' tenure to the age of, say, 80, is a definite second best, and with today's life expectancy and healthcare levels, it will in most cases achieve similar outcomes as life tenure for judges.

With the advent of social media and legal news reporting, constitutional courts in India have started receiving greater attention. Now people are often too quick to link judicial appointments made post-Independence to public-facing decisions by judges that have impacted the fate of governments in power. While such links may be dismissed as mere conjecture, it is hard to ignore the emotion behind the general public's craving for a truly independent judiciary.

By providing life tenure to judges, we tackle a number of problems at once, chief among them being the proper use of judicially active minds without interference from the political executive.

The modalities of such a system can be developed by creating an incentive structure that allows judges to retire voluntarily. By ensuring that the final years of judicial wisdom from Supreme Court judges are not expended in forums subordinate to the Supreme Court, we also solve the problem of unpredictable variance in judicial opinion. This variance may be assumed to result either from executive influence over judicial minds or from the sheer turnover of judges entering and leaving the Supreme Court in any given year. In 2023 alone, nine judges of the Supreme Court retired upon reaching the age of 65.[50] Every year, this exodus creates new avenues for governmental–judicial tussles over the Supreme Court collegium's suggestions for new appointees.

Appointment of judges for life will also reduce government influence over the court. Presently, every new government tries its own unique methods to appoint judges. The Chief Justice of India and the collegium have to spend a considerable amount of time tackling this issue. In a system with life tenure for judges, the reduced frequency of such appointments will calm the relationship between the executive and the judiciary. Contemporary scholars and journalists point to political appointments to the higher courts as examples of 'increasing' porousness in the political identity of judges, but this is an age-old problem. This can be understood by looking at the appointment of retired judges as governors of states. The first retired Supreme Court judge to be appointed as Governor was Justice S. Fazal Ali, who was made Governor of Assam in 1956 and remained in the post till 1959. There are many other examples over the decades, so this is not a problem that has arisen recently. In 1958, the 14th Report of the Law Commission of India discussed at length the issue of retired judges looking to be employed by the government. Describing the ethical issue involved, it noted that the government is a party in a large number of cases in the highest court and thereby the average citizen could get the impression that a judge who might hope to be employed by the government after retirement would not bring the 'detachment of outlook which is expected of a judge' in cases in which the government is a party.

Commenting on the procedure for selection of members to tribunals across the country, the 232nd Law Commission Report of 2009 further repeated the truth that judges do in fact 'seek' such appointments upon retirement. In his extensive study of the political ramifications of post-retirement appointments in India, legal scholar Shubhankar Dam has called this system of governmental posting 'institutional corruption'.[51] This is a term also used by Dennis Thompson, a political scientist and professor at Harvard University, in the context of external influences compromising the US Congress by creating an economy of influence, weakening public trust and institutional effectiveness.

As opposed to personal corruption, institutional corruption cannot be determined easily by any accountability mechanism in law, because it is difficult to make any real evidence-based arguments to demonstrate how a judge's judicial record in matters concerning the government influenced their chances of a post-retirement appointment. Institutional corruption might be entirely legal, but it corrupts the 'purpose' of the institution in question, which in this case is the Supreme Court's mandate of independent justice delivery. Incremental solutions such as cooling-off periods[52] will not change the institutional corruption that has crept into the Indian judiciary. However, life tenure will provide both ideological sincerity and transparency to judges while protecting them from any new governments that may come to power in the future.

The current mechanism for the removal of judges through impeachment as provided for in the Constitution will still serve as a viable mechanism to address individual judicial corruption. This process can be reformed to include the criterion of 'good behaviour' as is done in the US. The applicability of good behaviour has been a subject of debate as to whether the phrase elucidates a distinct standard for removal apart from the 'high crimes and misdemeanours' standard that is applicable to impeachment of other federal officers in the US.[53] In India, 'good behaviour' could be interpreted to mean that the individual in question is balanced, functional and does not engage in criminal activity. It would also include the individual's mental, physical and emotional ability to function as a judge. As the sole method for the removal of judges in the lifetime tenure system, the evaluation of good behaviour would be a genuine method for a government to actively combat individual judicial corruption. It should be specified what constitutes good behaviour and also how it will be monitored and evaluated.

In the collegium system, there is an informal disincentive structure that prevents the executive from forcing accountability on judges lacking 'good behaviour'. This is because the executive needs the cooperation of the collegium to continue to exert its influence over judicial appointments. When it has fewer chances to exert influence, it will be more interested in ensuring that valid reasons exist for the removal of judges lacking 'good behaviour' so that there are greater opportunities to appoint different judges during its term. However, the judges would also be able to withstand executive pressure and not have to worry about the impact that their attitude towards the government's suggestions would have on their own post-retirement careers.

Introducing the concept of lifetime tenure for judges would require relevant constitutional reform. However, at present, the Union government seems unlikely to consider even a small increase in the retirement age for judges. In 2022, former Law Minister Kiren Rijiju[54] informed a parliamentary panel considering the age of retirement for Supreme Court and high court judges that increasing the retirement age would benefit the 'non-performers' within the judiciary. He added that it would create a cascading effect, leading to similar demands from other categories of government employees. However, judges are not mere government employees, and the Central government does not have any authority to assess judicial performance outside of its role of vigilance.

By starting a conversation on lifetime tenure for judges, perhaps the demand for ineffective incremental tinkering with the retirement age can be reshaped into the more important question of why there should be any executive interference in the administration of justice in the higher judiciary at all. One hopes that better sense can prevail among the relevant stakeholders and that the question of judicial independence is posed more boldly through this debate. As a separate matter, the institutional economy of post-retirement appointments for judges must be stopped immediately. Of course, it is important for lifetime tenure to be granted to constitutional court judges before ending this system.

The Vidhi Centre for Public Policy pointed out in its 2016 report that the majority of post-retirement posts are creations of statute, so it is hard to fathom why a competent body for the appointment of members of tribunals cannot find legal talent outside the minuscule pool of retired judges. It was in this context that a bench of the Supreme Court responded to Senior Advocate Mukul Rohatgi's assertion that there exists a 'retired judge syndrome' by commenting that tribunals have become safe havens for retired judges and bureaucrats.[55] The appointment of retired judges to tribunals for the settlement of disputes in fields such as telecom, electricity or national company law does not match the needs of such specialist tribunals. More often than not, the judge spends their first few months in the role simply trying to understand the special laws applicable to the disputes presented before these tribunals.

Instead of appointing these old-timers, younger members of the bar or those belonging to appropriate professional fields should be considered. Such appointees would be able to provide longer years of service to these tribunals, thereby providing the highly sought-after institutional stability to these bodies. At present, the design of the statutes governing such tribunals is specific to retired judges, and thus the tribunals themselves become avenues for judicial delay in newer forms, functioning as they do with an ever-shifting roster of members with short tenures.

In 2021, the inefficient management of tribunals by the Central government was brought to the attention of the Supreme Court. Vacancies in the tribunals for real estate regulation, debt recovery and central administration were discussed. On then Chief Justice N.V. Ramana's directions, the Supreme Court registry noted that there were vacancies for 110 judicial members and 111 technical members across tribunals.[55] The vacancy issue is a persistent one, not only because of the bureaucratic process required to fill the vacancies but also because of the statutory design of these forums. Many such forums have to wait for the Central government to choose suitable judicial members from a relatively small pool of retired judges.

Because of the high number of vacancies regularly arising as a result of the short tenure of members, the tribunals lose out on effective, long-term administration. Additionally, the Central government's opinion of the judges becomes an inevitable factor for tribunal members to keep in mind while adjudicating cases in which the rights of citizens have been violated by the same government. This creates perverse incentives for judges in the administration of justice. Therefore, it is important to draw legal talent from outside the pool of retired judges of the superior courts to sit on the ever-increasing number of tribunals across the country.

A restriction on retired judges being part of such bodies should be combined with a re-imagination of the design of expert or subject-specific tribunals. This is to ensure a fair process that involves both the judiciary and the executive in the appointment of appropriate members to such tribunals. Once appointed, the members should also enjoy longer tenures to ensure the institutional growth and stability of the tribunals so that the purpose of speedy justice for which they were established is not lost in the constant hunt for retired judicial talent.

Overall, these measures will help improve the quality of the individuals who steer our courts and usher in greater levels of professionalism, independence and responsible judicial conduct.

6

Redefining Boundaries

We have discussed some large-scale changes to the Indian legal system that could bring about better delivery of justice and enforcement of law in the country. I still have other suggestions that defy neat categorisation, so in this final chapter let us explore some further fine-tuning of the legal principles underlying our judicial system. They will complement the changes suggested in the earlier chapters and hasten our move into an era of true decolonisation of Indian law.

Sovereign immunity

At present, government officials and judges cannot be held liable for any wrong decisions they may make in the course of their professional duties, provided those decisions are made in a bona fide manner. This is called 'sovereign immunity' and allows them to be answerable to no one and nothing but their own sense of professionalism and personal conscience. They are not accountable to the people they govern or sit in judgment over, who are also the recipients of their services. This means that government servants and judges suffer no professional consequences even if their mistakes result from negligence or lack of adequate effort on their part, unless their intentions are deemed malicious.

As a result, administrative or judicial decisions in India do not bear the burden of having to be correct, even though the consequences of any wrong decision have to be borne by the recipient. This illustrates why the principle of sovereign immunity is fundamentally at odds with the principles of constitutional accountability and due process of law. It is one of the vestiges of colonial India, spawned from the governance ideas of those times, and has no justifiable reason for continuing to exist. The question is, does it make sense for a modernising country, one that aspires to become a new India, to be a prisoner of this approach to governance and delivery of justice? Thus, the first among the additional suggestions we explore in this chapter is to reconsider the protection that sovereign immunity offers.

Limiting the question of sovereign immunity to the context of courts in India, we see that judges cannot be held personally liable for decisions that are subsequently overruled or set aside in challenge or for any mistake they might make.[1] This protection has been largely unquestioned in modern India, resulting in a few undesirable situations. The most negative aspect of this is the lack of judicial accountability. This is reflected in the inconsistency of judicial decisions in our country, the unreasonable delays, the deficiency of knowledge among judges, and elements of bias and prejudice in judicial pronouncements. We seem to accept that if a judge has financial integrity, then they don't need to face any consequences for other misdemeanours.

But let's reconsider this protection in the context of all other professions. The senior management of corporations, for example, is held accountable for all the decisions they take. If their decisions result in business growth, they benefit from that – but conversely, if they result in business disaster, they also have to face the consequences of those failures, which could happen even if the business leader was acting in the best interests of the firm. We need to take into account that success and failure are not just dependent on the quality of the decisions that lead to them, but also on factors outside, say, the leader's control, such as trends in the economy, government decision-making, policy changes, pandemics, wars, etc. Every decision-maker – whether in the public or private sector – is subject to scrutiny and judgment, particularly when their decisions impact the public at large. What, then, is so special about a government official or a judge that they must be protected from such scrutiny? The suggestion is not that judges be held to exactly the same standards as a business manager and be fired for making a wrong decision. However, they cannot enjoy complete protection from the consequences of wrong or bad decision-making.

At present, judges in India can continue in service regardless of the quality or timeliness of their decisions. We need to have a system to review all the judicial decisions made by a judge during a specific period, say a year, and evaluate them for efficiency and quality (that is, if they have been upheld through the appeal process). Then, the judge must be held accountable in some manner for their performance, such as having their remuneration, promotion and other career prospects linked to the outcome of their annual evaluation. Such analysis should also take into account the time a judge takes to decide a case and the adjournments that occur in the course of the case. The judge's performance must be aligned directly with the bonuses they receive over and above their basic pay, as well as with any raise in their remuneration. It is only prudent that judges are recognised for their service in delivering justice in the country, which is their most important function. The performance system for judges must include rewards for work of a high standard and disincentives for poor decision-making and a lack of professionalism.

In addition, if a litigant is seriously affected on account of any shortcoming on the part of a judge in court – including, but not limited to, insufficient knowledge of the law, delayed decision-making, poor professionalism, lack of effort or bias or prejudice – the affected litigant ought to be given the right to sue the judge for damages and compensation if their allegations can be proved. Today, this right is unavailable to litigants because of the sovereign immunity enjoyed by a judge. However, it is in keeping with the Indian philosophical idea that a king must be held liable for any wrong or slow decisions made by him, regardless of his motivations. The fear of consequences ensures that the king makes decisions cautiously but efficiently.

This idea is reflected in many Indian traditional legends, such as the story of King Dasharatha in the Ramayana. He had to bear the consequences[2] of mistakenly killing Shravan Kumar. In another Ramayana story, the Vanara king, Vali, was unable to avoid the consequences of having erroneously punished his brother Sugriva, even though there might have been a reasonable basis for him to assume foul play by Sugriva.[3] These tales reflect the Indian people's appreciation of the principle that every action has a consequence, and that even a sovereign acting in a bona fide manner cannot escape the consequences of a wrong or unjust act. There is no concept of immunity for certain individuals in our traditions, even if there are mitigating factors to consider. This concept is also seen further west in the case of Pontius Pilate, the Governor of Jerusalem who sentenced Jesus to death. He symbolically washed his hands in the hope of absolving himself of that sin, fearing the consequences of a decision that he knew was wrong. Clearly, he did not believe he had sovereign immunity.

History of sovereign immunity

The roots of sovereign immunity can be traced back to 1765 in England, when the decision in the *Entick v. Carrington*[4] case upheld that the government was subordinate to the law and that officials were permitted to act in the capacity they did only when it was derived from the law. However, any action taken in good faith could not be questioned. This theory relied on the notion that the king can do no wrong and extended to the king's officials acting within their authority. They too were considered incapable of committing any wrongdoing or causing any harm, even if there was evidence of misconduct or negligence on their part.

These principles were adapted into the realm of Indian law during the colonial period, with the first evidence of sovereign immunity seen in the *P&O Steam Navigation Company v. Secretary of State* case.[5] In issuing its judgment, the court carved out a distinction between the 'exercise of sovereign authority' and the 'exercise of non-sovereign authority' by state officials. The latter primarily pertained to the carrying out of undertakings by individuals in the employ of the state acting outside any official capacity, which is where liability arises.

The concept of judicial immunity was first propagated by Justice Lord Edward Coke in 1607 when he advocated the need for such protection for the judges of higher courts. He opined that the very nature of trials rendered one party the winner and the opposing party the loser. There was a likelihood that the losing party might hold the judge liable if it felt that the trial was unfair or did not consider material facts. This kind of persistent onslaught on the decision-making powers of judges created cracks in the independence of the judiciary, jeopardising the integrity of the entire system. For this reason, protection in the form of judicial immunity was extended to all judges.

Post-Independence, the concept of absolute sovereign immunity – implemented during the British Raj – did come up for challenge in the courts. After the Constitution came into effect, the first court decision dealing with the government's liability in tortious claims was the *State of Rajasthan v. Vidyawati*[6] case of 1962. In this case, the Supreme Court opined that the state was equivalent to any other employer. If an employer can be held responsible for its employees' tortious behaviour, then why should the government be considered an exception? Its liabilities must be viewed in the same way as those of a private entity and do not fall under sovereign immunity. This led to some dilution of the immunity available to government officials as compared to what was allowed under the British Raj.

Then, in 1985, the Judges (Protection) Act came into force. It directed that courts shall not entertain any civil or criminal proceedings against a person who is or was a judge for anything committed, done or spoken by them while discharging their official duties or functions.[7] It was clear from this ruling that whatever the actions of current or former judges, they would not be considered as serving any injustice or committing any malpractice. The fate of India's legal system was decided when sovereign immunity assumed a power for whose negative consequences the people had no remedy.

Upon first reading, the 1985 Act appears to provide blanket protection to judges under Section 3. However, on deeper scrutiny, it can be interpreted to mean that erring judges are liable for civil or criminal disciplinary actions, but only upon initiation of a valid sanction. This sanction rests on the recommendations of the high court in question, which has to advise the Governor to grant a sanction for the judge in question. To date, there has been no reported case of such a sanction being granted, and no situation in this matter has gone beyond hushed whispers and simmering discontent against the corrupt practices of the legal system. Effectively, therefore, the consequence of the act has been absolute sovereign immunity for judges in India.

In the *Veeraswamy v. Union of India* case,[8] the Supreme Court held that a judge may only be prosecuted with a sanction obtained from the President of India in consultation with the chief justice of India. Further, the Chief Justice of India can overrule the President, and the justice's final decision will be binding.[9] This means that the body being scrutinised for its actions is also the body that decides whether it is to be punished! How can accountability be fostered in a system such as this? Disciplinary action against a judge cannot be sanctioned by a member of their own fraternity.

Yet, Article 21 of the Indian Constitution states that when there is negligence to the detriment of the people or that endangers their lives, the individual guilty of that negligence cannot claim a defence under sovereign immunity.[10] Carelessness by government authorities is not protected under Indian law, and a citizen's fundamental rights can only be taken away by a process of law. No other act that infringes upon these rights will be considered valid under the law. Article 21 clearly holds that the statutory concept of sovereign immunity cannot supersede the provisions of the Constitution. However, this level of diligence is mandated only when the citizen stands to be deprived of life or liberty, and not in any other situation.

In India, lawyers often face injustice in courts when judges deliberately refuse to consider precedents presented with their arguments in a trial, despite precedents being paramount in judicial decision-making in the country. When judges fail to prioritise precedents, the resultant uncertainty and inconvenience not only flusters lawyers but also dissuades litigants from seeking justice because they perceive courts as applying the law inconsistently. This lack of predictability in judicial decision-making leaves a big question mark hanging over the integrity of our entire legal system.

If judges disagree with a prior judgment, they must be duty-bound to present firm reasons for this decision in their observations and judgments in open court, and to inform the concerned lawyers of the rationale behind their overruling of a precedent. The uncertainty faced by a lawyer presenting arguments in an Indian court goes against the very fundamentals of a common law system, and sovereign immunity only adds to the lawyers' distress as the judges cannot be questioned about their inconsistency.

In the UK, sovereign immunity is a centuries-old doctrine that dictates that the monarch and the government are protected against any civil legal action. This protection lies in the doctrine because there are no codified rules underpinning the concept. It stems from the idea that the monarch owns the court and is the source of justice in the country, and therefore cannot be made to appear in court or prosecuted for any actions. Specifically, Westminster law upholds 'crown immunity', which suggests that British law does not apply to the Crown. In 2017, the British Queen was granted an exemption from a law that allows police to initiate searches of private properties to investigate stolen cultural artefacts. Buckingham Palace simply stated that no such artefacts were within the premises, and no liability was pinned on the monarch.[11] However, the government may be sued for gross negligence or breach of contract. These are specific situations in which its officials can be held liable for their actions.

Countries such as the US, the UK, Germany, Canada, Australia, Sweden, Italy and South Africa provide legal avenues for individuals to sue the government for wrongful prosecution resulting in a miscarriage of justice. These claims are typically pursued through statutory compensation schemes, constitutional protections or human rights-based claims. The US prescribes sovereign immunity as a measure to prevent lawsuits against government entities.[12] This immunity has been extended to government officials and agencies to protect any actions carried out by them in their official capacity.

US law recognises two forms of sovereign immunity: absolute immunity and qualified immunity. The former refers to government agencies' immunity from being held accountable in court even for acts of malice or those done in bad faith. Under this immunity there are no repercussions for officials committing these acts irrespective of the effect of their actions. This concept stems from the traditional idea that a sovereign cannot be subjected to another's jurisdiction without the consent of the government. The near-absolute immunity enjoyed by judges in India is somewhat similar.

Qualified immunity shields law enforcement officers from personal liability in civil cases. Actions carried out in their official capacity by an officer while on duty are protected from being questioned in court as long as they have acted in good faith and have not breached 'clearly established' rights under the law. In recent years, this doctrine has faced increased scrutiny in the US due to its perceived abuse by officials.[13] In India, the immunity enjoyed by government officials is similar and is similarly abused. However, the US upholds the principle of suing officials for wrongful prosecution, which is not the case in India. This exception has been carved into US laws on sovereign immunity so that the government's power is not unfettered and liability can be imposed when acts are done mala fide.

In April 2022, US citizen Larry Thompson was subjected to malicious prosecution when he was imprisoned for two days after an unwarranted and violent entry into his home by the police.[14] Soon after, prosecutors dropped all charges against him. It was held that Thompson was not mandated to prove an 'affirmative indication of innocence'. The majority opinion declared that a plaintiff must only be required to show that the prosecution ended without a conviction of the defendant. This is unthinkable in India, which has one of the world's lowest conviction rates for major offences.

In the US, if an individual is falsely arrested and denied bail, they can sue the concerned officials and claim damages if the prosecution is unable to prove its case and the individual is released.[15] In the *State of North Carolina v. Henry Lee McCollum and Leon Brown* case of 1988,[16] two brothers were convicted of the rape and murder of a young girl in the North Carolina town of Red Springs. They had been arrested on the basis of rumours, and the police had then coerced them into giving false confessions. They were sentenced to death. However, in 2015, the discovery of DNA evidence proved that the crime had been committed by a convicted killer, which led to the brothers being declared innocent and subsequently released. They then sued the law enforcement officials and were awarded $75 million in compensation.

While the US and the UK have their own nuances in the way they approach the concept of immunity for law enforcement agencies and the government, the principle underlying this immunity remains the protection of government officials from certain legal actions. This protection, however, has faced criticism and scrutiny, particularly in the realm of law enforcement. If suing for wrongful prosecution were made available as an option to litigants in India, it would be a step in the right direction. At present, if charges against an individual are dismissed by a court, the wronged have no option for redress in our country. There are innumerable cases of prosecutors in India being unpunished for wrongfully arresting and torturing innocent citizens and then releasing them without charge.[17]

Ancillary litigations such as interim orders and adjournments happen so frequently and casually in our courts – leading to delays in the administration of justice – because judges cannot be held responsible for any failure on their part. There needs to be a judicial transformation to hold judges accountable for their actions and inactions, delays and judicial procrastination – even when the judges have acted in a bona fide manner. The common law system presumes that all judges and government officials act in good faith and with bona fide intentions.[18] This presumption needs to be diluted if our bureaucrats and judges are to be held liable for their actions. Irrespective of the intentions of the officials, it is important that their decisions are reasonable and aid in the delivery of justice.

Sovereign immunity has caused a slump in the Indian judicial system, leading to poor decisions such as awarding a disproportionately low amount to an aggrieved party after a successful case, leaving them in a losing position once the money and time spent on litigation are factored in.[19] A judge is assumed to be a perfect individual without any faults or biases, putting aside the fact that they are only human and exhibit frailties and desires like any other person. It is absurd to expect them to overcome these frailties, and it would be better instead to regulate around them. The extent of the consequences a judge must face for a mistake can be open to debate, but there can be no doubt that having such consequences in place would improve the quality of decision-making in the Indian judiciary.

It is crucial to initiate legal reforms that address the issue of sovereign immunity to bring about a radical change in the behaviour of judges, courts and the bureaucracy in India, orientating them towards working for the benefit of litigants. By reducing the scope of sovereign immunity or eliminating it altogether, the quality, consistency, transparency and timeliness of court decisions would improve significantly. The judicial system should no longer accommodate those lacking professionalism and integrity.

A modern vision

Many remnants of the British Raj still linger in the practice of law in India. The legal community continues to cling to archaic customs and beliefs that hinder judicial progress. It is time for a reimagining of the legal profession so that it reflects the needs and aspirations of a modern India.

Dress code

The idea of a uniform for the judiciary stems from a distinctly European tradition that no longer resonates in the Indian context. This may seem a minor detail, but it is a telling one, given that justice must not just be done but must be seen to be done as well. The dress code followed in our courts makes the lawyers and judges appear unrelatable to the ordinary litigant. The outdated black coats and gowns serve no real purpose but have an intimidating effect on litigants, witnesses and others who have to engage with the court system. Why shouldn't lawyers and judges wear normal attire, as long as it exudes dignity?

Courtroom language

Many lawyers only address judges as 'My Lord', fearing that deviating from this traditional form of address may jeopardise their case. However, they privately agree that judges should not be addressed in that manner. The archaic practices of using servile language – such as 'I humbly submit' or 'I beg to state' – have no place in a modern courtroom in a country of equals where justice must be delivered to fellow citizens as a service financed by the taxpayer.

Court proceedings should be conducted in simple, straightforward language and in a manner that everyone can understand.

Two-tiered bar

Designations within the legal profession – such as 'Senior Advocate' and 'Junior Advocate' – are relics of a British Raj culture that placed some lawyers on a pedestal. This caste-like hierarchy gives undue advantages to a select few and does not belong in a modern society. Senior Advocates in the superior courts of India are part of an exclusive club and enjoy special privileges such as being the first to be heard in the courtroom and having greater flexibility and space to make their arguments. They use this court-recognised status to demand higher fees from litigants and take on a large number of cases. This leads to delays and unequal treatment for litigants not using these lawyers. Prominent jurist Fali Sam Nariman has voiced strong reservations about this system, calling it a form of discrimination.[20] It is time to reevaluate these designations and embrace a more egalitarian approach, akin to the system in the US, which has no dual system and where lawyers are treated equally.

Professional constraints on lawyers

The notion of nobility associated with lawyering is another vestige of the colonial era. It is why lawyers in India are prohibited from running commercial websites or entering into multidisciplinary partnerships. These restrictions stifle modernisation in the legal field. Collaboration between lawyers and professionals from other domains such as accountants, tax advisers and PR specialists is essential in today's complex legal landscape. Yet, under the current rules, such multidisciplinary partnerships are prohibited in India. Doing away with these barriers would foster a more efficient and holistic approach to legal services in the country.

Countries such as the US, Canada, Australia and various European nations have embraced the multidisciplinary practice of law, recognising its value in providing comprehensive solutions to clients. It is time for India to follow suit and adopt this modern business model. The colonial mindset that segregates legal services into silos must be discarded so that the legal profession can embrace collaboration and innovation. In other countries, law firms are listed entities on the stock exchange, a concept yet to be embraced in India. Additionally, Indian law firms are barred from hiring foreign lawyers as partners, which limits their growth potential and prevents them from becoming multinational firms.

Change is never easy, especially when deeply entrenched customs and beliefs are involved. However, the legal profession must evolve to meet the needs of a rapidly changing world. By shedding the present fetters and embracing a modern vision, Indian law firms could open the doors to international collaboration and compete on the global stage. This, in turn, would result in their clients being better served and help create an environment of compliance with the rule of law in the country. It is only then that the legal profession in India would truly flourish and become capable of providing efficient, accessible and equitable justice to all.

Legal marketing

A commercial entity generally does not find it very difficult to find a capable lawyer when it needs one. That's because this need arises so often that the firm already knows the legal services market well. This gives them an advantage. However, it's very different for individuals and non-commercial organisations looking to find the right lawyer. Since they don't normally encounter legal issues, they are not familiar with the legal market. This leads them to hire a lawyer based on recommendations from friends and relatives, with little actual knowledge of the lawyer's calibre and speciality. Unfortunately, their chosen advocate is sometimes ill-equipped to handle their case or is too expensive. This happens because regulations make it hard for lawyers to put their skills and costing out in the public domain, thereby creating opacity when it comes to the search for legal talent.

This lack of knowledge of legal options among citizens exists because the current rules imposed by the Bar Council of India restrict advocates from publicising their services. These rules, rooted in Section 49 of the Advocates Act, 1961, impose strict guidelines on professional conduct and etiquette for lawyers. They prohibit lawyers from soliciting work or advertising their services, including by means of personal communication, advertisements and interviews. Even mentioning past associations or areas of specialisation by a lawyer is frowned upon. Violation of these rules can lead to serious consequences, including prosecution and disciplinary action. These stringent regulations suffocate Indian lawyers, leaving them with limited avenues to market themselves.

Lawyers in countries such as the US, Singapore, the UK, Australia and many European nations enjoy far more freedom to advertise their services under regulated frameworks. In the US, a landmark case[21] in 1977 upheld the right of lawyers to advertise. Their Federal Trade Commission recognises that advertising promotes healthy competition in the legal profession. Of course, the advertising must adhere to state and federal regulations, so each state's bar association prescribes specific rules for such advertising. In Singapore, specific legislation[22] allows advocates and solicitors to publicise their practice, subject to specific rules. Similarly in the UK, a solicitor's code of conduct permits lawyers to publicise their firms, provided they comply with the code's requirements. Lawyers in Australia and the European Union also have the liberty to advertise their services as long as their advertisements are not misleading.

Of course, marketing has the potential to be abused and mislead prospective customers to enhance sales and revenue. However, this is an evil that plagues all kinds of goods and services, yet there is no full ban on their advertising and marketing. This is because marketing also creates a certain level of transparency and informs prospective customers of the benefits of the product or service being marketed. So why must legal services be treated differently from other services or products? Should not the customer be entitled to learn about lawyers and legal firms, their expertise and fees, just as they do about other things on the market?

The obvious upside of allowing lawyers to market their experience and skills is that customers know more about the legal services available to them, which works to their benefit. If the Indian legal profession embraces modern marketing practices, citizens of our country would no longer have to look for legal help in the dark. If lawyers are allowed to showcase their expertise on websites and clients are allowed to review their services online, it would bring about greater transparency in the profession and in the justice system as a whole.

Accountability for lawyers

While Indian judges are not liable for any wrong decisions they may make, lawyers in the country face no legal liability for providing incorrect legal advice. I am yet to hear of a lawyer in India being successfully sued for such an error. Lawyers are duty-bound to advise their clients in a bona fide manner as they have 'an unremitting loyalty to the interests of a client' and a responsibility to act in a manner that would best advance the interests of the client.[23] However, does this standard of accountability suffice? Should a litigant accept that a lawyer they hire may claim that their actions or advice were bona fide and therefore cannot be held liable for them even if they turn out to be detrimental to the litigant?

The term 'advice' is relatively non-specific, so there cannot be a strict rule as to what constitutes 'wrong advice'. In the US, it applies to negligence and misconduct by a lawyer that causes harm or damage to the client.[24] It is the lawyer's professional obligation to provide clients with competent legal advice, and failure to do so could lead the litigant to raise a claim of legal malpractice against them. Wrong legal practices could include misquoting precedents or statutes from other jurisdictions, lack of proper communication with the client, inconsistencies in the drafting of contracts and failure to inform the client of appropriate filings and deadlines, among others.[25] Legal malpractice attorneys in the US specialise in identifying elements that constitute malpractice and advise clients on complex cases where facts and allegations against lawyers are convoluted or difficult to ascertain.

As a protective measure, lawyers may insure themselves against professional liabilities. Doing so can protect them if they are accused of negligence and claims are initiated against them. The insured would be indemnified against the loss they may incur from claims made against them for their conduct, which could include personal injury, copyright infringement, misrepresentation and inaccurate advice, among others.[26] In the US, the average cost of a full-rated policy with minimal limits for an attorney would be between $1,200 and $2,500 per year. Attorneys practising in higher-risk areas may expect to pay annual premiums in the range of $3,000 to $10,000, depending on their state of registration and any past claims against them.[27]

However, in India, the costs for a similar insurance cover range from 0.2 per cent to 2.5 per cent[28] of the indemnity limit (which generally falls between ₹17,000 and ₹25,000).[29] Thus, costs for insurance in India are much cheaper than in the US, and this is where the lack of accountability among Indian lawyers arises. Lawyers in India are not troubled by possible claims against them because their insurance helps them get away with giving wrong advice and causing harm to litigants.

There is a good case for raising the costs of professional liability insurance in India in order to deter lawyers from providing frivolous and baseless advice.

Lawyer accountability would be strengthened further if there were a mandate for performance reviews and client feedback. These reviews would not only ensure that lawyers offer a higher quality of service but also provide a reference point for potential clients when choosing a lawyer. In the US, there is legislation that requires federal agencies to set goals and measure their performance by reporting their accomplishments and accolades in an attempt to transition to a performance-based environment. This includes performance reviews of legal work done by the justice department.[30]

A standardised evaluation form can be circulated among judges, fellow lawyers and clients. Similar to the performance review for judges suggested earlier, this method of evaluation would allow lawyers to be assessed on their conduct and the service they provide – both in and out of the courtroom. Any errors or misdeeds would no longer go unnoticed, and they can be held accountable for their actions or lack thereof. Once lawyers are reviewed for their performance, the system can be audited for authenticity and perhaps some form of score or ranking for lawyers can be posted on a public platform. These could include statistical data on their general professionalism, timeliness, knowledge of law and advocacy skills. This would help prospective clients select a lawyer who has the appropriate expertise to handle their case.

Contingency fees

A contingency fee is a fee that is dependent on a specified and pre-agreed outcome. When applied to lawyers, it means a fee agreement in which the lawyer gets paid if the client wins, but not otherwise. However, Indian law prohibits such a fee system for lawyers. The Bar Council of India specifically disallows lawyers from charging fees that are dependent on the result of litigation. It also prevents them from sharing in any proceeds of litigation that accrue to their clients.[31] The origin of this rule can be found in an old-world understanding of law as a 'dispassionate' profession. However, times have changed, and we need to accept that most lawyers will deliver services in a manner that is aligned with their own financial interests.

If a 'success fee' is allowed, the lawyer stands to gain financially when their client wins the case and to lose when their client does. Therefore, it would make lawyers more mindful of resisting delays and adjournments to ensure that cases are decided more quickly. It will also mean that litigants need not take on the full burden of legal costs at the outset. Hence, it is in the interest of both lawyers and clients to adopt the system of contingency fees. Ironically, even the country that imposed this restriction on contingency fees upon us is slowly moving away from that stance. England first allowed lawyers to collect contingency fees in litigation and arbitration proceedings in 2013. They could also receive a share of the damages awarded.[32] Depending on the type of hearing, this was in the range of 25 to 50 per cent of the proceedings awarded to the client.

The reason for this policy shift in England was simply a recognition of the freedom of contract. If two contracting parties determine the nature of services to be provided by one to the other and the form of compensation for the said services to be paid to the providing party, the law should not come between them even if one of the parties were a lawyer and the service provided was legal in nature. England also recognises another form of contingency fee system in which legal fees are charged on the basis of the time spent by the lawyer on a trial under the condition that the lawyer would receive reduced or no fees if the case is lost. This is known as a 'conditional fee agreement' and has been permitted for a number of years now. However, it is seldom used in disputes arising under commercial litigation.

Safeguards can be woven into the policy to ensure that contingency fee arrangements do not encourage frivolous petitions and that the fee does not primarily become a vehicle for lawyers to enrich themselves. This can be done by capping the percentage payable as contingency fees according to the nature of the case. In the US, contingency fees are required to be specified in a signed agreement in which all potential expenses for the client must be listed. Upon the conclusion of the case, the lawyer is required to provide a written statement to the client stating the outcome of the matter. This kind of fee arrangement is particularly common in personal-injury cases, where the successful lawyer is awarded between 20 and 50 per cent of the recovery amount as fees. However, this levy of contingency fees is not unfettered, and contingency fees are usually not allowed for divorce cases or for the representation of a defendant in a criminal case.[33]

It has been found that individuals prefer a 'pure positive gamble' in which they would pay higher fees for a positive event – that is, winning the case – over a mixed gamble, where they pay a fixed fee to their lawyers whether they win their case or not. Research has suggested that well-informed clients with 'high-quality' cases (where the client has a high chance of winning) are willing to pay relatively high fees for a lawyer's service but a relatively low percentage as contingency fees. However, clients with 'low-quality' cases that are less likely to succeed prefer to pay a low fixed fee and a high contingency fee.[34] It has also been seen that loss aversion plays a major role in clients preferring to pay contingency fees.[35]

In India, the prohibition on contingency fees means that a lawyer's fee structure has three primary arrangements. The first is an upfront arrangement in which the client is presented with a fee schedule that is in accordance with a timeline. The fee is payable in tranches as per a schedule provided by the lawyer. The second is a time-based fee in which clients pay the lawyer based on the time they have spent on their case. In the third arrangement, the clients have to pay a fixed fee either in a single tranche before any legal services are provided to them, or in instalments spread over the duration of the case. This last arrangement is the one most commonly used in India.

In any of these fee structures, lawyers have little riding on the actual outcome of the trial and are financially detached from the dispute process. This detachment often works out to be counterproductive for the clients, who frequently complain that their lawyers deliberately prolong cases to get higher fees or lose interest in a case after most of their fees have been paid. There are also instances of lawyers advising clients to file enforcement proceedings even when their case is weak, or defending them in cases where their chances of winning are poor. Contingency fees could reduce the initial costs of litigation and also encourage due diligence by litigants and their lawyers on the quality of their case.

Currently, only individuals in the lowest socioeconomic strata are represented by legal aid, and this constitutes a minuscule percentage of people navigating the justice system. For all other persons, contingency fees will lower litigation costs. One contingency fee arrangement is having a substantial portion of the total legal fees held back until the conclusion of the dispute. This helps the client avoid delays in their trial and also avoid paying the entire fees in case they lose.[36] This can help people of meagre means enter into litigation even against large corporate entities. When the lawyer's fees are based on the outcome of a dispute, the disempowered may feel more emboldened to fight for a claim.[37] A success fee structure would push lawyers into evaluating the potential outcomes of the case more carefully, since both their fee and reputation would be contingent on their winning the case, and this pot of gold at the end of the rainbow would keep them motivated to achieve the predicted and desired outcome.[38]

India is opposed to the concept of contingency fees because it contradicts the principles of public policy and contravenes ethical conduct among lawyers.[39] It has been stated by various courts in India that rewarding an advocate with a part of the winnings in a case handled by them is against public policy, and for that reason, lawyers should not be engaged on a contingency fee.[40] Indian courts also consider the relationship between the lawyer and the client as highly fiduciary in nature and therefore believe that lawyers should be prevented from misusing the trust placed in them. This conclusion was based on the notion that contingency fees may compel a lawyer to take up cases that clearly have high chances of success, in turn limiting access to justice for litigants whose cases do not appear to have as good a chance of succeeding.

However, when courts in India decided against contingency fees, people were less aware of their rights and at the time the legislation may have been a necessity to prevent abuse of trust by lawyers. But the legislation must be modified to meet the needs of India's society today, a time when increased access to justice at lower costs is a necessity. This must be rightfully recognised by the courts in India and the law must reflect it. A direct impact of the introduction of contingency fees in India would be a sharp spike in class-action suits as seen in the US. This would result in a decrease in the rate of tortious crime in the country, as aggrieved parties would rightfully recover larger amounts as damages than they could earlier.

Take the 1992 case of *Stella Liebeck v. McDonald's Restaurants, P.T.S., Inc. et al,*[41] more popularly known as the 'McDonald's Hot Coffee Case'. Here, the plaintiff brought a claim against McDonald's after the hot coffee served to her by the food chain led to burn injuries. She successfully sued McDonald's for $125,000 for medical expenses, pain and suffering, mental anguish and loss of enjoyment of life. Since then, McDonald's and various other consumer-focused businesses have taken greater care in conducting their businesses.

The framework of contingency fees also puts a squeeze on unfair trade practices. Class-action suits would ensure that companies and other corporate entities refrain from illegal or unethical trade practices. This could also lead to the enforcement of product liability on manufacturers of goods, who will now have to hold greater responsibility for the goods they produce. If product liability is implemented, producers and sellers are held liable for what they produce and sell in the market. They are constantly under pressure to supply quality products for fear of becoming the target of class-action suits filed by aggrieved consumers. This would also lead to large-scale product recalls, as often seen in the US.

Contingency fees will also ensure that lawyers carefully assess cases for their likelihood of success so that even if the slightest chance of failure exists, they can take up such cases on a fixed, time-based or lump-sum fee structure. This is also a clear indication for the clients that their cases are relatively weak, though they are still being helped in exercising their right to seek justice and to be represented in court. Currently, lawyers often take on a case with a commercial mindset, focusing on profit-making despite knowing what the outcome of the trial is likely to be. This sometimes induces false hope and confidence in their clients. A change in this approach will lead to litigants perceiving the legal system as an approachable forum for dispute resolution where everyone's rights are protected at affordable costs. With the introduction of contingency fees, a wealthy entity or individual would not be able to get away with a crime just because the aggrieved party is not able to afford good representation in the courts.

India may also consider a ceiling on the contingency fees chargeable by a lawyer. The effect of contingency fees will also be seen in the duration of trials. Lawyers and clients will both seek to expedite trials, leading to lawyers resisting frivolous adjournments and delays during the process. This will reduce the cost of entry for litigants, who could then hire a lawyer for a minimal retainer fee. It allows for flexibility in the attorney–client relationship and compels the system to be more outcome-oriented. Lawyers will now be more responsible for the success of the cases they handle as their earnings hinge on that. Despite the historical opposition to this system in India, updating our laws to permit contingency fees will serve to empower litigants, incentivise due diligence and expedite trials while curbing frivolous litigation. Drawing on successful models from the US and the UK, India can enhance access to justice, deter wrongdoing and ensure fair compensation for aggrieved parties, ultimately helping foster a more legally compliant environment.

Right to bear arms

If someone suggests expanding the currently available legal right to defend oneself by allowing private citizens the right to carry weapons and to use violence to secure justice for themselves, many would baulk at the idea. It is natural to think that carrying guns and knives or taking the law into one's own hands to obtain justice will almost always increase the level of violence in society. But that is not entirely true. Let's examine the issue closely.

The first objection to such a right to private justice would be that if it is exercised by common people untrained in the basic aspects of civil and criminal law, it could end up subjecting a large number of innocent people to violence in the name of someone's pursuit of justice. The second objection would relate to the inability of common citizens to assess whether the punishment delivered by them is fair and proportionate to the offence. Both these possibilities would mean terrible outcomes for the rule-based society that this book argues for.

In this context, let's step back in history to the times when a king had limited abilities to enforce laws, prevent crime and deliver justice to victims of crime among his subjects. The people thus had no option but to obtain justice for themselves by using force as protection from crime. Common people would always be armed, and royalty or administration would not consider disarming the population or assuming exclusivity over violence. Sovereigns across the world accepted this approach.

Of course, those were times of excess and innocents were often put in harm's way by someone's misplaced sense of justice. Often, the punishment delivered by the victim of a crime was grossly disproportionate to the offence against them. To add to this, criminals could disguise their crimes as acts of defence or retaliation even when they had not been the target of any crime. Eventually, to prevent these injustices, the ruling administration modernised and built a more robust policing presence. This helped them arrogate to themselves the duty to protect their people, which led to the elimination or dilution of the age-old right of individuals to bear arms and defend themselves with weapons.

In the early 20th century, renowned German sociologist Max Weber articulated the idea of the State's monopoly on violence. He defined the 'State' as a community that claims the exclusive right to exercise legitimate physical force within its territory. This concept implied that the State was the only entity that could authorise the use of violence. So, if someone was the target of a crime, they had to complain to the State through the police. The latter were trained to deal with the situation and would investigate and prosecute the criminal. They could also complain to the courts, where professionals trained in matters of law and evidence appreciation would determine the facts and deliver justice.

Through this system, the State secured a monopoly on violence and ensured justice. Individuals were compelled to use the mechanisms of the State to seek justice. However, when it came to the right of an individual to carry and use weapons in defence, it was permitted 'whenever appropriate'. This was because many administrations knew that they lacked sufficient physical on-ground presence such as police personnel to completely prevent crime. However, any act of violence with the use of weapons had to be justified before the authorities or a court of law.

The idea of State monopoly over violence came to India with the British colonisers. The British introduced gun-control laws and restrictions on the carrying of sharp instruments such as long knives and swords by Indians. They used this emerging principle of State monopoly over violence to disempower the Indian people and protect themselves by taking away a citizen's right to carry weapons. This idea allowed the British to subjugate fierce independent communities such as the Rajputs, Sikhs and Marathas. It was a self-serving policy that benefited only the colonisers as it made armed resistance to British rule very difficult.

The Indian Arms Act of 1878 regulated the possession and carriage of firearms and prohibited Indians from possessing, carrying or selling any kind of weapon unless they held a license. However, licences were only issued sparingly to the elite of society or those loyal to the British. This weakened the ability of Indians to defend themselves against not just imperial power but also random criminal behaviour in society. The act was a significant legislative move and served as a stark reminder to common Indians of British dominion over India, highlighting the power disparity between the colonisers and the colonised. By controlling who could and couldn't bear arms, the British effectively restricted the ability of Indians to revolt against or resist British rule using force.[42]

For many martial communities in India, the bearing of arms was not just about defence but was also intertwined with their cultural identity, honour and pride. The Arms Act was therefore viewed by these communities as an attack on their honour and traditions.[43] The act possibly created a perception of helplessness among some sections of the Indian populace. By legally disarming Indians, the British likely instilled in them a sense of vulnerability and dependence. While the Indian spirit of resistance to imperial rule persisted, its expression evolved, sometimes manifesting in non-violent resistance and at other times in covert, armed rebellions employing the now illegal and difficult-to-procure arms.

Should not this disempowerment have then been reversed once India secured independence? By 1947, however, the new Indian leadership was already leaning towards establishing an Indian nation modelled on British principles, one in which the old coloniser's value systems prevailed. Our leadership believed in the British systems, in their governance models and in their approach to nation-building. Thus, the notion that the Indian population could not be trusted to carry weapons continued as a generally accepted idea. Many ideas such as this one were never challenged, questioned or reviewed. The Indians had become a compliant, subservient and easy-to-rule population. Our once fierce national personality was made pacifist, and we no longer have the physical or emotional strength to defend ourselves the way our ancestors did. A majority of the population today hopes that the government will defend them against crime, even though it often fails to do so.

If the government cannot defend, protect and deliver security to the Indian people, isn't it time to reconsider the restriction on bearing arms applied to our citizens? If someone disagrees, I ask them to think of the multiple injustices and crimes we face in daily life and our sense of helplessness in dealing with them. This is particularly true of the weaker and poorer sections of our society. They are neither able to prevent crimes nor seek recourse against them. Justice cannot be obtained within a reasonable timeframe or at an acceptable cost. The question to ask is whether this idea of State monopoly over both justice delivery and the right to carry weapons has not rendered the 'free' and innocent people of India powerless, particularly when they are unable to pursue legally acceptable remedies due to lack of economic resources or lack of institutional support, which are only theoretically available according to our books of law. Think of the hardship an ordinary citizen faces when trying to register a complaint with the police or have them intervene in situations of minor crime.

Of course, the idea of allowing a regular citizen to carry a weapon is only to enable them to defend themselves against crime when the State fails (particularly in emergency situations). Having said this, the emphasis is to enable citizens to defend themselves against crime and not to seek post facto remedy or recourse. Once a crime has already been committed, the victim should seek recourse through regular legal processes to obtain justice instead of trying to do so by themselves with the use of a weapon. If a person resorts to delivering justice on their own, it would amount to a violation of the law, even if they were the victim of a crime first. The right to carry firearms is not to be equated with the idea of permitting vigilante justice. It is to create fear in the minds of prospective criminals. The prospect of an intended victim being armed would serve as a good disincentive for attempting a crime.

If such a right is given to individuals to protect and defend themselves, the law would also need to include provisions against abuse of this right. One such provision would be to shift the burden of proof onto the individual exercising this right to establish that they did so in circumstances that were fair and acceptable. Another measure could be the denial of this right to carry weapons to persons with a criminal record or a history of grievous offences. There should be a blacklist preventing such individuals from owning and carrying firearms.

Supporters of the State monopoly on violence may raise concerns about the potential increase in violence if weapons are made more accessible to the people and argue that this might lead to a general increase in violence in the country. But they also need to consider that the current gun laws in the country inadvertently empower criminals while leaving their potential victims defenceless. We must ask ourselves if the notion of being a civilised and peaceful society is more important than actually being a society where security and justice prevail. Of course, in a utopian scenario we are civilised and peaceful but also safe and secure. But is such an idealistic situation possible?

All this must also be viewed in the context of the quality of justice delivery in India. Speaking at a public event in 2023, the Indian Home Minister admitted that India's conviction rate was abysmally low. It currently stands at about 50 per cent – in stark contrast to countries such as Israel and the US, which have conviction rates of 93 per cent and 90 per cent, respectively.[44] This means that criminals in India continue to commit crimes with little fear of punishment or prosecution, knowing that delivery of justice is a long-drawn procedure in our country. The opposition to my suggested change to remedy this situation will probably come from those who are uncomfortable with the idea of weapons among the general population. There is a fear that India will descend into a US-like situation, where there are shootings in schools and other public establishments.

However, there is a fair bit of statistical data in the public domain to support ownership of guns. While people have cited data to show that gun ownership does not prevent crime, some studies show that it does. In the US, gun-free zones are where criminals concentrate their activities. It is also pertinent to ask those in India who are hugely critical of the US for allowing its citizens the right to own or carry guns why they would then consider travelling to that country for leisure or even allowing their children to study there.[45] Is it because the US provides its citizens a higher level of justice and generally offers a better quality of life and work than India?

There was a period when I did a lot of grassroots politics, and at that time I would pose this question to many constituents to get a sense of what they thought of the matter. A vast majority of them, particularly in rural India and among the weaker sections of society (non-English speaking people), responded by saying they perceive ownership of weapons as allowing them protection from crime that the State cannot provide. There can be no doubt that most individuals would feel a heightened sense of security when they are armed compared to when they are not. It is exactly this sentiment that forms the underlying basis of support for gun ownership in the US.

To assess the validity of the concern of increased violence with more weapons present in society, we can take a closer look at the communities in India that have always had access to guns and long knives through legal exemptions. One such community is the Kodava tribe, also known as the Coorgis or the Kodavas. The martial tribe from Kodagu (earlier Coorg) in southwest Karnataka is known for its unusually high gun ownership and gun culture. The Kodavas, who have a population of about 4,00,000, have been exempt from the Arms Act from the time of its introduction. Nearly every family in that community keeps guns, and cartridges are sold in public markets there.

The Kodavas live in an area where predators such as tigers, panthers and wild boars are found in the wild. The tribespeople were known as adept hunters until their hunting practices were curtailed by the Wildlife Preservation Act of 1973. Every year, the Kodavas worship arms in a special festival called Kiel Poldu, which also includes a sharpshooting competition.[46] In 2021, the exemptions granted to the Kodavas were held constitutionally valid by the Karnataka High Court. Rejecting a challenge to the exemption, the High Court observed that the martial community has rightly been granted exemption from the Arms Act, noting that the exception period is not indefinite but valid for ten years, with extensions permitted subject to certain terms and conditions.[47]

Another community receiving exemptions from the Arms Act is the Sikh religious group. Their tenets require the carrying of a 'kirpan', which is a short, curved sword worn around the waist. Most religious Sikhs possess and carry kirpans, but the exemption does not extend to the manufacture of such swords. Both the Kodavas and the Sikhs are perceived to be people of high integrity and are not viewed as violent or criminal communities. Access to guns and knives does not make them murderers. This is the same logic used in the US by those against gun control laws – simply possessing a gun does not make a person a killer. This is not to say that certain individuals would not use a readily accessible gun to commit murder, but it is not access to a weapon that makes them a murderer. In other words, guns do not kill people – it is people who kill people. Further, if one takes into account that a criminal is almost always armed and a victim is not, we can ask if a crime would still have been committed if the criminal were aware that the intended victim carried a gun. The danger lies in the intention to kill and not in a lethal device by itself.

How long will the people of our nation have to live with an administration incapable of adequately protecting them? Would the ailing criminal justice system of our country benefit if citizens had the right to defend themselves? It bears repeating that an individual would need to justify to the authorities any use of arms and face punishment if the court finds the explanation unacceptable. So, the right to bear arms would not be a free permit for trigger-happy individuals but would serve to create a responsible society capable of private defence.

Of course, the process established by law ought to be the only means of securing justice should one be the victim of a crime nonetheless. Citizens must not resort to any form of vigilante justice. But when it comes to protection and defence, they must be allowed to carry weapons to create trepidation, doubt and fear in the minds of criminals about a weaponised pushback by a victim.

Enforcement agency powers

The success of a country's criminal justice system is widely understood to be a combination of many factors, chief among them being its conviction rates.[48] Although this notion may be a manifestation of the 'crime control' model of criminal justice[49] ingrained into Indian society, this perception is very real and exists in the collective consciousness of the country. It is created by the collective distrust in the law enforcement mechanism and in the criminal justice system.[50] The obvious method to rectify this distrust is the right to bear arms as a constitutional right.

However, a compromise could be found by expanding the scope of powers of law enforcement through widening the right to use firearms for law enforcement personnel. It may offer a solution to improve criminal justice in India that comes without the drawbacks of allowing people to arm themselves. It would serve to appease the widespread craving for instant justice among our population. A criminal being shot by the police offers immediate and visible justice and is widely cheered. In contrast, a police officer who arrests a criminal and follows the legal process is often met with less enthusiasm, as that path is seen as offering opportunities for the criminal to evade punishment. The public consciousness of India desires and celebrates instant retribution over delayed remedy.

In 2022, the country saw this sort of 'instant justice' when four individuals accused of rape and murder were killed by the police in Hyderabad.[51] This incident was widely celebrated by the general public, who saw it as the speedy delivery of justice to the victims and as well-deserved punishment for the criminals.[52] Similar measures in Uttar Pradesh also found their way into the hearts of many common Indians. This kind of 'instant justice' has its roots in the retributive school of punishment. It is a legitimate school of thought that in ancient times was believed to be the very reason for the existence of a justice system wherein actions have punitive consequences.

The expansion of the powers of law enforcement personnel required to deliver this form of justice would need to have a number of checks and balances in place to prevent its abuse. It would also necessitate better training for police officials and the removal of any form of immunity available to them. In the European Union,[53] law enforcement personnel are trained to adjudicate the existence of a crime or a criminal only when it is prima facie seen to exist before any sort of measure for instant justice can be taken. There should be severe penalties for any misuse of the power to use firearms granted to law enforcement officials. The officials should be held liable under the normal penal provisions of the country should any abuse of this power be proven.

Women empowerment

There are certain specific forms of injustice that are unique to women. While most are aware of these injustices, I list here some of the major ones that need urgent fixing. The three significant items on the list would be (i) women being subjected to physical and emotional sexual harassment; (ii) the disadvantages they suffer in workplaces; and (iii) the cultural injustices they face, including within their own homes and families. The Indian government has traditionally attempted to deal with these issues through statutes and cultural campaigns. The question is whether this approach has had the desired effect. There is no doubt that Indian women today are more empowered than they were at the time of Independence, but would another 75 years of the same approach solve all their problems? If not, then there is a need to consider innovations or even an evolution in the approach taken in the past.

In looking for possible solutions, we have to keep in mind that excessive affirmative action can be counterproductive. This can be illustrated through the parable of the hunter who in an act of kindness picks up some baby birds that fell out of their nest and places them back in it. While the baby birds are comforted, they never learn to fly – because only in their efforts to get back into the nest would they have learned that skill so essential for their lives. Eventually, a predator comes to their nest and the birds could not escape by flying away. The hunter's act of kindness eventually leads to their death. What we can learn from this story is that to make any section of society resilient, it must be allowed the freedom to fail and thereby learn – but maybe not to the extent that the freedom and failure lead to fatality. The suggestion therefore is to limit affirmative action for women to instances of real need and avoid a general application to all women in all circumstances, which would be excessive.

We also have to evaluate whether our society sets expectations for our women without regard to their natural talents and abilities. Has our quest for gender equality resulted in imposing masculine standards on women? Men are never judged by feminine standards. Should the different genders be judged by different standards? Biologically, there are things men are naturally better at, and there are other things that women are better at. We should allow women to pursue occupations more aligned with their femininity without concern that this may result in their delivering lesser economic value than traditionally masculine occupations. Of course, individuals of either gender who desire to pursue professions not aligned with their own gender should also have the right to do so.

Victorian ideals continue to cast a dark shadow over women's lives in India. The legal system and societal perceptions deny women the freedom to express their true selves and their sexuality. In ancient India, women were celebrated for their grace and beauty, and their attire allowed for free expression of their sexuality, unhindered by the judgmental attitude and restrictions of Victorian sensibilities. In the Vedic system, men were obliged to protect the women, and the women in turn were tasked with nurturing the family.[54] However, in the tantric[55] and tribal systems, the woman was unbounded and free, and expressed herself openly. This was shown in the form of the goddess Devi and her consort, Shiva, who was openly accepting of her freedom and rarely tried to rein it in.

Yet, as the Vedic system grew in influence, segregation of occupations and tasks on the basis of gender grew entrenched in various sections of Indian society. This was still viewed as segregation and not suppression. Tales from the Puranas that describe societal behaviour during those periods are replete with exceptions in which an individual crosses the gender divide and takes up an occupation seen as suitable for the other gender. There are stories about men in the kitchen and women in the battlefield and in politics. Societal behaviour that is now recognised as suppression is a later phenomenon, one that begins in the medieval period with the invasions from Central Asia.

As time passed, the influence of Victorian ideas seeped deeply into our culture, bringing with it the repression of many natural human behaviours, in particular those relating to sexuality. We used to be a society that celebrated the fullness of human experience – where women once roamed bare-chested or wearing minimal clothing – but have now become one that forces sexuality into hiding and views such behaviour as lewd. Religious prophets in India never advocated for such repression, but certain monastic orders within Hinduism, Buddhism and Jainism sought to control and streamline the expression of natural feelings. However, their influence was limited when compared with the lasting impact of the ideas that arrived with the British colonials.

Even after Independence, India has struggled to shed the shackles of the colonial mindset. Today, when a girl is born to a Hindu family, the celebratory chants are about the goddess Lakshmi. There is never a mention of a goddess such as Devi, also known as Parvati. I would imagine that this is because the goddess Lakshmi is typically depicted as serving her husband and tending to his needs by pressing his feet, while Parvati is depicted as an equal to her husband, Shiva. Devi does not let the man in her life change the power and control she possesses, which is why Indian society does not want a woman to be like her.

We often hear stories of horrific crimes committed against women in India. The 'Nirbhaya' case[56] of 2012 – which involved the brutal rape and torture of a young woman in Delhi – sent shockwaves through the nation. It was a stark reminder that women in India were unsafe under the patriarchal gaze of our people. This includes not just men but also a vast number of compliant women, who are major contributors to the lack of safety of fellow women in India. Indian women sometimes have to endure uncomfortable situations such as being stared at lewdly or suffering derogatory comments. Some even experience sexual aggression in the form of groping and molestation. This makes them feel vulnerable and insecure.

The strength and courage of the women of India have been showcased by historical figures such as Rani Lakshmi Bai and, in independent India, Indira Gandhi. Despite its rich history of powerful and accomplished women, our country has become increasingly unsafe for women, who continue to face discrimination and disrespect in their everyday lives. Our society must prioritise the independence, safety and empowerment of our women and take proactive steps to ensure that women can live their lives without fear in our country. Education will play a crucial role in challenging societal norms and breaking down the barriers faced by women.

Both sex and sex education need to be destigmatised. Open discussions on sex-related topics can dispel myths and create a healthier understanding of human sexuality. Through awareness and empowerment, the women of this country can reclaim their rights and demand the respect they deserve. The media too has a significant role to play in this narrative. It has the power to raise awareness, sensitise the public and exert pressure on decision-makers. The journey towards a more inclusive and empowered future for Indian women must begin with a collective recognition of traditional Indian values, which held that human sexuality should never be suppressed but embraced as an integral part of one's identity.

The legal system must also contribute to this revolution by undergoing appropriate reforms to recognise the importance of women's safety and their right to be seen as equal to men in every aspect of their lives. The first change on the legal front that can expedite the empowerment of Indian women is the explicit legalisation of prostitution. The second is to truly recognise women as independent adults with their own agency, who are capable of making their own choices in every aspect of their lives.

Explicit legalisation of prostitution

Prostitution is a centuries-old practice in India. Kings, feudal lords and rich merchants often patronised prostitutes. In fact, in ancient India, prostitution used to be a recognised profession that was controlled and regulated by both men and women.[57] Some courtesans such as Amrapali[58] from the kingdom of Vaishali – which corresponds to modern-day Bihar – attained great renown around 500 BCE. Most women who entered this line of work at that time did so of their own free will. Free from the restrictions of society, they willingly became prostitutes.

Sexual harassment and oppression of women are modern-day issues that stem primarily from built-up sexual frustration in men in society today. The clear solution to this societal issue is to legalise prostitution in a controlled manner while also ensuring that the women who enter the profession are consenting adults. It is futile to discuss the morality of prostitution when we are tasked with something far greater and more pressing. Prostitution can curb sexual oppression and relieve the inequalities faced by women in society every day. However, this does not mean that we are deflecting any of this oppression onto sex workers. That is why it is important to ensure that the women in the profession are there of their own will.

Some studies have found that countries where sex trade is illegal are more likely to suffer violence in society. There is also lower use of contraception by illegal sex workers, who have higher rates of contracting diseases such as HIV. PLOS Medicine[59] conducted a study in 33 countries between 1990 and 2018 and found that sex workers who were exposed to repressive policing such as arrests and detention were more likely to face violence from their clients, partners and others. However, prostitutes who were not treated in this brutal manner were half as likely to contract fatal diseases and were approximately 30 per cent more likely to use contraceptive measures.[60]

There is a peculiar aversion within Indian society towards prostitution, and most of the opposition comes from men. It is a puzzling anomaly, because those in favour of it agree that by providing a regulated and safe environment for the fulfilment of sexual desires, many social problems could be alleviated. Legalisation of prostitution would not only reduce incidents of sexual harassment in society but also empower women to take control of their own bodies; it is a matter of their right and liberty.

Why do I ask for *explicit* legitimisation of prostitution? The reason is that prostitution is not actually illegal in India today. Our country only penalises prostitution-related activities such as soliciting, kerb-crawling, trafficking and other non-consensual acts that force women into prostitution.[61] But since we also don't have a law explicitly stating that prostitution itself is legal, public authorities such as the police have turned it into a dirty, immoral act, in effect making it illegal. It means that some Indians consider it acceptable and not immoral that women are regularly harassed and exploited in our country, but decriminalised, controlled prostitution with the consent of women is seen as a crime. It is a contradictory viewpoint, to say the least.

Countries such as Canada, Thailand and Japan have identified a need to legalise controlled prostitution. In Canada, there are strict regulations under the Protection of Communities and Exploited Persons Act that allow communication for selling sex. However, the regulations under the House Government Bill C-36 of 2014 disallow communications intended to get people to buy or purchase sex services. In other words, sex workers are permitted to advertise their own services, but one cannot advertise such services on their behalf. It is also illegal to sell these services in areas where a minor could reasonably be expected to be found, such as playgrounds or in the vicinity of schools. Germany has one of the most organised and progressive approaches to prostitution.[62] It legalises and taxes the practice while also allowing brothels to advertise and process jobs in the profession through human resource companies. Germany passed the Prostitutes Protection Act in 2016 in an attempt to protect the legal rights of sex workers. The legislation includes provisions such as the issuance of permits to engage in the sex trade and even registration certificates for prostitutes.

In Mexico, prostitution is legal under federal laws, and 13 Mexican states allow and regulate prostitution. Some cities have designated 'tolerance zones' to act as red-light districts. The activity of prostitutes in those areas is regulated by the authorities.[63] In the UK, activities such as kerb-crawling, use of force or threat to access prostitutes and trafficking are illegal. In Northern Ireland, the buying of sex is illegal but the selling of it is legal. A government report titled 'Prostitution: Third Report of Session 2016–17'[64] states that the sale and purchase of sexual services are allowed in England and Wales, but related activities such as trafficking and maintaining a brothel are illegal.

Taking cues from these countries, India too must introduce unambiguous legalisation of prostitution. It would be a step in the right direction towards bringing back some of the values of India's 'Golden Age', when women were not judged or violated on the basis of their clothing or demeanour or whom they chose to have sex with. Sexual permissiveness cannot completely eradicate gender inequality, but a lack of it will most definitely induce it in society.

I tested the idea of legalising prostitution while attempting to establish a classical liberal political party. Not a single woman I spoke to was against the idea of legalising prostitution, and most even spoke of it as a natural thing to do. This was probably on account of their belief that autonomy over a woman's body rests solely with the woman herself rather than with societal norms. However, many men were against the idea.

Treating women as equals

Many of our laws have been weighted in favour of women based on the presumption that they are the 'weaker' gender and thereby need the benefits of affirmative action to gain social respect. These laws cover sexual harassment of women at the workplace, the social evil of dowry and the grant of maintenance in divorce cases.

Sexual harassment: One must note that various forms of conduct that amount to sexual harassment at the workplace would also be offences under ordinary criminal law. This includes rape, assault, outraging the modesty of women and criminal intimidation. Since these conducts are dealt with under regular criminal laws, we should focus on conducts that are not considered offences under criminal law but are illegal acts in the workplace. This includes acts such as bullying or discrimination, which are faced equally by men.

The suggestion here is to decriminalise the law while keeping such acts illegal, thereby making them subject to civil remedies. Hence an act that constitutes a criminal offence will continue to be a crime and be addressed under existing criminal law provisions. However, an illegal act that is not a crime will give the victim a right to make a civil claim. When an act is criminalised, the law can be misused by unscrupulous persons in any workforce as a tool for harassment or retaliation. By decriminalising such acts while retaining their illegal character and addressing them through civil and administrative remedies, the law achieves a more balanced and proportionate approach. This ensures that genuine victims have access to effective redressal mechanisms, while protecting individuals from potential abuse of the process. In this way, decriminalisation maintains accountability and deterrence without creating a system that is draconian or prone to misuse.

Dowry: The Anti-Dowry Law has existed since the 1950s, when Indian women were not as empowered as they are today. Today's laws must reflect today's reality, and in that vein, the State needs to consider the enhancement in women's empowerment that has taken place over the last few decades since Independence. The law is now often abused through the filing of false complaints, so we need to consider decriminalising it while keeping the act of demanding dowry illegal. Dowry can be viewed in contractual terms of freedom of choice. Even if we decriminalise the law, it should continue to have civil consequences as an illegal act. Instead of imprisoning the husband and his parents, imposing severe financial penalties could serve as a more effective deterrent. A woman may choose to pursue a civil monetary claim on the grounds of dowry demands, and the court would have the authority to award exemplary damages. This will also help prevent the rampant abuse of today's anti-dowry laws.

That being said, the regular laws that criminalise physical assault, torture, murder, etc. would continue to apply, and if such a crime is committed against a woman by her husband or in-laws, they would face legal consequences whether the actions were connected to a dowry demand or not. But other forms of unacceptable behaviour towards her – even if perpetrated by the same people on the same grounds – should be treated as a civil wrong. The idea remains the same, that is, to decriminalise the act, but to retain its illegality. A woman should be offered help to separate from her husband, seek a divorce and then claim financial compensation if applicable. Such a policy would help women stand up against unacceptable social behaviour even within their own families and foster a culture of intolerance for dowry-related matters in society.

Maintenance after divorce: The presumption that a man carries the responsibility of taking care of the financial needs of his spouse – or former spouse – originates from a time when separated or divorced women had next to no opportunities to generate an income by themselves and needed greater economic protection than they do today. But now Indian women are significantly better educated, experienced and confident, particularly in urban areas. Therefore, they are in a much better position to take care of themselves economically than women of past generations.

Given this change, should former wives continue to be ringfenced from the responsibility of taking care of their own economic needs? At a time when women legitimately seek equality with men in society, their efforts to that end are delegitimised when they simultaneously push the burden of economic well-being onto their husbands. In the age of quality, we need to revisit the presumption that the man has to bear the entire economic burden of his family. This would also empower women to think of their own financial stability should their marriages end in divorce. It would also lead to a social movement in which families with daughters put in the same level of effort to empower their daughters as they do for their sons.

Other measures: We should consider the provision of financial support specifically for women as well as government-sponsored training so that they can pursue specialised professions that financially empower them. I also suggest that a cadre of female police officers be present at police stations and in courts to deal with gender-based crimes against women.

7

Looking Ahead: Through the Eyes of the Common Person

Phase 1: Year 2028 – The first glimpses of change after implementation of suggestions in chapters 1 and 2

Digitising justice

Priya, a small-town litigant, no longer needs to travel miles or brave intimidating courtrooms. She watches her hearing livestreamed at home with her family beside her, able to see her lawyer's performance and the judge's conduct in real time. This transparency makes her feel empowered to demand higher standards.

Behind the scenes, judges and lawyers draw upon an online knowledge grid that instantly provides updated case law and statutes. Outdated precedents no longer derail proceedings. Priya's case moves faster, and decisions are based on law and substance, not on the personality or prestige of lawyers. Qualitatively, decisions of lower courts are of higher quality, similar to the quality one might expect in a higher court, and as a result, it has become difficult to successfully appeal decisions of the lower courts. Workload on the higher courts is consequently reduced.

Within a few years, virtual courts and AI-powered case analysis further cut costs and delays, making justice more predictable and citizen-friendly.

Only a few years earlier, Priya would have endured crowded, opaque courtrooms, uncertain whether her lawyer was diligent or whether the judge had access to the right information, and she would have doubted the quality of judicial decision-making. This is no longer the case.

Business environment reforms

Nilanjana, who runs a modest restaurant, contracts a logistics vendor, Rohit, to supply essential goods. He does his best to avoid breaching the contract, since the consequences could result in severe damages and costs for him. The other side of the coin is that Rohit no longer fears the prospect of not getting paid, for were that to happen, the consequences of non-payment would mean penal damages imposed on Nilanjana. Hence, with contractual certainty, the speed of business or the speed of money circulation has gone up. India's GDP has seen a manifold jump.

If Rohit defaults, Nilanjana can swiftly sue him, win damages and refocus on growing her business rather than battling procedural delays. Strengthened laws now make non-compliance expensive. Courts impose significant financial penalties, contingency fees reduce upfront costs of lawyers and fast-track commercial courts resolve disputes swiftly.

Frivolous injunctions too are a thing of the past, since vacation of an injunction results in high costs for the person who obtained the injunction in a frivolous manner.

Meanwhile, whistle-blowers in large corporations feel safe to expose fraud, pushing companies towards compliance. This has forced a rethink on the part of the promoter and owner community: they now live in fear of an insider exposing their wrongdoing. Hence, the environment of compliance has improved. In the past whistle-blowers feared retaliation from both their employers and the system.

The new order signals to entrepreneurs like Nilanjana that integrity and fairness are rewarded, not punished.

And lastly, with a higher ease of doing business, fewer permits and licences, Nilanjana can focus on and expand her business rapidly. She started as a small-time entrepreneur, focused on the business and now has a multi-city enterprise. A higher level of legal compliance will kick in after a few years, once her business is sufficiently large, and she can afford consultants and has sufficient personal wealth.

Phase 2: Year 2030 – Deeper structural shifts

Harmonising law with the Indian mind

Suraj, an honest street-food vendor working hard to make ends meet, once lived in fear of his business being impeded by obscure health regulations he never knew existed, and of being extorted by lower officials for this failing. Under the old system, ignorance was no defence, and prosecutions were arbitrary.

Today, the prosecution must prove that Suraj knew or had a reasonable opportunity to know the law before he can be penalised. Laws are published, publicised and explained in accessible formats. Courts adopt a victim-oriented approach: Suraj's rights are safeguarded while ensuring fairness to the accused.

Criticising judicial conduct is no longer dangerous; reformed contempt laws allow citizens to question judgments without fear. This has strengthened public trust in the judiciary and brought the law closer to the people it serves.

And last but not least, when a litigant goes to court, she goes to an inquisitional court that attempts to determine the truth and deliver justice in the manner the judge feels appropriate in the circumstances of the case. This judge is no longer a prisoner of having to choose which lawyer makes a more convincing argument, regardless of the truth, and is no longer bound by past decisions that the judge feels are incorrect or must be inapplicable in the present case.

Constitutional reforms

Naina, once trapped in the backlog of appeals before the Supreme Court, now sees a leaner apex court focused exclusively on constitutional questions. Everyday appeals are swiftly handled by a final court of appeals.

Judges are chosen through open parliamentary scrutiny, their performance reviewed not only by peers but also by citizens like Naina. Incentives are tied to the quality and speed of justice. Articles 136 and 142, once stretched to cover wide swathes of litigation, are redefined to limit judicial overreach. Public interest cases are heard in specialised tribunals, freeing the Supreme Court to guard constitutional principles.

For Naina, justice is no longer a distant hope – it is timely, accessible and rooted in accountability.

Judges have also become more independent-minded. They no longer have to consider post-retirement occupations for themselves. However, judges are now more accountable than ever before – for any unjustified or incorrect decisions. Sovereign immunity is no longer available. Ajay, once a victim of poor judgments and endless delays, can now seek recourse against judicial negligence. Sovereign immunity is rebalanced: judges and officials are accountable for egregious errors or misconduct. This has fostered professionalism and diligence across the system.

Out-of-the-box ideas

Monarch, a young advocate, begins his career in a transformed legal profession. Gone are archaic dress codes and medieval language barriers. Lawyers openly market their services, purchase professional insurance and negotiate contingency fees. Advocacy is driven by both conscience and aligned financial incentives, elevating the quality of representation. Clients encounter a significantly higher level of professionalism at the hands of lawyers.

The disadvantage of being a young lawyer, in terms of both how he is received in court and how clients perceive him, is a thing of the past. Merit has become more important in this reformed world of lawyers.

For citizens, safety no longer depends solely on the State. Carefully regulated reforms allow individuals limited rights to self-defence, reducing petty crime and easing pressure on courts.

Women feel this change most profoundly. Diya, a corporate employee, walks home with greater confidence. Civil remedies for dowry demands, targeted financial support in marital disputes and stronger women's police and judicial presence reinforce her independence. Sex work, once criminalised and unsafe, is now legalised and regulated to protect consenting adults like Kalki, who now has access to support services and legal safeguards. This has contributed to less sexual harassment than women of the past faced in their daily lives.

The cumulative effect is a society where dignity, equality, and accountability are not just ideals but lived realities.

A break from the past

What unites these stories – from Priya's digital hearing to Nilanjana's fast-track commercial case, from Suraj's protection against arbitrary prosecution to Naina's empowered role in constitutional reform – is the sense that justice has finally become citizen-centred.

The reforms dismantle a system once mired in opacity, delay and elitism. They replace it with one that values transparency, accountability and efficiency. Citizens see tangible improvements, such as:

i. speed and predictability in justice delivery,
ii. accessibility through technology and cost reforms,
iii. fairness in laws that respect context and reality,
iv. accountability of judges, officials and corporations alike, and
v. empowerment of women, workers, small entrepreneurs and vulnerable groups.

Closing reflection

India's legal journey is not about cosmetic tweaks but about a profound rebalancing of power, away from institutions and elites, and towards the citizen.

The common litigant, the street vendor, the small entrepreneur, the young lawyer, the working woman – all now see law as a tool for dignity, not intimidation. They live in a system where compliance is natural, accountability is real and justice is not delayed into irrelevance.

The reforms envisioned in this book are not utopian dreams but pragmatic steps, each rooted in international best practice and tailored to Indian realities. Together, they sketch a future in which every citizen, whether rich or poor, powerful or powerless, feels the law is on their side.

The new order is not defined by fear of authority but by trust in justice. It unlocks an India where opportunity is matched with fairness, where power is balanced by accountability and where the everyday citizen finally stands at the centre of the nation's legal universe.

Acknowledgements

My immense appreciation and profound thanks to the people without whom this book would not have got off the ground. They helped with research, writing, editing and making the book accessible to lay readers. So thank you, Nilanjana Ghosh, Stuti Agrawal and Yash Vijay – all advocates; Capt. Sanjay Gahlot, IRS (Retd); Varun Sen Bahl, lawyer and policy professional; Sabir Hussain, journalist; and last but not least, Kripa Raman, my editor.

Thanks also to the team at Bloomsbury India for all the help. Their edits made the book so much lighter to read.

And a shoutout once more to my buddy Capt. Sanjay Gahlot, who helped put together the cartoons for the book.

Notes

CHAPTER 1 THE FROG ON A SLOW BOIL: A QUEST FOR TRUE FREEDOM

1 Association of Democratic Reforms, National Survey, 2019. Available online: https://adrindia.org/content/jobs-health-care-and-drinking-water-top-priorities-voters-govt-performance-scored-below (accessed on 1 February 2025).

2 A. Sekhri and A. Gupta, 'Section 66A and Other Legal Zombies', Internet Freedom Foundation Working Paper No. 2/2018. Available online: https://papers.ssrn.com/sol3/papers.cfm?abstract_id=3275893 (accessed on 1 February 2025).

3 As per data released in 2020 by the National Crime Records Bureau, over 76 per cent of prison inmates in India were undertrials. '4.83 Lakh Indians in Jail up to 2020-end, Less Than One-Fourth Convicts: Data', *Economic Times*, 3 February 2022.

4 According to the Supreme Court's website, there were 67,898 cases pending in the apex court as of 1 May 2021. The pendency of cases in the high courts and district courts is even higher. On 20 June 2021, the National Judicial Data Grid (NJDG) statistics showed that more than 58 lakh cases were pending in high courts and over 3.8 crore in district courts across the country. Available online: https://scdg.sci.gov.in/scnjdg/ (accessed on 1 February 2025).

5 'Strategy for New India @75', NITI Aayog, 2018, p. 180. Available online: https://niti.gov.in/sites/default/files/2019-01/Strategy_for_New_India_0.pdf (accessed on 1 February 2025).

6 This phrase encapsulates four different approaches to achieving a goal or resolving a matter. 'Saam' means a peaceful and amicable resolution; 'Daam' refers to using economic means to reach a desired goal; 'Dhand' denotes the use of force or punishment; and 'Bhed' involves creating differences to achieve a goal. Also see: 'What Is Sam-Dan-Dhanda-Bhed?', *Hinduism*

Stack Exchange, 2023. Available online: https://hinduism.stackexchange.com/questions/54423/what-is-sam-dan-danda-bhed (accessed on 1 February 2025).

7 'Ram Rajya' was a period in ancient Indian tradition when justice prevailed and every citizen was content with the manner of governance, with King Rama as the ruler as depicted in the Ramayana.

8 The Constitution of India, 1949.

9 *Vishwa Hindu Adhivakta Sangh and Ors. v. Union of India and Ors.* 1993 (1) UPLBEC 501.

10 M.K. Gandhi, 'The UP Tour', *Young India*, 305 (Gujarat: 1929).

11 *Kesavananda Bharati Sripadagalvaru v. State of Kerala* AIR 1973 SC 1461; *Indira Nehru Gandhi v. Raj Narain and Ors.* AIR 1975 SC 2299; *S.G. Jaisinghani v. Union of India and Ors.* AIR 1967 SC 1427; *Justice K.S. Puttaswamy and Ors. v. Union of India and Ors.* (2017) 10 SCC 1.

12 Harish Narasappa, *Rule of Law in India: A Quest for Reason* (Oxford University Press, 2018).

13 N.A. Deshpande, 'The Importance of Keeping Promises', *The Wisdom Library*. Available online: https://www.wisdomlib.org/hinduism/book/the-padma-purana/d/doc365310.html.

14 1 John 2:5, NIV, The Holy Bible. Available online: https://www.biblegateway.com/passage/?search=1%20John%202%3A5&version=NIV (accessed on 1 February 2025).

15 'No Greater Sin Than a Promise Not Kept', *The Morning Call*, 5 October 2021. Available online: https://www.mcall.com/2011/01/14/faith-column-no-greater-sin-that-a-promise-not-kept/#:~:text=In%20Islam%2C%20keeping%20one's%20word,%E2%80%9CO%20you%20who%20believe (accessed on 1 February 2025).

16 Prevention of Money Laundering Act, 2002.

17 *Anderson, et al v. Pacific Gas & Electric Company*, Superior Court for the County of San Bernardino, Barstow Division, File BCV 00300 (1993).

Chapter 2 Digitising Justice: Advancing Courtroom Technology

1 *Swapnil Tripathi and Ors. v. Union of India and Ors.* (2018) 10 SCC 639.

2 S.R. Gupta and U. Sharma, 'Live-Streaming and Courts: Accessible, Affordable and Accountable Judiciary', *SCC Blog Online*, 23 June 2021. Available online: https://blog.scconline.gen.in/post/2021/06/23/live-streaming-n-courts-accessible-affordable-and-accountable-judiciary-part-2/ (accessed on 1 February 2025).

3 'Model Rules for Live Streaming and Recording of Court Proceedings'. Available online:https://cdnbbsr.s3waas.gov.in/s388ef51f0bf911e452e8dbb1d807a81ab/uploads/2021/06/2022091599.pdf (accessed on 1 February 2025).

4 J. Battle, 'Open Justice, Court Reform', *The Bar Council of UK*, 9 November 2022. Available online: https://www.barcouncil.org.uk/resource/open-justice-court-reporting-and-the-rule-of-law.html (accessed on 1 February 2025).

5 *Scott v. Scott* [1913] AC 417 (HL).

6 A few oft-cited rulings on the open court principle are *Scott v. Scott* [1913] AC 417 (HL). (House of Lords, UK) and *Attorney General (Nova Scotia) v. MacIntyre* [1982] 1 SCR 175 (Supreme Court of Canada). On the principle in India, see *Swapnil Tripathi and Ors. v. Union of India* (2018) 10 SCC 639.

7 J. Rawls, *A Theory of Justice*, Rev. Ed., p. 75 (Harvard University Press, 1971). Available online: https://giuseppecapograssi.files.wordpress.com/2014/08/rawls99.pdf (accessed on 1 February 2025).

8 'Inefficiency and Judicial Delay: New Insights from the Delhi High Court', Vidhi Centre for Legal Policy, 29 March 2017. Available online: https://vidhilegalpolicy.in/research/2017-3-29-inefficiency-and-judicial-delay-new-insights-from-the-delhi-high-court/ (accessed on 1 February 2025).

9 S. Upadhyay, 'Misbehaviour with Lady Judge: Allahabad High Court Orders Examination of CCTV Footage of the Incident', *LiveLaw*, 20 July 2023. Available online: https://www.livelaw.in/high-court/allahabad-high-court/allahabad-high-court-advocates-misbehaviour-lady-judge-forensic-examination-cctv-footage-incident-233223 (accessed on 1 February 2025).

10 S. Rautray, '70K Pending Cases: Supreme Court Blames It on Adjournments', *Economic Times*, 20 April 2022. Available online: https://economictimes.indiatimes.com/

news/india/70k-pending-cases-supreme-court-blames-it-on-adjournments/articleshow/90943695.cms?from=mdr (accessed on 1 February 2025).

11 'Inefficiency and Judicial Delay: New Insights from the Delhi High Court', Vidhi Centre for Legal Policy. Available online: https://vidhilegalpolicy.in/research/2017-3-29-inefficiency-and-judicial-delay-new-insights-from-the-delhi-high-court/ (accessed on 1 February 2025).

12 V.A. da Silva, 'Big Brother Is Watching the Court: Effects of TV Broadcasting on Judicial Deliberation', *Verfassung und Recht in Übersee/ Law and Politics in Africa, Asia and Latin America*, 51 (4): 437–55. Available online: https://www.jstor.org/stable/26745776 (accessed on 1 February 2025).

13 Argument Audio, Supreme Court of the US of America. Available online: https://supremecourt.gov/oral_arguments/argument_audio/2023#:~:text=The%20public%20may%20either%20download,recording%20oral%20arguments%20in%201955 (accessed on 1 February 2025).

14 'SC Expresses Concerns over Frivolous Appeals Clogging the System', *The Leaflet*, 16 March 2022. Available online: https://theleaflet.in/sc-expresses-concern-over-frivolous-appeals-clogging-the-system/ (accessed on 1 February 2025).

15 'Live Streaming of Court Proceedings Are Being Misused, Lawyers Body Expresses Concern', *Latest Laws*, 11 July 2022. Available online: https://www.latestlaws.com/latest-news/live-streaming-of-court-proceedings-are-being-misused-lawyers-body-expresses-concern-187162 (accessed on 1 February 2025).

16 *Swapnil Tripathi and Ors. v Union of India and Ors.* (2018) 10 SCC 639.

'Indubitably, live streaming of court proceedings has the potential of throwing up an option to the public to witness live court proceedings which they otherwise could not have due to logistical issues and infrastructural restrictions of courts; and would also provide them with a more direct sense of what has transpired.'

17 In *Justice K.S. Puttaswamy and Ors. v. Union of India* (2017) 10 SCC 1 the Supreme Court of India delivered a landmark judgment on the 'right to privacy'. The court

held that the right to privacy is 'intrinsic to life and personal liberty' and is therefore inherently protected under Article 21 of the Constitution of India as well as being part of the fundamental freedoms guaranteed under Part III of the Constitution.

18 The Judiciary, Government of India. Available online: https://legalaffairs.gov.in/sites/default/files/chapter%207.pdf (accessed on 1 February 2025).

19 'Breaking Up Judge's Isolation, Guidelines to Improve the Judges Skills and Competences, Strengthen Knowledge Sharing and Collaboration, and Move Beyond a Culture of Judicial Isolation', European Commission for the Efficiency of Justice, 6 December 2019. Available online: https://rm.coe.int/cepej-2019-15-en-knowledge-sharing/16809939e4 (accessed 1 February 2024).

20 Judges for Democracy (Juezas y Jueces *para la* Democracia). Available online: www.juecesdemocracia.es (accessed on 1 February 2025).

21 The European e-Justice Portal. Available online: https://e-justice.europa.eu/home?plang=en&action=home (accessed on 1 February 2025).

22 A. Aswathappa, 'The Parliamentary Standing Committee on Virtual Courts in India', DAKSH, 16 September 2020. Available online: https://www.dakshindia.org/the-parliamentary-standing-committee-on-virtual-courts-in-india/ (accessed on 1 February 2025).

23 J. Clark, 'Evaluation of Remote Hearing During the COVID-19 Pandemic', HM Courts & Tribunals Service, December 2021. Available online: https://assets.publishing.service.gov.uk/government/uploads/system/uploads/attachment_data/file/1040183/Evaluation_of_remote_hearings_v23.pdf (accessed on 1 February 2025).

24 M. Legg and A. Song, 'The Courts, the Remote Hearing and the Pandemic: From Action to Reflection', *UNSW Law Journal*, 44 (1): 126–66. Available online: https://www.unswlawjournal.unsw.edu.au/wp-content/uploads/2021/04/04-Legg-Song.pdf (accessed on 1 February 2025).

25 J. Raczynski, 'The Current Status of the (Virtual) Courts', *Thomson Reuters*, 22 July 2020. Available online: https://

www.thomsonreuters.com/en-us/posts/legal/virtual-courts/ (accessed on 1 February 2025); and 'How Courts Embraced Technology, Met the Pandemic Challenge, and Revolutionized Their Operations', *Pew Trusts*, 1 December 2021. Available online: https://www.pewtrusts.org/en/research-and-analysis/reports/2021/12/how-courts-embraced-technology-met-the-pandemic-challenge-and-revolutionized-their-operations (accessed on 1 February 2025).

26 K. Sloan, 'Beam Me Up, Counselor. Are Hologram Witnesses Headed to Court?', Reuters, 17 May 2023. Available online: https://www.reuters.com/legal/government/beam-me-up-counselor-are-hologram-witnesses-headed-court-2023-05-16/ (accessed on 1 February 2025).

27 'Turning 50: Delhi High Court Looks at Future and Hologram Technology', *Financial Times*, 28 October 2016. Available online: https://www.financialexpress.com/india-news/turning-50-delhi-high-court-looks-at-future-and-hologram-technology/432749/ (accessed on 1 February 2025).

28 D. Braue, 'VR to Overhaul Court Rooms: Walk-throughs to Help Jurors Find Consensus', *Information Age*, 26 July 2021. Available online: VR to overhaul court rooms | Information Age | ACS (accessed on 1 February 2025).

29 R.S. Spandana, 'AI and the Law: A New Era in the Justice System', *Supreme Court Observer*, 25 February 2023. Available online: https://www.scobserver.in/journal/ai-and-the-law-a-new-era-in-the-justice-system/ (accessed on 1 February 2025).

30 R.E. Stern, B.L. Liebman, et al., 'Automating Fairness? AI in the Chinese Court', *Columbia Journal of Transnational Law*, 59: 515 (2021). Available online: https://scholarship.law.columbia.edu/cgi/viewcontent cgi?article=3946&context=faculty_scholarship (accessed on 1 February 2025).

31 B. Harris, 'Could an AI Ever Replace a Judge in Court?', World Governments Summit, 7 November 2017. Available online: https://live.worldgovernmentsummit.org/observer/articles/2017/detail/could-an-ai-ever-replace-a-judge-in-court (accessed on 1 February 2025).

32 R.S. Spandana, 'AI and the Law: A New Era in the Justice System?', *Supreme Court Observer*, 25 February 2023. Available

online: https://www.scobserver.in/journal/ai-and-the-law-a-new-era-in-the-justice-system/ (accessed on 1 February 2025).

33 Ibid.

Chapter 3 Revamping India's Commercial Legal System

1 'World Bank Poverty and Inequality Portal and Macro Poverty Outlook', World Bank Group, 16 September 2024. Available online: https://www.worldbank.org/en/country/india/overview (accessed on 1 February 2025).

2 'Social Security Welfare Schemes', Ministry of Labour and Employment. Available online: https://eshram.gov.in/social-security-welfare-schemes#:~:text=Benefits,6000%2F%2D%20monthly%20pension%20jointly (accessed on 1 February 2025).

3 R. Desai, U. Chachra, et al., 'India Equity Strategy and Economics', *Morgan Stanley Research*, 29 May 2023. https://www.flame.edu.in/pdfs/fil/presentations/Ridham-Desai-India-Equity-Strategy-and-Economics-FIL-With-The-Masters-June2023.pdf (accessed on 1 February 2025).

4 'Indian Unicorns: The Torchbearers of the Indian Economy', Invest India, 27 July 2022. Available online: https://www.investindia.gov.in/team-india-blogs/indian-unicorns-torchbearers-indian-economy (accessed on 1 February 2025).

5 Ibid.

6 U. Misra, 'Why Improving on World Bank's Ease of Doing Business Rankings Might Have Hurt Economies', *Indian Express*, 23 May 2023. Available online: https://indianexpress.com/article/explained/explained-economics/world-bank-ease-of-doing-business-rankings-gdp-impact-explained-8623891/ (accessed on 1 February 2025).

7 A. Magazine and P. Mukul, 'World Bank to Stop Ease of Doing Business Report as Probe Finds Data Juggling', *Indian Express*, 18 September 2021. Available online: https://indianexpress.com/article/business/economy/world-bank-to-stop-ease-of-doing-business-report-as-probe-finds-data-juggling-7516537/ (accessed on 1 February 2025).

8 EIU Business Environment Rankings, Economist Intelligence. Available online: https://www.eiu.com/n/global-themes/

business-environment-rankings/ (accessed on 1 February 2025).

9 S. Chadha, 'Explained: Why India Now Ranks Above China in Global Business Environment Ranking', *Times of India*, 27 December 2022. Available online: https://timesofindia.indiatimes.com/business/india-business/explained-why-india-now-ranks-above-china-in-a-global-business-environment-ranking/articleshow/96535024.cms (accessed on 1 February 2025).

10 M. Mittal, 'India Turns 3rd Most Improving Market in Business Environment Ranking: EIU Report', *MoneyControl*, 15 November 2024. Available online: https://www.moneycontrol.com/news/business/economy/india-turns-3rd-most-improving-market-in-business-environment-ranking-eiu-report-12867978.html (accessed on 1 February 2025).

11 'India's Richest 1% Has Highest Concentration of Wealth in Decades, Study Shows', Reuters, 20 March 2024. Available online: https://www.reuters.com/world/india/indias-richest-1-has-highest-concentration-wealth-decades-study-shows-2024-03-20/ (accessed on 1 February 2025).

12 *Hadley & Anr. v. Baxendale & Ors.* [1854] EWHC Exch J70.

13 *Rookes v. Barnard* [1964] UKHL 1.

14 *BMW of North America, Inc. v. Gore*, 517 U.S. 559 (1996).

15 'BNP Paribas Agrees to Plead Guilty and to Pay $8.9 Billion for Illegally Processing Financial Transactions for Countries Subject to U.S Economic Sanctions', US Department of Justice, 30 June 2014. Available online: https://www.justice.gov/archives/opa/pr/bnp-paribas-agrees-plead-guilty-and-pay-89-billion-illegally-processing-financial

16 *Adobe Systems v. P. Bhoominathan* (2009) 39 PTC 658 (Del); and A. Jain and G. Gokhale, 'India: A Pinch for Privacy- Punitive Penalty Is the Court's Way', *Mondaq*, 4 April 2019. Available online: www.mondaq.com/india/copyright/794742/a-pinch-for-piracy---punitive-penalty-is-the-courts-way (accessed on 1 February 2025).

17 P. Pawar and S.C. Irani, 'Costs Regime in Civil Litigation in India: A Paper Tiger', JSA Advocates & Solicitors, 8 June 2021. Available online: https://www.jsalaw.com/articles-publications/costs-regime-in-civil-litigation-in-india-a-

paper-tiger/#:~:text=Sections%2035%2C%2035A%2C%20and%2035B%20of%20the%20Code%20stipulate%20provisions,costs%20for%20delay%E2%80%9D%2C%20respectively (accessed on 1 February 2025).

18 Costs in Civil Litigation, Report No. 240, Law Commission of India. Available online: https://cdnbbsr.s3waas.gov.in/s3ca0daec69b5adc880fb464895726dbdf/uploads/2022/08/2022081077-3.pdf (accessed on 1 February 2025).

19 *Ashok Kumar Mittal v. Ram Kumar Gupta and Ors.* (2009) 2 SCC 656.

20 *Sanjeev Kumar Jain v. Raghubir Saran Charitable Trust* (2012) 1 SCC 455.

21 *Manindra Chandra Nandi v. Aswini Kumar Acharjya* ILR (1921) 48 Cal 427.

22 *Vinod Seth v. Devinder Bajaj* (2010) 8 SCC 1.

23 *Salem Advocate Bar Association, Tamil Nadu v. Union of India* AIR 2005 SC 3353.

24 *Vinod Seth v. Devinder Bajaj* (2010) 8 SCC 1.

25 Ibid.

26 Costs in Civil Litigation, Report No. 240, Law Commission of India. Available online: https://cdnbbsr.s3waas.gov.in/s3ca0daec69b5adc880fb464895726dbdf/uploads/2022/08/2022081077-3.pdf (accessed on 1 February 2025).

27 *G.T. Girish v. Y. Subba Raju (D) By LRS and Anr.* [2022] 8 SCR. 991.

28 'Late Commercial Payments: Charging Interest and Debt Recovery', Government of UK. Available online: https://www.gov.uk/late-commercial-payments-interest-debt-recovery/charging-interest-commercial-debt (accessed on 1 February 2025).

29 Justice S.S. Dhavan, 'The Indian Judicial System: A Historical Survey', Allahabad High Court. Available online: https://www.allahabadhighcourt.in/event/TheIndianJudicialSystem_SSDhavan.html (accessed on 1 February 2025).

30 M. Chakraborty, '1899–1996: Tracing the Course of Codification of Arbitration Law in India', VIA Mediation and Arbitration Centre. Available online: https://viamediationcentre.org/readnews/Mjc2/1899-1996-tracing-the-course-of-codification-of-arbitration-law-in-India (accessed on 1 February 2025).

31 Ibid.
32 Practise Notes, 'Ad Hoc Arbitration: An Introduction to the Key Features of Ad Hoc Arbitration', *LexisNexis*. Available online: https://www.lexisnexis.co.uk/legal/guidance/ad hoc-arbitration-an-introduction-to-the-key-features-of-ad hoc-arbitration (accessed on 1 February 2025).
33 The Arbitration and Conciliation Act 1996, s. 9(2).
34 Notification dated 3 June 2024, Department of Expenditure, Procurement Policy Division, Ministry of Finance, No.F.1/2/2024-PPD.
35 A. Kumar and A. Hansaraman, 'Institutional Arbitration: The Right Choice for Arbitration Users in India', *Bar and Bench*, 29 September 2022. Available online: https://www.barandbench.com/columns/institutional-arbitration-the-right-choice-for-arbitration-users-in-india (accessed on 1 February 2025).
36 Ibid.
37 *Afcons Infrastructure Ltd. and Ors. v. Cherian Varkay Construction Co. (P) Ltd. and Ors.* (2010) 8 SCC 24.
38 T. Ollapally, A. Sreehari and S. Ramakrishnan, 'The Mediation Gap: Where India Stands and How Far It Must Go', DAKSH. Available online: https://www.dakshindia.org/Daksh_Justice_in_India/14_chapter_04.xhtml#:~:text=The%20non%2Dappearance%20of%20parties,per%20cent%20of%20such%20cases.&text=In%20comparison%2C%20in%20Delhi%2C%2056,terminated%20prior%20to%20mediation%20commencing (accessed on 1 February 2025).
39 'National Conference on Mediation', *SCC Online*, 15 April 2023. Available online: https://www.scconline.com/blog/post/2023/04/15/national-conference-on-mediation-at-the-dawn-of-golden-age/ (accessed on 1 February 2025).
40 G. Agarwal, 'From Conflict to Collaboration: Pre-Litigation Mediation After the Mediation Act, 2023', *NLIU Law Review*, 12 November 2024. Available online: https://nliulawreview.nliu.ac.in/blog/from-conflict-to-collaboration-pre-litigation-mediation-after-the-mediation-act-2023/#:~:text=Over%2050%2C000%20cases%20have%20been,April%202022%-20and%20June%202023 (accessed on 1 February 2025).
41 S. Rajendran, 'Mediation Finding Favour in Dispute Settlement', Hindu Centre for Politics and Public Policy,

13 June 2020. Available online: https://www.thehinducentre.com/the-arena/current-issues/article31810363.ece (accessed on 1 February 2025).

42 S. Tigga, 'Change in Mindset Crucial for Success of Mediaton Processes: Bombay HC Chief Justice Upadhyaya', *Indian Express*, 15 October 2023. Available online: https://indianexpress.com/article/cities/pune/change-mindset-crucial-success-mediation-processes-bombay-hc-chief-justice-upadhyaya-8983959/ (accessed on 1 February 2025).

43 S. Rajendran, 'Mediation Finding Favour in Dispute Settlement', Hindu Centre for Politics and Public Policy, 13 June 2020. Available online: https://www.thehinducentre.com/the-arena/current-issues/article31810363.ece (accessed on 1 February 2025).

44 'The Tenth Mediation Audit', Centre for Effective Dispute Resolution. Available online: https://www.cedr.com/wp-content/uploads/2023/02/Tenth-CEDR-Mediation-Audit-2023.pdf (accessed on 1 February 2025).

45 L. Sridharan, 'What, How, Where, When and Why of the Mediation Act, 2023', Lakshmikumaran & Sridharan Attorneys. Available online: https://www.lakshmisri.com/newsroom/news-briefings/what-how-where-when-and-why-of-the-mediation-act-2023/ (accessed on 1 February 2025).

46 There may be no data to track this behaviour but practising commercial lawyers who regularly negotiate contracts often observe such resistance during contractual negotiations.

47 B. Debroy and S. Jain, 'Strengthening Arbitration and Its Enforcement in India', National Institute of Urban Affairs. Available online: https://smartnet.niua.org/sites/default/files/resources/Arbitration.pdf (accessed on 1 February 2025).

48 'Of Flawed Considerations and Failed Legislations: Observations From the Implementation of the Commercial Courts Act, 2015', *Bar and Bench*, 16 June 2020. Available online: https://www.barandbench.com/columns/the-commercial-courts-act-2015-notes-on-considerations-and-observations-from-its-implementation (accessed on 1 February 2025).

49 Law Commission of India, 188th Report on the Constitution of Hi-tech Fast Track Commercial Divisions in High Courts. Available online: http://lawcommissionofindia.nic.

in/reports/188th%20report.pdf (accessed on 1 February 2025); and Law Commission of India, 253rd Report on Commercial Division, Commercial Appellate Division and Commercial Courts Bill, 2015. Available online: http://lawcommissionofindia.nic.in/reports/Report_No.253_Commercial_Division_and_Commercial_Appellate_Division_of_High_Courts_and__Commercial_Courts_Bill._2015.pdf (accessed on 1 February 2025).

50 Ibid.

51 V. Mishra and A. Jauhar, 'Commercial Courts: A Failure in Implementation', NDTV Profit, 21 June 2019. Available online: https://www.bqprime.com/opinion/commercial-courts-a-failure-in-implementation (accessed on 1 February 2025).

52 S. Krishnaswamy and V.M. Aithala, 'Commercial Courts in India: Three Puzzles for Legal System Reform', *Journal of India Law and Society*, 2 September 2020.

53 Reforms in the Judiciary: Some Suggestions', Report No. 230, Law Commission of India, August 2009.

54 National Judicial Data Grid, High Courts of India. Available online: https://njdg.ecourts.gov.in/hcnjdg_v2/ (accessed on 1 February 2025).

55 *Union of India v. R. Gandhi* (2010) 11 SCC 1.

56 M. Neelakantan, 'Indian Tribunals: Is the Patch to Hell Paved with Good Intentions?', *SCC Times*, 6 July 2021. Available online: https://www.scconline.com/blog/post/2021/07/06/indian-tribunals-is-the-path-to-hell-paved-with-good-intention/ (accessed on 1 February 2025).

57 'The Tribunal System in India', PRS India. Available online: https://prsindia.org/billtrack/prs-products/the-tribunal-system-in-india-3750#_edn19 (accessed on 1 February 2025).

58 P. Mohanty, 'The Feats and Failures of IBC: Why It Must Change', *Fortune India*, 29 October 2021. Available online: https://www.fortuneindia.com/opinion/the-feats-failures-of-ibc-why-it-must-change/106119 (accessed on 1 February 2025).

59 'Financial Haircuts Under IBC Process and Government Measures', Taxguru, 28 November 2024.

Available online: https://taxguru.in/corporate-law/financial-haircuts-ibc-process-government-measures.html (accessed on 1 February 2025).

60 'Videocon Insolvency: Creditors to Take 96% Haircut on Dues; NCLT Requests Increase in Pay-Out', *Economic Times*, 16 June 2021. Available online: https://economictimes.indiatimes.com/news/company/corporate-trends/videocon-insolvency-creditors-to-take-96-haircut-on-dues-nclt-requests-increase-in-pay-out/articleshow/83561586.cms.

61 'Ruchi Soya: Lenders to Take 52% Haircut as Patanjali's Plan Gets Green Signal', *Moneycontrol*, 2 May 2019. Available online: https://www.moneycontrol.com/news/business/companies/ruchi-soya-lenders-to-take-52-haircut-as-patanjalis-plan-gets-green-signal-3921981.html#:~:text=With%20Patanjali%20Ayurved%20acquiring%20debt-ridden%20oil%20firm%20Ruchi,National%20Company%20Law%20Tribunal%20%28NCLT%29%20on%20May%207; also see: 'Patanjali Secures Rs 3,200 Crore Loan from Banks to buy Ruchi Soya', *Economic Times*, 29 November 2019. Available online: https://economictimes.indiatimes.com/industry/services/retail/patanjali-secures-rs-3200-crore-loan-from-banks-to-buy-ruchi-soya/articleshow/72296548.cms.

62 'Implementation of Insolvency and Bankruptcy Code: Pitfalls and Solutions', Report No. 32, Standing Committee on Finance, Lok Sabha (2020–21). Available online: https://eparlib.sansad.in/bitstream/123456789/811572/1/17_Finance_32.pdf (accessed on 1 February 2025).

63 *Gujarat Bottling Co. Ltd v. The Coca Cola Company and Ors.* AIR 1995 SC 2372.

64 *Best Sellers Retail (India) Pvt. Ltd v. Aditya Birla Nuvo Ltd and Ors.* AIR 2012 SC 2448; and *Morgan Stanley Mutual Fund and Ors. v. Kartick Das and Ors.* (1994) 4 SCC 225.

65 The Specific Relief (Amendment) Act, 2018.

66 The Specific Relief (Amendment) Act, 2018, s. 10; and the Specific Relief Act, 1963, s. 20A.

67 'Specific Relief Act 1963 Amendment', Shardul Amarchand Mangaldas, 1 October 2018. Available online: https://www.amsshardul.com/insight/specific-relief-act-1963-amended-w-e-f-1-october-2018/ (accessed on 1 February 2025).

68 R. Chakrabarti, et al., 'India: The Specific Relief (Amendment) Act, 2018: Overview & Implications', Mondaq, 17 September 2018. Available online: https://www.mondaq.com/india/contracts-and-commercial-law/736966/the-specific-relief-amendment-act-2018-overview--implications. (accessed on 1 February 2025).

69 *Shivashakti Sugars Limited v. Shree Renuka Sugar Limited and Ors.* (2017) 7 SCC 729.

70 'Economic Impact of Court Judgments (Part 1): Legally Speaking with Tarun Nangia', *NewsX Live,* 7 March 2020. Available online: https://www.youtube.com/watch?v=jCpFaO24KgI (accessed on 1 February 2025).

71 J. Boehm and E. Oberfield, '(Un)ease of Doing Business: How Congested Courts Hinder Firm Productivity', *VoxDev*, 7 September 2019. Available online: https://voxdev.org/topic/institutions-political-economy/unease-doing-business-how-congested-courts-hinder-firm (accessed on 1 February 2025).

72 'Role of MSME Sector in the Country', Government of India Public Information Bureau, 7 August 2023. Available online: https://pib.gov.in/PressReleseDetailm.aspx?PRID=1946375#:~:text=2023%2C%20as%20per%20Udyam%20Registration,are%20attached%20as%20annexure%20I (accessed on 1 February 2025).

73 Ibid.

74 'Matrices of State Rules and Schemes Under the Street Vendors Act, 2014', Centre for Civil Society, 6 March 2020. Available online: https://ccs.in/matrices-state-rules-and-schemes-under-street-vendors-act-2014 (accessed on 1 February 2025).

75 'Crony Capitalism Needs to Be Kept Under Watch', *Mint*, 7 May 2023. Available online: https://www.livemint.com/opinion/online-views/the-big-mac-index-a-handy-snapshot-of-crony-capitalism-india-ranks-10th-highest-in-billionaire-overload-and-rent-seeking-sectors-11683482939941.html. (accessed on 1 February 2025).

76 F. Schauer, *The Force of Law* (Harvard University Press, 2015); C. Bezemek and N. Ladavac, *The Force of Law Reaffirmed: Frederick Schauer Meets the Critics* (Switzerland: Springer, 2016).

77 R. Parloff, 'How VW Paid $25 Billion for "Dieselgate"—and Got Off Easy', *Fortune*, 6 February 2018. Available online:

https://fortune.com/2018/02/06/volkswagen-vw-emissions-scandal-penalties/ (accessed on 1 February 2025).

78 Ibid.

79 'Whistleblower Laws Around the World', National Whistleblower Centre. Available online: https://www.whistleblowers.org/whistleblower-laws-around-the-world/ (accessed on 1 February 2025).

80 Ibid.

81 M. Datta, 'Whistleblowing in India', *Lexology*, 2 August 2024. Available online: https://www.lexology.com/library/detail.aspx?g=98144dab-784a-4a98-9cb0-8150d2db9b84 (accessed on 1 February 2025).

82 'Bihar Govt Wakes Up to IITian's Murder', *Rediff*, 6 December 2003. Available online: https://www.rediff.com/news/2003/dec/05bihar1.htm (accessed on 1 February 2025).

83 'Staff, Whistleblower Pays with Life', *The Hindu*, 12 July 2016. Available online: https://www.thehindu.com/news/national/karnataka/whistleblower-pays-with-life/article3438966.ece (accessed on 1 February 2025).

84 D. Rana, 'Whistleblowers Protection Act, 2014: A Cracked Foundation?', Mondaq, 4 October 2021. Available online: https://www.mondaq.com/india/whistleblowing/1118060/whistle-blowers-protection-act-2014-a-cracked-foundation (accessed on 1 February 2025).

85 'SEC Issues Largest-Ever Whistleblower Award', US Securities and Exchange Commission, 5 May 2023. Available online: https://www.sec.gov/news/press-release/2023-89#:~:text=Whistleblower%20awards%20can%20range%20from,could%20reveal%20a%20whistleblower's%20identity (accessed on 1 February 2025).

86 Ibid.

87 P. Gratton, 'Securities and Exchange Commission (SEC) Defined: How It Works', Investopedia, 26 April 2025. Available online: https://www.investopedia.com/terms/s/sec.asp (accessed 1 July 2025).

88 'Sarbanes–Oxley (SOX) Corporate Whistleblower Protection Law', Zuckerman Law. Available online: Sarbanes-Oxley (SOX) Corporate Whistleblower Protection Law - Zuckerman Law (accessed on 1 February 2025).

89 Chapter IIIA of SEBI (Prohibition of Insider Trading) Regulations, 2015; and A. Garg and K. Malpani, 'SEBI's Attempt to Blow the Whistle on Insiders', *Law School Policy Review*, 17 May 2020. Available online: https://lawschoolpolicyreview.com/2020/05/17/sebis-attempt-to-blow-the-whistle-on-insiders/ (accessed on 1 February 2025).

90 'SEBI Makes Reward for Whistleblowers on Insider Trading More Attractive', *Economic Times*, 29 June 2021. Available online: https://economictimes.indiatimes.com/markets/stocks/news/sebi-makes-reward-for-whistleblowers-on-insider-trading-more-attractive/articleshow/83953473.cms?utm_source=contentofinterest&utm_medium=text&utm_campaign=cppst (accessed on 1 February 2025).

91 'SEBI's Recent Amendments of Clause 49', KPMG, 17 September 2014. Available online: https://assets.kpmg.com/content/dam/kpmg/pdf/2014/09/FirstNotes-17Sept14.pdf (accessed on 1 February 2025).

92 SEBI (Listing Obligations and Disclosure Requirements) Regulations 2015, Reg. 16(1)(c).

93 SEBI (Listing Obligations and Disclosure Requirements) Regulations 2015, Reg. 24(1).

94 SEBI (Listing Obligations and Disclosure Requirements) Regulations 2015, Reg. 62L.

95 A. Laskar, 'SEBI Tells Listed Firms to Provide Annual Information Memorandum', *Mint*, 18 February 2014. Available online: https://www.livemint.com/Money/ZNTbe0IShW3aDIAVgDY6dJ/Sebi-tells-listed-firms-told-to-provide-annual-information-m.html (accessed on 1 February 2025).

96 SEBI (Listing Obligations and Disclosure Requirements) Regulations, 2015.

97 'Business Extent of Disclosure Index', World Bank, 2021.

98 'Facebook to Pay $100 Million for Misleading Investors About the Risks It Faced from Misuse of User Data', U.S. Securities and Exchange Commission, 24 July 2019. Available online: https://www.sec.gov/news/press-release/2019-140 (accessed on 1 February 2025).

99 'Bureau, Whistleblower Group Accuses Infosys CEO of "Unethical Practices" to Boost Numbers', *The Hindu Business Line*, 7 December 2021. Available online: https://

www.thehindubusinessline.com/info-tech/infosys-was-indulging-in-unethical-practices-to-boost-revenues-allege-whistleblower/article62237810.ece (accessed on 1 February 2025).

Chapter 4 Harmonising Indian Law with the Indian Sense of Justice

1 D.R. Davis Jr., 'Hinduism as a Legal Tradition', *Journal of the American Academy of Religion,* 75 (2): 241–67. Available online: https://www.jstor.org/stable/40006370 (accessed on 1 February 2025).

2 B.A. Brody, 'Law and Morality', in S.G. Post (ed.), *The Encyclopaedia of Bioethics*, 1375–80 (New York: Macmillan, 2004).

3 S. Bhavya, 'Dharma Under Indian Jurisprudence', *Indian Journal of Law and Legal Research,* 5 (2). Available online: https://heinonline.org/HOL/LandingPage?handle=hein.journals/injlolw11&div=239&id=&page= (accessed on 1 February 2025).

4 M.K. Gandhi, *An Autobiography or The Story of My Experiments with Truth*, (Critical Edition), translated by M. Desai, p. 259 (Yale University Press). Available online: https://www.sas.upenn.edu/~cavitch/pdf-library/Gandhi_Autobiography.pdf (accessed on 1 February 2025).

5 W. Doniger, 'Veda', Britannica. Available online: https://www.britannica.com/topic/Veda (accessed on 1 February 2025).

6 S. Sarkar, 'Manusmriti: A Critical Analysis', *International Journal of Humanities & Social Science Studies*, 8 (6): 255–60. Available online: https://www.ijhsss.com/files/25.-Satarupa-Sarkar.pdf (accessed on 1 February 2025).

7 'Yuga', Britannica. Available online: https://www.britannica.com/topic/yuga (accessed on 1 February 2025); and P. Thakur, 'Mysteries of the Yuga Cycle: Kali Yuga to End in 2025?', The Speaking Tree, 2 February 2016. Available online: https://www.speakingtree.in/allslides/when-will-kali-yuga-end. (accessed on 1 February 2025).

8 C.M. Agrawal, *Golu Devta: the God of Justice of Kumaun Himalayas*, (India: Shree Almora Book Depot, 1996); and M. Baindur, 'Goludev of Chitai: Practices and Rituals',

Sahapedia. Available online: https://www.sahapedia.org/goludev-of-chitai (accessed on 1 February 2025); and R. Singh, 'Goludev', Justice Adda, Available online: https://www.justiceadda.com/goludev (accessed on 1 February 2025).

9 Ibid.

10 K. Ravindran, 'Where Gods Descend on Humans', *Times of India*, 12 July 2015. Available online: https://timesofindia.indiatimes.com/blogs/tracking-indian-communities/where-gods-descend-on-humans/ (accessed on 1 February 2025).

11 S. Tamilponni, 'Judicial Administration of the Imperial Cholas', *Journal of Emerging Technologies and Innovative Research*, 6 (2): 272–81. Available online: https://www.jetir.org/papers/JETIR1902C46.pdf (accessed 1 February 2019).

12 A.A.A. Fyzee, 'Muhammadan Law in India: Comparative Studies in Society and History', 5 (4): 401–15 (Cambridge: Cambridge University Press). Available online: https://www.cambridge.org/core/journals/comparative-studies-in-society-and-history/article/abs/muhammadan-law-in-india/ACF16F0DE95EB7454035755BF90B8AE1 (last accessed on 1 February 2025).

13 S. Neill, *A History of Christianity in India: The Beginnings to AD 1707*, 68–86 (Cambridge: Cambridge University Press, 1984). Available online: https://www.cambridge.org/core/books/abs/history-of-christianity-in-india/christians-in-the-indian-middle-age/8C30F43BED4A37117F92B67112D2B2A4 (accessed on 1 February 2025); and R.E. Frykenberg, 'Christian History Timeline: Christianity in India', Christian History Institute. Available online: https://christianhistoryinstitute.org/magazine/article/christianity-in-india (accessed on 1 February 2025).

14 S. Chandra, *Medieval India: From Delhi Sultanate to the Mughals (1206–1526): Part 1* (New Delhi, India: Har-Anand Publications, 1997); and M. Mahajan, 'Islam and the Mughal Empire in South Asia: 1526–1857', *Education about Asia*, 28 (1). Available online: https://www.asianstudies.org/publications/eaa/archives/islam-and-the-mughal-empire-in-south-asia-1526-1857/ (accessed on 1 February 2025).

15 'Judicial Administration in Ancient India', Ithihas. Available online: https://ithihas.wordpress.com/2013/10/08/judicial-

administration-in-ancient-india/ (accessed on 1 February 2025).

16 H. Kabir, 'Influence of Islamic Culture on Indian Life', *Annals of the American Academy of Political and Social Science,* 233: 22–29. Available online: https://www.jstor.org/stable/1025818 (accessed on 1 February 2025).

17 M.P. Singh and N. Kumar, 'Tracing the History of the Legal System India', *The Indian Legal System: An Enquiry*, 1–22 (Delhi: Oxford University Press). Available online: https://academic.oup.com/book/32396/chapter-abstract/268688552?redirectedFrom=fulltext (accessed on 1 February 2025)

18 J.M. Gest, 'The Influence of Biblical Texts upon English Law', *University of Pennsylvania Law Review and American Law Register*, 59: 15–38. Available online: https://archive.org/details/jstor-3307668 (accessed on 1 February 2025); and A.M. Tier, 'The Evolution of Personal Laws in India and Sudan', *Journal of the Indian Law Institute*, 26 (4): 445–517. Available online: https://www.jstor.org/stable/43950945 (accessed on 1 February 2025).

19 J.R. Schmidhauser, 'Legal Imperialism: Its Enduring Impact on Colonial and Post-Colonial Judicial Systems', *International Political Science Review*, 13 (3): 321–34. Available online: https://doi.org/10.1177/019251219201300307 (accessed on 1 February 2025).

20 Ibid.

21 S.E. Merry, 'Law and Colonialism', *Law & Society Review*, 25 (4): 889–922. Available online: https://doi.org/10.2307/3053874. (accessed on 1 February 2025).

22 B.Z. Tamanaha, 'Postcolonial Legal Pluralism', *Legal Pluralism Explained: History, Theory, Consequences*, pp. 55–96 (New York, 2021; online edn, Oxford Academic, 18 March 2021). Available online: https://doi.org/10.1093/oso/9780190861551.003.0003 (accessed 13 February 2025).

23 J.R. Schmidhauser, 'Legal Imperialism: Its Enduring Impact on Colonial and Post-Colonial Judicial Systems', *International Political Science Review*, 13 (3): 321–34. Available online: https://doi.org/10.1177/019251219201300307 (accessed on 1 February 2025).

24 Ibid.

25 Ibid.

26 J. Flint, 'Planned Decolonization and Its Failure in British Africa', *African Affairs*, 82 (328): 389–411. Available online: http://www.jstor.org/stable/722072. (accessed on 1 February 2025).

27 K. McBride, 'Colonialism and the Rule of Law', *Mr. Mothercountry: The Man Who Made the Rule of Law*, pp. 10–33 (New York, 2016; online edn, Oxford Academic, 22 September 2016). Available online: https://doi.org/10.1093/acprof:oso/9780190252977.003.0002 (accessed on 1 February 2025).

28 J.R. Schmidhauser, 'Legal Imperialism: Its Enduring Impact on Colonial and Post-Colonial Judicial Systems', *International Political Science Review*, 13 (3): 321–34. Available online: https://doi.org/10.1177/019251219201300307 (accessed on 1 February 2025).

29 M. Zavala, 'Decolonizing Knowledge Production', *Encyclopedia of Educational Philosophy and Theory*, edited by M.A. Peters, pp. 375–82 (Singapore: Springer). Available online: doi:10.1007/978-981-287-588-4_508.

30 T.R.S. Allan, 'First Principles: The Rule of Law and Separation of Powers', *Constitutional Justice: A Liberal Theory of the Rule of Law*, pp. 31–60 (Oxford, 2003; online edn, Oxford Academic, 1 January 2010). Available online: https://doi.org/10.1093/acprof:oso/9780199267880.003.0002 (accessed 1 February 2025).

31 R.J. Miller, 'The Doctrine of Discovery: The International Law of Colonialism', *The Indigenous Peoples' Journal of Law, Culture & Resistance*, 5: 35–42. Available online: https://www.jstor.org/stable/48671863 (accessed on 1 February 2025).

32 A.L. Conklin, 'Colonialism and Human Rights, a Contradiction in Terms? The Case of France and West Africa, 1895–1914', *American Historical Review*, 103 (2): 419–42. Available online: https://doi.org/10.2307/2649774 (accessed on 1 February 2025).

33 R. Michaels, 'The Legal Legacy of the Colonial Era', Max Planck Forschung, 4: 16–21. Available online: https://www.mpg.de/18486977/W001_Viewpoint_016-021.pdf (accessed on 1 February 2025).

34 P. Koch, 'How Should We Balance Morality and the Law?', Center for Medical Ethics and Healthy Policy, 20 December

2019. Available online: https://blogs.bcm.edu/2019/12/20/how-should-we-balance-morality-and-the-law/ (accessed on 1 February 2025).

35 J. Hare and J. Herdt, 'Religion and Morality in Western Philosophy', *The Stanford Encyclopedia of Philosophy* (Winter 2024 Edition). Available online: https://plato.stanford.edu/entries/religion-morality/ (accessed on 1 February 2025).

36 P.M. Sandler, 'The Common Law', *The Fine Art of Trial Advocacy: A Young Lawyer's Resource for Success* (Chicago: American Bar Association Book Publishing, 2021). Available online: https://www.americanbar.org/content/dam/aba-cms-dotorg/products/inv/book/417398552/chptr1_1620816_trialadvocacy.pdf (accessed on 1 February 2025).

37 *Fida Hussain v. Moradabad Development Authority* (2011) 12 SCC 615.

38 A.K. Awasthi, 'Stare Decisis and Supreme Court', *JTRI Journal*, Institute of Judicial Training and Research, Issue 30: 77-81. Available online: https://ijtr.nic.in/2008%20Dec.pdf; also available here: https://ijtr.nic.in/webjournal/8.htm (accessed on 1 February 2025).

39 *State of Orissa v. Sudhansu Sekhar Misra and Ors* (1968) 2 SCR 154.

40 K. Buchanan, 'The Civil Law System: Global Legal Collection Highlights', *Library of Congress Blogs*, 28 July 2015. Available online: https://blogs.loc.gov/law/2015/07/the-civil-law-system-global-legal-collection-highlights/ (accessed on 1 February 2025).

41 'Law of the Twelve Tables: Roman Law,' Britannica. Available online: https://www.britannica.com/topic/Law-of-the-Twelve-Tables (accessed on 1 February 2025).

42 'The Common law and Civil Law Traditions', *The Robbins Collection*, 2010. Available online: https://www.law.berkeley.edu/wp-content/uploads/2017/11/CommonLawCivilLawTraditions.pdf (accessed on 1 February 2025).

43 *Nordally v. Attorney General* [1986] MR 204; *The State v. Abdul Rashid Khoyratty* [2006] UKPC 13.

44 Lord Mance, 'Should the Law Be Certain?', The Oxford Shrieval Lecture delivered at the University Church of St Mary the Virgin, Oxford, on 11 October 2011. Available online: https://

supremecourt.uk/uploads/speech_111011_342362219c.pdf (accessed on 1 February 2025).

45 Lord Reid, 'The Judge as Law Maker', *Journal of the Society of Public Teachers of Law* (New Series), 12 (1): 22–29. Available online: https://heinonline.org/HOL/LandingPage?handle=hein.journals/sptlns12&div=10&id=&page= (accessed on 1 February 2025).

46 Anirudh, 'Does Judiciary "Make Laws"?', *PRS India*, 20 April 2011. Available online: https://prsindia.org/theprsblog/does-the-judiciary-%E2%80%9Cmake-laws%E2%80%9D?page=3&per-page=1#:~:text=The%20eventual%20outcome%20of%20the,legislating%E2%80%9D%20rather%20than%20interpreting%20laws (accessed on 1 February 2025).

47 *Vishaka and Ors. v. State of Rajasthan and Ors.* AIR 1997 SC 3011.

48 *Suraz India Trust v. Union of India and Anr.* (2012) 13 SCC 497.

49 Anirudh, 'Does Judiciary "Make Laws"?', *PRS India*, 20 April 2011. Available online: https://prsindia.org/theprsblog/does-the-judiciary-%E2%80%9Cmake-laws%E2%80%9D?page=3&per-page=1#:~:text=The%20eventual%20outcome%20of%20the,legislating%E2%80%9D%20rather%20than%20interpreting%20laws (accessed on 1 February 2025).

50 *Peninsular and Oriental Steam Navigation Company v. Secretary of State for India* (1861) 5 Bom. H.C.R. Appendix A- 1.

51 G.C. Hazard Jr. and A. Dondi, 'Responsibilities of Judges and Advocates in Civil and Common Law: Some Lingering Misconceptions Concerning Civil Lawsuits', *Cornell International Law Journal*, 39: 59–70 (2006). Available online: https://scholarship.law.upenn.edu/faculty_scholarship/1094 (accessed on 1 February 2025).

52 'Adversarial Versus Inquisitorial Legal Systems', United Nations Office on Drugs Crime, May 2018. Available online: https://www.unodc.org/e4j/en/organized-crime/module-9/key-issues/adversarial-vs-inquisitorial-legal-systems.html#:~:text=The%20inquisitorial%20process%20can%20be,defence%20to%20determine%20the%20facts.of (accessed on 1 February 2025).

53 'Difference Between Adversarial and Inquisitorial System'. Available online: https://moodle.pmaclism.catholic.edu.au/

mod/resource/view.php?id=13369 (accessed on 1 February 2025).

54 Justice Abdul Nazeer, Speech on 'Decolonisation of the Indian Legal System', delivered at the 16th National Council Meeting of the Akhil Bharatiya Adhivakta Parishad, Hyderabad, *LiveLaw*, 26 December 2021. Available online: https://www.livelaw.in/pdf_upload/lectureofjusticesabdulnazeer-406739.pdf (accessed on 1 February 2025); also see: Mehal Jain, 'Neglect of Ancient Indian Legal Giants Like Manu, Kautilya & Adherence to Colonial Legal System Detrimental to Constitutional Goals: Justice Abdul Nazeer', *LiveLaw*, 27 December 2021. Available online: https://www.livelaw.in/top-stories/justice-abdul-nazeer-ancient-indian-jurisprudence-manu-kautilya-colonial-legal-system-188437?from-login= (accessed on 1 February 2025).

55 'Apex Court's Views on Indianisation of the Legal System', *Freelaw*, 30 December 2021. Available online: https://www.freelaw.in/legalnews/Apex-Court-s-views-on-Indianisation-of-the-legal-system (accessed on 1 February 2025).

56 V. Halvorsen, 'Is It Better That Ten Guilty Persons Go Free Than That One Innocent Person Be Convicted?', *Criminal Justice Ethics*, 23 (2): 3–13. Available online: https://www.ojp.gov/ncjrs/virtual-library/abstracts/it-better-ten-guilty-persons-go-free-one-innocent-person-be (accessed on 1 February 2025).

57 J. O'Rahilly-Hadley, 'Beyond Reasonable Doubt', Hugo Law Group, 13 February 2023. Available online: https://hugolawgroup.com.au/insights/beyond-reasonable-doubt/#:~:text=Blackstone's%20principle%20remains%20influential%20in,'beyond%20a%20reasonable%20doubt' (accessed 1 February 2021).

58 A. Keane and P. McKeown, 'Time to Abandon "Beyond Reasonable Doubt" and "Sure": The Case for a New Description of the Criminal Standard of Proof and an Explanation of Why and How It Should Be Used', Centre for the Study of Legal Professional Practice. Available online: https://www.city.ac.uk/__data/assets/powerpoint_doc/0010/425377/Time-to-abandon-beyond-reasonable-doubt-and-sure.pptx (accessed on 1 February 2025).

59 'Record of Discussion of the Interaction between the NHRC, India, and the UN Special Rapporteur on Extrajudicial, Summary or Arbitrary Executions, held on 22 March 2012 at 11:30 hrs in the NHRC Conference Room', National Human Rights Commission of India. Available online: https://nhrc.nic.in/sites/default/files/Record%20Note-%20UN%20Spl.Rapporteur%20on%20Extra-Judicial%20Powers.pdf (accessed on 1 February 2025).
60 E. Shapiro, 'A Timeline of OJ Simpson's Life and the Sensational Trial', *ABC News*, 12 June 2025. Available online: https://abcnews.go.com/US/key-moments-oj-simpsons-life/story?id=48724637 (accessed 25 June 2025).
61 M. Ajmera and M. Patel, 'Victimization and Administration of Criminal Justice in India', *International Journal Law Review*, 1 (1): 33.
62 A. Kumar, 'Need for Victim-Oriented Criminal Justice System', *Times of India Opinion Blog*, 7 May 2021. Available online: https://timesofindia.indiatimes.com/blogs/voices/need-for-victim-oriented-criminal-justice-system/ (accessed on 1 February 2025).
63 Ibid.
64 J. Bajoria, 'Why India Needs a Victim and Witness Protection Law, Could Delhi's Witness Protection Scheme Be a Template for a Nationwide Law?', Human Rights Watch, 19 December 2017. Available online: https://www.hrw.org/news/2017/12/19/why-india-needs-victim-and-witness-protection-law (accessed on 1 February 2025).
65 *Rattan Singh v. State of Punjab* AIR 1980 SC 84.
66 *Nirmal Singh Kahlon v. State of Punjab and Ors.* AIR 2009 SC 984.
67 Crime Victims' Rights Act (CVRA) (18 U.S.C. § 3771).
68 C. Doyle, 'Crime Victims' Rights Act: A Summary and Legal Analysis of 18 U.S.C. §3771'. Washington, DC: Congressional Research Service, 9 December 2015. Available online: https://fas.org/sgp/crs/misc/RL33679.pdf (accessed on 1 February 2025).
69 Code of Practice for Victims of Crime in England and Wales (Victims' Code), Supreme Court of the UK. Available online: https://assets.publishing.service.gov.uk/media/60620279d3bf7f5ceaca0d89/victims-code-2020.pdf

(accessed on 1 February 2025).

70 'Average 82 Murders a Day, 11 Kidnappings, Abduction Every Hour in India in 2021: NCRB Data', *The Hindu*, 31 August 2022. Available online: https://www.thehindu.com/news/national/average-82-murders-a-day-11-kidnappings-abduction-every-hour-in-india-in-2021-ncrb-data/article65833404.ece#:~:text=An%20average%20of%2082%20people,Records%20Bureau%20(NCRB)%20report (accessed on 1 February 2025).

71 'Central Indiana Man Sentenced to 200 Years in Prison for Sexually Exploiting Minors, Possessing Child Pornography', US Immigration and Customs Enforcement, 8 January 2020. Available online: https://www.ice.gov/news/releases/central-indiana-man-sentenced-200-years-prison-sexually-exploiting-minors-possessing (accessed on 1 February 2025).

72 J. Andenaes, 'The General Preventive Effects of Punishment', *University of Pennsylvania Law Review*, 114 (7): 949–83. Available online: https://www.jstor.org/stable/3310845 (accessed on 1 February 2025).

73 H.A. Bedau, 'Retribution and the Theory of Punishment', *Journal of Philosophy*, 75 (11): 601–20. Available online: S%20RETRIBUTIVE%20THEORY%20INVOLVES%20A,OF%20RETURNING%20SUFFERING%20FOR%20MORAL (accessed on 1 February 2025).

74 S. Chinda, 'Reformative Theory of Punishment: Analysing the Status in India', *International Journal of Law Management and Humanities*, 4 (3): 1114–119. Available online: https://ijlmh.com/paper/reformative-theory-of-punishment-analyzing-the-status-in-india/ (accessed on 1 February 2025).

75 The Contempt of Courts Act 1971, s. 2(b).

76 Ibid., s. 2(c).

77 M. Safi, 'India's Top Judges Issue Unprecedented Warning over Integrity of Supreme Court', *Guardian*, 12 January 2018. Available online: https://www.theguardian.com/world/2018/jan/12/india-supreme-court-judges-integrity-dipak-misra (accessed on 1 February 2025).

78 'Truth Is a Valid Defence in Contempt Proceedings Only if It Is Bonafide and in Public Interest: SC [Read Judgment]', *LiveLaw*, 31 August 2020. Available online: https://www.livelaw.in/top-

stories/truth-valid-defence-in-contempt-only-if-bonafide-public-interest-162197?infinitescroll=1 (accessed on 1 February 2025).

Chapter 5 Constitutional Reforms

1 *Surya Prakash Khatri & Anr. v. Madhu Trehan and Others* 2001 Cri LJ 3476.

2 A.A. Choudhary, 'Many Inefficient Judges Were Appointed by Collegium, Centre Tells SC', *Times of India*, 11 June 2015. Available online: https://timesofindia.indiatimes.com/india/many-inefficient-judges-were-appointed-by-collegium-centre-tells-sc/articleshow/47614579.cms (accessed on 1 February 2025).

3 Mehal Jain, 'The Need of the Hour Is the Indianisation of Our Legal System: Chief Justice NV Ramana', *LiveLaw*, 18 September 2021. Available online: https://www.livelaw.in/top-stories/the-need-of-the-hour-is-the-indianisation-of-our-legal-system-chief-justice-nv-ramana-181912?from-login=699367&token=RDWEBQS5U9RFDZG6YOZ3EKTW7JT2FTDZAHSSO (accessed on 1 February 2025).

4 American Bar Association Guidelines for the Evaluation of Judicial Performance, Special Committee on Evaluation of Judicial Performance. Available online: https://www.americanbar.org/content/dam/aba/publications/judicial_division/aba_blackletterguidelines_jpe_wcom.pdf (accessed on 1 February 2025); and 'Black Letter Guidelines for the Evaluation of Judicial Performance', American Bar Association, 2005. Available online: https://www.americanbar.org/content/dam/aba/publications/judicial_division/aba_blackletterguidelines_jpe.pdf (accessed on 1 February 2025).

5 R.W. Berch and E.N. Bass, 'Judicial Performance Review in Arizona: A Critical Assessment', *Arizona Law Review*, 56 (2): 353–81.

6 'International Framework for Court Excellence', International Consortium for Court Excellence (Third Edition), 2020. Available online: https://www.asean-ifce.com/files/ifce/english-international-framework-3rd-edition.pdf (accessed on 1 February 2025).

7 'Judges Face Performance Appraisals', *BBC News*, 30 December 2013. Available online: https://www.bbc.com/news/uk-25550587 (accessed on 1 February 2025).
8 P. Manivannan, S. Thomas and B.Z. Shah, 'Evaluating Contract Enforcement by Courts in India: A Litigant's Lens', XKDR Forum, 21 November 2022. Available online: https://xkdr.org/paper/evaluating-contract-enforcement-by-courts-in-india-a-litigants-lens (accessed on 1 February 2025).
9 Ibid.
10 D. Kumar and R.M. Singh, 'Exploring Court Performance and Developing Its Scale', *International Journal for Court Administration*, 13 (1): 3–19. Available online: https://doi.org/10.36745/ijca.399 (accessed on 1 February 2025).
11 W.C. Prillaman, *The Judiciary and Democratic Decay in Latin America: Declining Confidence in the Rule of Law* (Westport: Praeger, 2000); and J.L. Staats, S. Bowler and J.T. Hiskey, 'Measuring Judicial Performance in Latin America', *Latin American Politics and Society*, 47 (4): 77–106. Available online: https://doi.org/10.1111/j.1548-2456.2005.tb00329.x (accessed on 1 February 2025).
12 A. Vora, 'Pendency Increases by over 1,600 Cases in May 2024 as the Supreme Court Commences Its Summer Break', *Supreme Court Observer*, 12 June 2024.
13 'India Overtakes China as the World's Most Populous Country', United Nations Department of Economic and Social Affairs, 24 April 2023. Available online: Policy Briefs | UN DESA Publications (accessed on 1 February 2025).
14 'History', Supreme Court of India. Available online: https://www.sci.gov.in/about-department/history/ (accessed on 1 February 2025).
15 Ibid.
16 'Apex ("Supreme") Courts', *Judiciaries Worldwide*. Available online: https://judiciariesworldwide.fjc.gov/apex-supreme-courts.
17 D. Mahapatra, 'SC: Doubling Number of Judges Not a Solution to Tackle Pendency', *Times of India*, 30 November 2022. Available online: https://timesofindia.indiatimes.com/india/sc-doubling-number-of-judges-not-a-solution-to-tackle-pendency/articleshow/95866366.cms (accessed on 1 February 2025).

18 'Pendency and Vacancies in the Judiciary' PRS Legislative Research. Available online: https://prsindia.org/policy/vital-stats/pendency-and-vacancies-in-the-judiciary (accessed on 1 February 2025).

19 Sumeda, 'Explained: The Clogged State of the Indian Judiciary', *The Hindu*, 13 May 2022.
Available online: https://www.thehindu.com/news/national/indian-judiciary-pendency-data-courts-statistics-explain-judges-ramana-chief-justiceundertrials/article65378182.ece (accessed on 1 February 2025).

20 D. Mahapatra, 'SC: Doubling Number of Judges Not a Solution to Tackle Pendency', *Times of India*, 30 November 2022. Available online:
https://timesofindia.indiatimes.com/india/sc-doubling-number-of-judges-not-a-solution-to-tackle-pendency/articleshow/95866366.cms (accessed on 1 February 2025).

21 'Pendency in Supreme Court Dips by 4K in 13 Days Under New CJI', *Times of India*, 16 September 2022. Available online: https://timesofindia.indiatimes.com/india/pendency-in-supreme-court-dips-by-4k-in-13-days-under-new-cji/articleshow/94232688.cms (accessed on 1 February 2025).

22 M. Gupta, 'Is the Global Reputation of India's Supreme Court in Decline?', *Article 14*, 30 November 2020. Available online: https://article-14.com/post/is-the-global-reputation-of-india-s-supreme-court-in-decline (accessed on 1 February 2025).

23 'Venkaiah Naidu Bats for Bifurcation of Supreme Court, Says This Will Ensure Speedy Disposal of Cases', *Indian Express*, 28 September 2019. Available online: https://indianexpress.com/article/india/venkaiah-naidu-supreme-court-bifurcation-justice-delivery-6036330/ (accessed on 1 February 2025).

24 'SC Vacations: Comparing India to Other Countries', *Supreme Court Observer*, 13 March 2020. Available online: https://www.scobserver.in/journal/sc-vacations-comparing-india-to-other-countries/ (accessed on 1 February 2025).

25 Ibid.

26 *N. Suriyakala v. A. Mohandas and Ors.* (2007) 9 SCC 196.

27 *Jamshed Hormusji Wadia v. Board of Trustees of Port of Mumbai* (2004) 3 SCC 214.

28 *P.N. Kumar v. Municipal Corporation of Delhi* (1988) 1 SCR 732.
29 Adoption of Draft Article 118, Constituent Assembly Debates, Vol. 8, 27 May 1949. Available online: https://www.constitutionofindia.net/debates/27-may-1949/#8.93.243 (accessed on 1 February 2025).
30 *Union Carbide Corporation and Ors. v. Union of India and Ors.* AIR 1992 SC 248.
31 *Manoharlal Sharma v. The Principal Secretary* (2014) 9 SCC 516.
32 *State of Tamil Nadu and Ors. v. K. Balu and Ors.* (2017) 2 SCC 281.
33 P. Bharadwaj, 'Highway Liquor Sale Ban', *SCC Online*, 1 April 2017. Available online: https://www.scconline.com/blog/post/2017/04/01/highway-liquor-sale-ban-the-500-metre-distance-direction-issued-on-15-12-2016-modified-for-areas-with-less-population-and-hilly-terrain/ (accessed on 1 February 20255).
34 *M. Siddiq (D) thr. L.Rs. v. Mahant Suresh Das and Ors.* (2020) 1 SCC 1.
35 *In Re: The Delhi Laws Act, 1912* AIR 1951 SC 332.
36 *M.C. Mehta v. Union of India (UOI) and Ors.* (2020) 7 SCC 530.
37 A. Saraogi and G. Kashyap, 'The Court Receives over 25,000 PILs a Year', *Supreme Court Observer*, 22 June 2021. Available online: https://www.scobserver.in/journal/on-an-average-the-court-receives-over-25000-pils-a-year/ (accessed on 1 February 2025).
38 'Uttarakhand High Court Seeks Immediate Steps to Stop Mechanized Mining from Rivers in the State', *India Legal*, 29 December 2022. Available online: https://www.indialegallive.com/top-news-of-the-day/news/uttarakhand-high-courtstop-mechanized-mining-rivers-state/ (accessed on 1 February 2025).
39 A.G. Noorani, 'Judges and Their Bogus Collegium', *Frontline*, 27 August 2022. Available online: https://frontline.thehindu.com/the-nation/state-of-judiciary-in-india-judges-and-their-bogus-collegium/article65790536.ece (accessed on 1 February 2025).
40 *S.P. Gupta v. Union of India and Ors.* AIR 1982 SC 149.
41 *Supreme Court Advocates-on-Record Association and Ors. v. Union of India* (1993) 4 SCC 441.

42 *In Re: Appointment and Transfer of Judges* AIR 1999 SC 1.

43 *Supreme Court Advocates-on-Record Association and Ors. v. Union of India* (2016) 5 SCC 1.

44 'SC Entrusts Ex-Judge Rao with Task of Preparing Report on Finalization of AIFF Constitution', *Times of India*, 2 May 2023. Available online: https://timesofindia.indiatimes.com/sports/football/top-stories/sc-entrusts-ex-judge-rao-with-task-of-preparing-report-on-finalisation-of-aiff-constitution/articleshow/99940078.cms (accessed on 1 February 2025).

45 K. Rajagopal, 'Supreme Court Constitutes Committee to Look into Jail Reforms', *The Hindu*, 25 September 2018. Available online: https://www.thehindu.com/news/national/supreme-court-constitutes-committee-to-look-into-jail-reforms/article25035259.ece (accessed on 1 February 2025).

46 'Law in Numbers: Evidence Based Approaches to Legal Reform', Vidhi Centre for Legal Policy, 12 August 2016. Available online:
https://www.documentcloud.org/documents/3234234-Vidhi-Briefing-Book-Law-in-Numbers-2 (accessed on 1 February 2025); and P. Shrivastava, '70% Retired SC Judges as of Feb 16 Already in Quasi-Judicial & Other Posts', *Legally India*, 7 December 2016. Available online: https://www.legallyindia.com/tag/vidhi-centre-for-legal-policy (accessed on 1 February 2025).

47 Ibid.

48 A. Mandhani, 'Ranjan Gogoi RS Seat Made Big News in 2020, but He Is Among 70% SC Judges with Retirement Gigs', *The Print*, 4 January 2021. Available online: https://theprint.in/judiciary/ranjan-gogoi-rs-seat-made-big-news-in-2020-but-he-is-among-70-sc-judges-with-retirement-gigs/576154/ (accessed on 1 February 2025).

49 U. Poddar, 'Could Post-Retirement Benefits for Supreme Court Judges Hamper Judicial Independence?', *Scroll.in*, 3 September 2022. Available online: https://scroll.in/article/1031816/can-post-retirement-benefits-for-supreme-court-judges-hamper-judicial-independence. (accessed on 1 February 2025).

Note: The salary of the chief justice of India is slightly higher, at ₹33.6 lakh per year, which is reduced to ₹16.8 lakh annually after retirement.

50 P. Sharma, 'Nine Supreme Court Judges to Retire in 2023', *LiveLaw*, 1 January 2023. Available online: https://www.livelaw.in/top-stories/nine-supreme-court-judges-to-retire-in-2023-217815 (accessed on 1 February 2025).

51 S. Dam, 'Active After Sunset: The Politics of Judicial Retirement in India', *Federal Law Review*, 51 (1): 31–57. Available online: https://journals.sagepub.com/doi/10.1177/0067205X221146335 (accessed on 1 February 2025).

52 V. Venkatesan, 'Justice S. Abdul Nazeer's Appointment as the Governor Without a Cooling-Off Period Brings It Under Scrutiny', *LiveLaw*, 13 February 2023. Available online: https://www.livelaw.in/columns/justice-sabdul-nazeers-appointment-as-the-governor-without-a-cooling-off-period-brings-it-under-scrutiny-221476 (accessed on 1 February 2025).

53 'Overview of Good Behaviour Clause', *Constitution Annotated: Analysis and Interpretation of the US Constitution*. Available online: https://constitution.congress.gov/browse/essay/artIII-S1-10-2-1/ALDE_00000684/ (accessed on 1 February 2025).

54 'Justice Department Says Raising Judges' Retirement Age May Benefit Non-Performers', *The Hindu*, 25 December 2022. Available online: https://www.thehindu.com/news/national/raising-judges-retirement-age-could-extend-service-of-non-performers-justice-dept-to-parliamentary-panel/article66304237.ece (accessed on 1 February 2025).

55 R.M. Biju, 'Tribunals Have Become a Haven for Retired Judges and Bureaucrats', *LiveLaw*, 1 February 2023. Available online: https://www.livelaw.in/top-stories/supreme-court-judge-sk-kaul-tribunals-must-have-specialists-as-members-220477 (accessed on 1 February 2025).

56 K. Tripathi, 'Sorry State of Tribunals: How Mounting Vacancies Are Affecting Litigation', *The Quint*, 10 August 2021. Available online: www.thequint.com/news/law/sorry-state-of-tribunals-how-mounting-vacancies-are-affecting-litigation#read-more (accessed on 1 February 2025).

Chapter 6 Redefining Boundaries

1 Judges (Protection) Act, 1985, s. 3.
2 'The Story of Shravan Kumar', *Eduindex News,* 2 July 2021. Available online: https://eduindex.org/2021/07/02/the-story-of-shravan-kumar/#:~:text=With%20his%20dying%20breath%2C%20Shravan,(shrine)%20dedicated%20to%20Shravana. (accessed on 1 February 2025).
3 S. Mishra, 'Vali and Sugriva', *Amar Chitra Katha*, 15 September 2020. Available online: https://www.amarchitrakatha.com/mythologies/vali-and-sugriva/?srsltid=AfmBOooMrqeoah1oVGvi2C4X_PTOWoa8hXxsEIfzu1DziZN-PA7UxPRd (accessed on 1 February 2025).
4 *Entick v. Carrington* (1765) EWHC KB J98.
5 *Peninsular and Oriental Steam Navigation Company v. Secretary of State for India* (1861) 5 Bom. H.C.R. Appendix A- 1.
6 *The State of Rajasthan v. Vidyawati and Ors.* AIR 1962 SC 933.
7 B. Indulia, 'Can a Judge Be Sued for Any Act Done or Ordered to Be Done by Him in Discharge of His Judicial Duty? HC Discusses Provision', *SCC Online*, 21 September 2020. Available online: https://www.scconline.com/blog/post/2020/09/21/gau-hc-can-a-judge-be-sued-for-any-act-done-or-ordered-to-be-done-by-him-in-discharge-of-his-judicial-duty-hc-discusses-provision/ (accessed on 1 February 2025).
8 *K. Veeraswami v. Union of India and Ors.* (1991) 3 SCC 655.
9 Justice K.S. Rao, 'Can Judges Get Blanket Protection?', India Legal, 22 August 2016. Available online: https://www.indialegallive.com/top-news-of-the-day/legal-eye-articles/judges-protection-high-court-president/ (accessed on 1 February 2025).
10 *State of Andhra Pradesh v. Challa Ramakrishna Reddy and Ors.* AIR 2000 SC 2083
11 R. Evans, D. Pegg and S. Carrell, 'What Does the Queen's Legal Immunity Mean?', *Guardian*, 14 July 2022. Available online: https://www.theguardian.com/uk-news/2022/jul/14/what-does-queen-legal-immunity-mean-british-laws (accessed on 1 February 2025).
12 Sovereign Immunity Law and Legal Definition, US Legal. Available online:

https://definitions.uslegal.com/s/sovereign-immunity/ (accessed on 1 February 2025).

13 S.A. Keller, 'Qualified and Absolute Immunity at Common Law', *Stanford Law Review*, 73: 1337–1400. Available online: https://review.law.stanford.edu/wp-content/uploads/sites/3/2021/06/Keller-73-Stan.-L.-Rev.-1337.pdf (accessed on 1 February 2025).

14 *Thompson v. Clark et al.* (2022) 142 S. Ct. 1332.

15 42 U.S. Code § 1983.

16 *State of North Carolina v. Henry Lee McCollum and Leon Brown* (1988) 321 N.C. 557.

17 N. Totenberg, 'Supreme Court Makes it Easier to Sue the Police for Malicious Prosecution', *NPR*, 4 April 2022. Available online: https://www.npr.org/2022/04/04/1090857790/supreme-court-malicious-prosecution-sue-thompson (accessed on 1 February 2025).

18 S.A. Keller, 'Qualified and Absolute Immunity at Common Law', *Stanford Law Review*, 73: 1337–1400. Available online: https://review.law.stanford.edu/wp-content/uploads/sites/3/2021/06/Keller-73-Stan.-L.-Rev.-1337.pdf (accessed on 1 February 2025).

19 'Costs in Civil Litigation', Law Commission of India. Available online: https://cdnbbsr.s3waas.gov.in/s3ca0daec69b5adc880fb464895726dbdf/uploads/2022/08/2022081077-3.pdf (accessed on 1 February 2025).

20 S. Sirohi, 'Section 16 (2) Violates Article 14: Fali S. Nariman', *Legal India*, 4 May 2021. Available online: https://www.legalindia.com/senior-designations-advocates-act-introduced-a-caste-system-section-16-2-violates-article-14-fali-s-nariman/ (accessed on 1 February 2025).

21 *Bates v. State Bar of Arizona* (1977) 433 US 350.

22 The Legal Profession Act, 1966.

23 D. Mahapatra, 'Supreme Court: Can't Sue Lawyers for Wrong Advice', *Times of India*, 22 September 2012. Available online: https://timesofindia.indiatimes.com/india/supreme-court-cant-sue-lawyers-for-wrong-advice/articleshow/16497152.cms (accessed on 1 February 2025).

24 'Does Bad Advice Constitute Legal Malpractice?', Robbins Law Group, 30 January 2022. Available online: https://

www.robbinslaw.com/does-bad-advice-constitute-legal-malpractice (accessed on 1 February 2025).

25 'Bad Lawyer Advice Is Legal Malpractice', Stanger Law LLC. Available online: https://www.stangerlaw.com/professional-malpractice/legal-malpractice/bad-advice/#:~:text=Based%20Law%20Firm.-,Bad%20Lawyer%20Advice%20Is%20Legal%20Malpractice,pursue%20a%20legal%20malpractice%20claim (accessed on 1 February 2025).

26 'What Is Professional Liability Insurance Coverage?', *The Hartford*. Available online: https://www.thehartford.com/professional-liability-insurance (accessed on 1 February 2025).

27 'Attorney Malpractice Insurance Average Premium', L Squared Insurance Agency. Available online: https://www.l2insuranceagency.com/blog/attorney-malpractice-insurance-average-premium/ (accessed on 1 February 2025).

28 'Guide to Lawyer's Indemnity Insurance', Insuropedia, 20 December 2022. Available online: A Guide to Lawyers' Indemnity Insurance - Insuropedia (accessed on 1 February 2025).

29 'Lawyers Professional Indemnity Insurance', Ethika. Available online: https://www.ethika.co.in/professional-indemnity-insurance-lawyers/ (accessed on 1 February 2025).

30 'Legal Malpractice Insurance: Cost and Coverage Trends', US Government Accountability Office, 28 May 2004. Available online: https://www.gao.gov/products/gao-04-422 (accessed 1 March 2025).

31 Bar Council of India Rules on Standards of Professional Conduct and Etiquette, Part VI, Chapter II, Rule 20.

32 Legal Aid, Sentencing and Punishment of Offenders Act, 2012, s. 45; and 'Litigation: Asset or Liability? How Contingency Fees Could Change Commercial Litigation', Herbert Smith Freehills Kramer, 25 January 2012. Available online: https://www.hsfkramer.com/notes/litigation/2012-01/litigation-asset-or-liability-how-contingency-fees-could-change-commercial-litigation (accessed on 1 February 2025).

33 'Contingency Fee', Legal Information Institute. Available online: https://www.law.cornell.edu/wex/contingency_fee#:~:

text=Upon%20the%20conclusion%20of%20a,bear%20in%20 a%20particular%20case (accessed on 1 February 2025).

34 D.L. Rubinfeld and S. Schotmer, 'Contingent Fees for Attorneys: An Economic Analysis', *RAND Journal of Economics*, 24 (3): 343–56. Available online: https://www.jstor.org/stable/2555962 (accessed on 1 February 2025).

35 E. Zamir and I. Ritov, 'Revisiting the Debate over Attorneys' Contingent Fees: A Behavioural Analysis', *Journal of Legal Studies*, 39 (1). Available online: https://www.journals.uchicago.edu/doi/10.1086/605510 (accessed on 1 February 2025).

36 N. Rickman, 'The Economics of Contingency Fees in Personal Injury Litigation', *Oxford Review of Economic Policy*, 10 (1): 34–50.

37 S. Maheshwari, 'Allowing Lawyers to Charge Contingency Fees: Impact on the Legal Services Market', *GNLU Journal of Law and Economics*, 2: 79–92. Available online: https://gjle.in/wp-content/uploads/2019/12/Allowing-Lawyers-to-Charge-Continency-Fees-Impact-on-the-Legal-Services-Market.pdf (accessed on 1 February 2025).

38 Ibid.

39 *Ganga Ram v. Devi Dasi* (61 P.R. (of 1907) p. 280).

40 *Kathu Jairam Gujar v. Vishvanath Ganesh Javadekar* AIR 1925 Bom 470.

41 *Stella Liebeck v. McDonald's Restaurants, P.T.S., Inc. et al* 1995 WL 360309.

42 B.D. Metcalf and Thomas R. Metcalf, *A Concise History of Modern India* (Cambridge University Press, 2006).

43 J.M. Brown, *Gandhi's Rise to Power: Indian Politics 1915–1922* (Cambridge University Press, 1972).

44 'Union Home Minister Amit Shah Stresses on Need to Increase Conviction Rate in Country', *Times of India*, 28 January 2023. Available online: https://timesofindia.indiatimes.com/india/union-home-minister-amit-shah-stresses-on-need-to-increase-conviction-rate-in-country/articleshow/97399073.cms (accessed on 1 February 2025).

45 '35% More Indian Students Travelled to the US for Higher Education in 2022–23 When Compared to the Previous Year', *The Hindu*, 13 November 2023. Available online: https://www.thehindu.com/news/national/tamil-nadu/35-more-indian-

students-travelled-to-us-for-higher-education-in-2022-23-when-compared-to-previous-year/article67529045.ece#:~:text=Around%2011.6%25%20wanted%20to%20pursue,in%20the%20U.S.%2C%20she%20said (accessed on 1 February 2025).

46 Raj Chengappa, 'Kodavas: One of the Few Tribes in India Allowed to Possess a Gun Without a Licence', *India Today*, 30 June 1981. Available online: https://www.indiatoday.in/magazine/living/story/19810630-kodavas-one-of-the-few-tribes-in-india-allowed-to-possess-a-gun-without-a-licence-773011-2013-11-20 (accessed on 1 February 2025).

47 *Capt. Chetan Y.K. v. Union of India* (2021) WP 11948/2021 (GM-RES-PIL).

48 'Conviction Rate Has to Go up if India's Law and Order Situation Is to Improve, Says Amit Shah', *Economic Times*, 29 January 2023. Available online: https://economictimes.indiatimes.com/news/elections/assembly-elections/karnataka/conviction-rate-has-to-go-up-if-indias-law-order-situation-has-to-improve-says-amit-shah/articleshow/97403881.cms?from=mdr (accessed on 1 February 2025).

49 R.M. Rich, 'Crime Control: A Theoretical View', *Essays on the Theory and Practice of Criminal Justice* (US of America: United Press of America, 1977). Available online: https://www.ojp.gov/ncjrs/virtual-library/abstracts/crime-control-theoretical-view-essays-theory-and-practice-criminal (accessed on 1 February 2025).

50 N. Mannathukkaren, 'How Did the State Come to Legitimise Vigilante Action?', *The Wire*, 9 January 2020. Available online: https://thewire.in/law/jnu-caa-protests-abvp-bjp (accessed on 1 February 2025).

51 'All 4 Accused in Hyderabad Rape-Murder Case Killed in Encounter: Telangana Police', *Economic Times*, 6 December 2019. Available online: https://economictimes.indiatimes.com/news/politics-and-nation/all-4-accused-in-hyderabad-gang-rape-murder-shot-dead/articleshow/72393178.cms?from=mdr (accessed on 1 February 2025).

52 N.C. Asthana, 'Police Encounters: What Makes Indian Society Celebrate "Instant Justice"?', *The Quint*, 17 September 2021. Available online: https://www.thequint.com/opinion/police-

encounters-what-makes-indian-society-celebrate-instant-justice (accessed on 1 February 2025).

53 G. Dagorn and D. Jullien, 'Nanterre Police Shooting: Under What Circumstances Are Police Officers Allowed to Use Firearms?', *La Monde*, 1 July 2023. Available online: https://www.lemonde.fr/en/les-decodeurs/article/2023/06/29/nanterre-police-shooting-under-what-circumstances-are-police-officers-allowed-to-use-firearms_6039450_8.html (accessed on 1 February 2025).

54 Shashiprabha Kumar, 'Persona of Women in the Vedas', Vedic Heritage Portal. Available online: https://vedicheritage.gov.in/pdf/Persona_of_Women_in_Veda.pdf (accessed on 1 February 2025).

55 Swami Satyananda Saraswati, 'Role of Woman in Tantra', *Yoga Magazine*. Available online: http://www.yogamag.net/archives/2010s/2012/1208/1208role.html (accessed on 1 February 2025).

56 *Mukesh and Ors. v. State of NCT of Delhi and Ors.* (2017) 6 SCC 1.

57 S.W. Chitale, 'Ganikas: Prostitution in Ancient India', Wisdom Library. Available online: https://www.wisdomlib.org/hinduism/essay/kathasaritsagara-cultural-study/d/doc1474015.html (accessed on 1 February 2025).

58 P. Kumar, 'Monarch Turned Ganika Amrapali Turned Buddhist Monk', *Arunachal Observer*, 7 October 2024. Available online: https://arunachalobserver.org/2024/10/07/monarch-turned-ganika-amrapali-turned-buddhist-monk/ (accessed on 1 February 2025).

59 L. Platt, P. Grenfell, R. Meiksin, et al., 'Associations Between Sex Work Laws and Sex Worker Health: A Systematic Review and Meta-Analysis of Quantitative and Qualitative Studies', *PLOS Medicine*, 11 December 2018. Available online: https://journals.plos.org/plosmedicine/article?id=10.1371/journal.pmed.1002680 (accessed on 1 February 2025).

60 U. Bacchi, 'Legalizing Prostitution Lowers Violence and Disease, Report Says', Reuters, 12 December 2018. Available online: https://www.reuters.com/article/world/legalizing-prostitution-lowers-violence-and-disease-report-says-

idUSKBN1OA28M/#:~:text=The%20research%2C%20published%20in%20journal,streets%20for%20prostitutes%20%2D%20are%20illegal (accessed on 1 February 2025).

61 Immoral Trafficking Act of 1956, s. 3, 4, 5, 6, 7 and 8.

62 'Countries Where Prostitution Is Legal in 2024', World Population Review. Available online: https://worldpopulationreview.com/country-rankings/countries-where-prostitution-is-legal (accessed on 1 February 2025).

63 Ibid.

64 'Prostitution: Third Report of Session 2016–17', House of Commons Home Affairs Committee. Available online: https://publications.parliament.uk/pa/cm201617/cmselect/cmhaff/26/26.pdf (accessed on 1 February 2025).

Bibliography

Agrawal, C.M. *Golu Devta: The God of Justice of Kumaun Himalayas*. India: Shree Almora Book Depot, 1996.

Allan, Trevor. *Constitutional Justice: A Liberal Theory of the Rule of Law.* Oxford: Oxford University Press, 2003.

Bezemek, Christoph and Nicoletta Ladavac. *The Force of Law Reaffirmed: Frederick Schauer Meets the Critics.* Switzerland: Springer, 2016.

Brody, B.A. 'Law and Morality'. In *The Encyclopaedia of Bioethics*, edited by S.G. Post, 1375–1380. New York: Macmillan, 2004.

Brown, Judith Margaret. *Gandhi's Rise to Power: Indian Politics 1915–1922.* India: Cambridge University Press, 1972.

Chandra, Satish. *Medieval India: From Delhi Sultanate to the Mughals (1206–1526): Part 1.* New Delhi: Har-Anand Publications, 1997.

Gandhi, Mohandas Karamchand. *An Autobiography or The Story of My Experiments with Truth* (Critical Edition), translated by Mahadev Desai. London: Yale University Press, 2018.

McBride, Keally. 'Colonialism and the Rule of Law'. In *Mr. Mothercountry: The Man Who Made the Rule of Law*. New York: Oxford University Press, 2016.

Metcalf, Barbara and Thomas Metcalf. *A Concise History of Modern India*. UK: Cambridge University Press, 2006.

Narasappa, Harish. *Rule of Law in India: A Quest for Reason.* India: Oxford University Press, 2018.

Neill, Stephen. *A History of Christianity in India.* UK: Cambridge University Press, 1984.

Rawls, John. *A Theory of Justice* (Revised Edition). US of America: Harvard University Press, 1999.

Sandler, Paul Mark. *The Fine Art of Trial Advocacy: A Young Lawyer's Resource for Success*. Chicago: American Bar Association Book Publishing, 2021.

Schauer, Frederick. *The Force of Law*. England: Harvard University Press, 2015.

Singh, Mahendra Pal and Niraj Kumar. *The Indian Legal System: An Enquiry*. Delhi: Oxford University Press, 2019.

Tamanaha, Brian. *Legal Pluralism Explained: History, Theory, Consequences*. New York: Oxford University Press, 2021.

Index

About the Author

Anand Prasad is a corporate and commercial lawyer with more than three decades of experience representing both domestic and international clients on a wide range of legal and commercial issues within and outside India. He is a co-founder of Trilegal, one of the country's premier commercial law firms. He left Trilegal in 2017 to establish a new political party founded on classical liberal values. In 2019, he returned to the practice of law and helped co-found the firm AP&Partners, Advocates.